Suffering and Evil in the Plays of

Christopher Marlowe

SUFFERING AND
EVIL IN THE PLAYS OF
Christopher
Marlowe

By DOUGLAS COLE

PRINCETON, NEW JERSEY
PRINCETON UNIVERSITY PRESS
1962

Publication of this book has been aided by
the Ford Foundation program to support publication,
through university presses, of work in the
humanities and social sciences

*

Printed in the United States of America

To Ginny

NON È L'AFFEZÏON MIA SÌ PROFONDA,

CHE BASTI A RENDER VOI GRAZIA PER GRAZIA.

ACKNOWLEDGMENTS

THE playwright who may draw from a rich heritage of varied dramatic traditions is fortunate indeed; but even more fortunate is the scholar or critic whose subject has been given intelligent and illuminating treatment by his predecessors and contemporaries. To acknowledge adequately my indebtedness to those who have written on Marlowe and the Elizabethan theater would be impossible, but I should like to mention those whose work has most influenced my understanding and treatment of Marlowe's drama: M. M. Mahood, Harry Levin, Hardin Craig, Willard Farnham, and Bernard Spivack.

I am also happy to record my special debts of gratitude to Mr. John Bakeless, for bibliographical advice; to the Rev. William T. Costello, S.J., for information about the curriculum at sixteenth-century Cambridge and about matters theological; to Mr. Richard Vaughan, Librarian of Corpus Christi College, Cambridge, for kindly supplying me with a microfilm of the manuscript catalogue of printed books in the Corpus Library during Marlowe's university years; and to Mrs. Baldwin Smith for rescuing my typescript from its more serious lapses into awkwardness.

This book is a revision of a doctoral dissertation submitted to Princeton University in 1960. In its original form it was read by Professor Alan S. Downer, who, even before his helpful suggestions for improving the manuscript, had already provided me with one major approach to my subject by his infectious enthusiasm for the theatrical dimensions of dramatic art. At every stage of its development, my study has benefited immeasurably from the unfailing guidance and encouragement of the man to whom I owe my greatest debt of thanks—Professor Gerald Eades Bentley.

DOUGLAS COLE

Yale University
January 1962

ABBREVIATIONS

EETS	Early English Text Society
ELH	*Journal of English Literary History*
LCL	Loeb Classical Library
MLN	*Modern Language Notes*
MLQ	*Modern Language Quarterly*
MLR	*Modern Language Review*
MSR	Malone Society Reprints
PMLA	*Publications of the Modern Language Association of America*
PQ	*Philological Quarterly*
QRL	*Quarterly Review of Literature*
RES	*Review of English Studies*
SP	*Studies in Philology*
SQ	*Shakespeare Quarterly*
SR	*Sewanee Review*
TFT	Tudor Facsimile Texts
TLS	*[London] Times Literary Supplement*

CONTENTS

· ix ·

CONTENTS

Suffering and Evil in the Plays of
Christopher Marlowe

PROLOGUE

Art a Painter? Canst paint me a teare, or a wound,
A groane, or a sigh? ...

—THE SPANISH TRAGEDIE (1602)

*D*RAMA is made from actions and ideas; when those actions and ideas focus on problems of suffering and evil, drama enters the realm of the tragic. In the development of tragedy on the English stage, Christopher Marlowe holds a position of crucial importance; his name is a hallmark of the creative genius of the English Renaissance. By examining the representation of suffering and evil in Marlowe's plays, and by relating this aspect of his dramaturgy to the theatrical and ideological backgrounds of his time, this book seeks to clarify both the measure of Marlowe's artistic originality and the nature of his tragic vision. This has necessarily involved the study of the broader context of Marlowe's plays, the context provided by such varying elements as the dramatic traditions influential in sixteenth-century England, the theatrical practice of Marlowe's immediate contemporaries in serious drama, the character of Marlowe's source materials, the prevailing ideological currents in Elizabethan England, and more particularly the heritage of theological thought which Marlowe himself must have encountered during his six years as a scholar ostensibly preparing for holy orders at Cambridge University. My primary method has been to introduce relevant areas of this background material into the close examination of the treatment of suffering and evil in each of Marlowe's plays. So complex and important, however, is the background of dramatic traditions in Marlowe's time that I have thought it best to introduce the study with a review of the major methods used by Marlowe's predecessors to stage the human experience of suffering and evil.

The spectacle of human suffering is an integral and essential element in dramatic tragedy, an element which presents the dramatist with a central problem in technique and the critic with a central problem in interpretation. The technical problem involves the mode of representation, on stage, of human pain and anguish, both physical and mental, with special concern for the effects and functions of such representation within the play as a whole. The interpretative problem involves the analysis of response to the dramatist's representation of suffering, with special concern for its implications of meaning within the "universe" of the play.

It is always dangerous, as F. L. Lucas reminds us, to generalize too precisely about the spirit of tragedy. But, he adds, we can at least say that in tragedy "the problem of evil and of suffering is set before us; often it is not answered, but always there is something that makes it endurable."[1] There are two important implications here. The first is that the tragedian's treatment of suffering and of evil will be such as to present these things *as problems*; mere representation of suffering is not of itself "tragic," not adequate to provoke the question, however implicitly, "Why suffering?" The same holds true of the depiction of evil, in whatever form it takes. It is the *mode* of representation that can give to suffering and evil a tragic dimension; hence the importance of the dramatist's technique. The second implication is that part of the tragedian's art is to provide some means of balance which will render his depiction of suffering and evil bearable. This is to recognize that at least part of the complex emotional effect of dramatic tragedy is some sense of equilibrium; here again, to reach the cause or causes of such equilibrium, we are led to the examination of the artist's technique.

The dramatic artist has a complex medium at hand, a medium which allows him the simultaneous use of sight and sound.

---

[1] *Tragedy: Serious Drama in Relation to Aristotle's Poetics* (London, 1957), p. 77.

His effects are produced through a combination of scene, atmosphere, action, speech, and the weight of actuality brought to bear by the presence of living actors. We are always at a disadvantage, therefore, in trying to analyze the dramatist's art through the text of the play alone, yet even on this basis much can be done. Consider, for instance, the possibilities of representing suffering through action or scene—the visible terms of the dramatic medium. There is, first of all, the obvious and common device of having events of a physically painful nature take place on stage. This can happen either suddenly and without preparation—an effective shock technique—or at the end of a period of strained expectancy, in which case a sense of the inevitability of destruction carries with it possibilities for dramatic irony. The scope of manipulating such external and physical suffering is broad indeed, ranging from sheer sensationalism through emblematic situations and actions to the subtler effects achieved by ironic juxtaposition of scenes, movements, or deeds. But however effective the representation of external suffering may be, the expression of inward pain and anguish often proves the most enduring and evocative element in tragedy. There suffering takes on the specifically human dimension. The chief tool for dramatic representation of such suffering, besides the variable capabilities of actors themselves, is, of course, language: representation through thought and sound. The skillful dramatist is able to build his emotional effects by means of prosodic variation, imagery, descriptive diction, and irony of statement or context. In the art of dramatic language, Marlowe has received his greatest recognition; without doubt, his "mighty line" brought new strength and influence to the English tragic stage. Yet in his treatment of suffering there is evident a wide range of devices and techniques which make his plays more powerful than could his mastery of dramatic blank verse alone.

Beyond the dramaturgical problems involved in the representation of suffering lie the ideological problems concerning evil, and the causes of evil, which determine the conceptual framework of the tragic play. They are inescapable, for deep in the roots of human suffering, whether in life or in art, there is always the mystery of evil. In the history of Western civilization dramatic tragedy, more than any other art form, has addressed itself most directly to the expression and the probing of this mystery. Inevitably, the tragedian in his approach to the problem of evil is dependent on the ideas and concepts of the philosophies and theologies of his age. Therefore, in my endeavor to establish the nature of Marlowe's vision of evil, I have been led from the themes embedded in his plays to the possible sources of those themes in his own formal intellectual training at Cambridge in the 1580's. It seemed inconceivable that there should be but a slight relationship between the author of *Doctor Faustus* and the Archbishop Parker Scholar of Cambridge University who, as F. S. Boas tells us, as a six-year student "apparently destined to take holy orders must have been supposed to give the first place to divinity in his academic curriculum."[2] When one adds to this the knowledge that theology was the most important of the graduate studies in the Cambridge of Marlowe's day, that undergraduates not even preparing for divinity attended both the long and systematic Sunday sermons and the divinity disputations which were the acme of the school exercises, that the hottest issues at Cambridge were theological ones,[3] and finally that Marlowe's own college, Corpus Christi, had recently acquired one of the finest collections of theological books from the private library of Archbishop Parker,[4] it is only reasonable to expect

[2] *Christopher Marlowe: A Biographical and Critical Study*, rev. ed., (Oxford, 1953), p. 20.

[3] See William T. Costello, S.J., *The Scholastic Curriculum at Early Seventeenth-Century Cambridge* (Cambridge, Mass., 1958), pp. 107-112; and H. C. Porter, *Reformation and Reaction in Tudor Cambridge* (Cambridge, 1958), *passim*.

[4] John Strype, *The Life and Acts of Matthew Parker* (London, 1711), p. 518 (Uuu3ᵛ). For the regulations concerning the use of this library see H. P. Stokes, *Corpus Christi* (London, 1898), pp. 185-187. The complete

that Marlowe came away from Cambridge with more theological sophistication than is ordinarily supposed. It goes without saying that the body of his theological learning would have involved much concerning the nature of man and the problem of evil, much, in other words, that could contribute to his artistic vision of tragedy. That it did so contribute, particularly in the most memorable of his tragedies, *Doctor Faustus*, but also throughout his dramatic work, is one of the major arguments of this study.

Marlowe has long been considered one of the great originating spirits of Elizabethan tragedy. The surge of his blank verse, the vigor and intensity of his central conceptions and characters, the drive and reach of his imagination have established him firmly as a leader in the poetic drama of his age. The precise nature of his achievement in tragedy, however, has been somewhat blurred by three prevalent tendencies: first, to see his work as the beginning of a totally new movement; second, to see it only in the light of what we know, or think we know, about Marlowe's personal life; and last, to consider it primarily as a preparation for the greater work of Shakespeare. The limitations of such perspectives may be avoided if we keep in mind that the plays are first of all dramatic actions which present significant experiences in objective form, that they must depend in one way or another on the conventions of the particular theatrical tradition in which they arise, and that they are worth experiencing for their own sake.

A play is not created *ex nihilo*. No dramatist who writes for the stage can separate himself completely from the conventions of his tradition; even the most rebellious attests to convention by trying the exact opposite, the complete reversal, of what is expected or assumed to be normal. The great playwright is like the master craftsman who uses the same tools as the journeyman, but with more skill and ingenuity; most

contents of the Parker bequest are listed in Corpus Christi College Library MS. 575.

· 7 ·

important, he shapes his material according to his own vision. But our appreciation of his art is enhanced if we understand the nature of his material and of his tools. Therefore, to realize how Marlowe's predecessors came to grips with suffering and evil is to be able to measure more accurately the true achievement of his tragic art, and to distinguish more clearly the marks of his vision of tragedy. Accordingly, our study begins with a survey of the characteristic techniques and ideas underlying the representation of suffering and evil in the more important dramatic traditions available to Marlowe: the heritage of the mystery-cycles, the morality plays, the drama of Seneca and of Seneca's English imitators; it also includes the significant tradition of non-dramatic tragedy in *De Casibus* literature, and Thomas Kyd's influential contemporary play, *The Spanish Tragedy*.

CHAPTER I · THE BACKGROUNDS OF MARLOVIAN TRAGEDY

Come giue vs a tast of your quality;
come, a passionate speech.—HAMLET

CHAPTER I · THE BACKGROUNDS
OF MARLOVIAN TRAGEDY

I. THE MEDIEVAL MYSTERY-CYCLES:
THE COMEDY OF EVIL

H E distance between Marlowe's plays and the mystery-cycles of the medieval Church is not so great as one might at first assume. It was not until 1569-1580, the decade before young Marlowe went up to Cambridge, that the traditional performances of the craft cycles were finally suppressed by the stringent regulations of the English Reformation.[1] Furthermore, one notices certain similarities of emotion and behavior between the stock figures of the cycle plays and some of Marlowe's characters. The tyrant Herod, with his extravagant boasts and cruel deeds, has been seen as a dramatic prototype of Marlowe's Tamburlaine.[2] Like Herod before him, Tamburlaine orders a massacre of innocents, swears oaths by Mahomet, makes claims of world mastery and of superhuman powers. But unlike his medieval counterpart, Tamburlaine succeeds in the purpose of his massacre, turns his connection with Mahomet into one of daring defiance, and fulfills most of his martial boasts. Both Herod and Tamburlaine, however, are confronted with shocking proof of the limitations of their power, and their common reaction is wild rage. One does not easily forget the extraordinary wrath of Tamburlaine when confronted with the death of Zenocrate:

> What, is she dead? *Techelles*, draw thy sword,
> And wound the earth, that it may cleaue in twaine,

[1] Harold C. Gardiner, S.J., *Mysteries' End: An Investigation of the Last Days of the Medieval Religious Stage*, Yale Studies in English, Vol. 103 (New Haven, 1946), p. 72.

[2] Harry Levin, *The Overreacher: A Study of Christopher Marlowe* (Cambridge, Mass., 1952), p. 31.

> And we discend into th'infernall vaults,
> To haile the fatall Sisters by the haire,
> And throw them in the triple mote of Hell,
> For taking hence my faire *zenocrate*.
>
> . . . .
>
> Behold me here diuine *zenocrate*,
> Rauing, impatient, desperate and mad,
> Breaking my steeled lance . . .[3]

With allowances for the great difference in language, is there not a prefiguration of such dramatic behavior in the violent reaction of Herod to the news that the Magi have escaped his plot?

> A-nothur wey? owt! owt! owtt!
> Hath those fawle traytvrs done me this ded?
> I stampe, I stare, I loke all abowtt!
> Myght I them take, I schuld them bren at a glede!
> I rent! I rawe! and now run I wode![4]

Not all Herods express their suffering in rant. In the dying speech of the Herod in the Chester cycle one finds the conventional theme of despair linked with damnation that will still echo in the famous final monologue of Doctor Faustus:

> Alas! what the devill is this to mone?
> Alas! my daies bene nowe done;
> I wotte I muste dye sone:
> Bottles is me to make mone,
> For dampned I muste be;
> My legges rotten and my armes,
> I have done so manye harmes,

[3] *Tamburlaine the Great* (London, 1590), G8. Readex Microprint of the Huntington Library copy in *Three Centuries of Drama: English, 1512-1641*, ed. Henry W. Wells (New York, 1953).

[4] *Two Coventry Corpus Christi Plays*, ed. Hardin Craig, 2nd ed., EETS, ex. ser. LXXXVII (London, 1957), p. 27.

That nowe I see of feindes swarmes,
From hell cominge after me;
I have done so moche woe,
And never good seith I mighte goe,
Therefore I see cominge my foe,
To feche me to hell.
I bequeath heare in this place
My soule to be with Sathanas.
I dye nowe, alas! alas!
I maie no longer dwell.[5]

The distinctions in expression are even more important, however, than the conventions held in common. The dying words of Faustus communicate a sense of inevitable and unendurable loss which is a much more powerful rendering of the damnation theme than anything in the mystery plays. So, too, the testimony of torment that is wrung from the inner being of Marlowe's Mephostophilis:

Why this is hell: nor am I out of it.
Think'st thou that I that saw the face of God,
And tasted the eternall Ioyes of heauen,
Am not tormented with ten thousand hels,
In being depriu'd of euerlasting blisse?
O *Faustus* leaue these friuolous demandes,
Which strikes a terror to my fainting soule.[6]

The contrast in tone with the following "agony" of Lucifer's fall in the *Ludus Coventriæ* or Hegge cycle is a total one:

Now I am a devyl ful derke,
That was an aungelle bryht.
Now to helle the wey I take,
In endeles peyn ther to be pyht.

[5] *The Chester Plays*, ed. Thomas Wright, Shakespeare Society, 2 vols. (London, 1843 and 1847), I, 185-186. Lines 7 and 8 in the above quotation are transposed in some versions of the text.
[6] *Marlowe's "Doctor Faustus" 1604–1616*, ed. W. W. Greg (Oxford, 1950), B-text ll. 301-307.

For fere of fyre a fart I crake;
In helle donjoone myn dene is dyth.[7]

The difference is governed not merely by language, but by an entire attitude. For Lucifer's plight, at once serious in nature and ludicrous in expression, is representative of the general dramatic situation in which the evil characters of the cycle plays find themselves. Herod's rage and Pharao's boasting, Pilate's pride and Cain's obscenity—all are indications of serious moral disorder and herald a foreknown destruction, and yet at the same time they are made ridiculous by their dramatic context and expression. This curious juxtaposition of elements has been aptly characterized by the phrase, the medieval comedy of evil.

This association of evil and the comic, which is everywhere characteristic of medieval art and letters, and which is indeed perpetuated in plays of the English Renaissance, has been the subject of some probing scholarly speculation. Willard Farnham has suggested one good reason for the presence of grotesque comedy in the most serious of religious art: "The reason seems to be that the Middle Ages found it good for man's soul to be taken down a peg whenever it started to soar. They seem to have been keenly aware that man's soul can soar much too cheaply and easily, and to have felt that man in the flesh must never forget the natural lout that is in him, ready to make him ridiculous or even to mark him for Hell. . . . Both gargoyle and fool, we must assume, made sport of the thoughtless and cured pride for the thoughtful."[8]

This tempering quality is not the whole reason, however. Charlotte R. Kesler, in her consideration of the medieval drama,[9] has made some thoughtful suggestions which take

[7] *Chief Pre-Shakespearean Dramas*, ed. Joseph Quincy Adams (New York, 1924), p. 87.

[8] "The Mediæval Comic Spirit in the English Renaissance," *Joseph Quincy Adams Memorial Studies*, ed. James G. McManaway et al. (Washington, D.C., 1948), p. 434.

[9] "The Importance of the Comic Tradition of English Drama in the

into account medieval philosophical concepts. One such concept is the *speculum* approach to reality, regarding the totality of the natural universe and of history as the mirror of the divine purpose. When all things are to be accounted for, both the comic and the grotesque must be included (the selectivity of classical decorum is obviously out of the question here); and if all things are also to be taken as *exempla* for moral and religious ideas, the comic furnishes a ready vehicle for the reflection of man's moral limitations and absurdities. A second concept is intimately connected with this notion of limitation: the metaphysical concept of evil as privation, an absence or a lack of proper being. This idea arises from the proposition that all being is ultimately good, since God has brought it into existence. Hence, it is only by virtue of a lack of being, a default of being, or a denial of being that evil can be explained. And if the nature of evil is privative, if evil itself has no true reality on the metaphysical level, the manifestations of evil on the physical plane can become objects of mockery, for they are in a sense temporal delusions. Furthermore, from the perspective of eternity, all nature and all history take part in a universal Divine Comedy, the glorious and just end of which is determined by the providence of God. In the long-range divine scheme of things, evil is essentially both impotent and vulnerable; hence the possibility of looking at it as a laughable degradation.

This last principle seems to be most relevant to the treatment of suffering and evil in the mystery plays. In the great sweep and expanse of the cyclical structure of these plays, the sweep that takes in all Christian history from the creation of the angels to the last judgment, a dramatic context is provided which establishes the viewpoint from which the audience may judge and interpret each incident or pageant in the whole.

Interpretation of Marlowe's *Doctor Faustus*," unpublished Ph.D. dissertation (University of Missouri, 1954), chs. i and ii.

Since this dramatic context is the artistic representation of the context of divine providence itself, a factor of necessary limitation is imposed directly on whatever suffering and evil takes place: the basic plot is known from the start; the representatives of the forces of evil and destruction are doomed before they begin; the more confident and boastful they are, the more ludicrous they become; any suffering they experience is but just and deserved; if it is expressed in vulgar terms, the association with the base animal limitations of human life is at least appropriate to what is bad and temporal. At the same time, the suffering of innocent figures in the cycle plays is mitigated in the eyes of the audience by the secure knowledge that the ultimate outcome will be more than just compensation for the travails involved. The catastrophic and primeval fall of man becomes the *felix culpa*; even the harsh cruelties of the Passion of Christ are made bearable by the universal conviction that the *via dolorosa* is the way to the world's redemption. In short, the medieval audience of the mystery-cycles was assured, as was St. Augustine, that all things work together unto good—suffering, evil, even sin.

If the dramatic context of the mystery-cycle provided the essential clue for the interpretation of evil and suffering, the solidity and permanence of that context was responsible for the unshakeable conventions which governed the expression of suffering and evil. The *dramatis personae* are the Biblical figures of Christian revelation; those who stood in the Scriptures as the enemies of God, of the Chosen People, or of Christ, became the inevitable villains of the medieval drama. But they were villains who were made not so much to be feared as to be scorned. Lucifer and the devils, the persistent supernatural agents of evil and destruction, act but to their own discomfiture and only within the limits established by God. Their characteristic expression—"Out! harrow!"—is the essential note of defeat which initially appeared in the vernacular version of probably the first staged depiction of the devils in religious drama, the Harrowing of Hell.[10] Pharao, Herod, Octavian, and Pilate are all developed in the same manner for the same effect: they appear making the most boastful and ridiculous claims of power and pride in a context which implicitly undercuts everything they have to say since it foreshadows a victory for the forces of spiritual good. Pharao's pride must give way before the Exodus; Herod's ranting boasts must fade to ridiculous nonsense in light of the birth of the King of Kings; Pilate's loud demands for peace and order are put to scorn by the Prince of Peace he sends to Calvary. What is emphasized again and again is the essential ineffectiveness of these pompous characters, the inevitable frustration and insignificance of the great material power they profess and wield. The details of their pride and possessiveness are at the same time exemplary faults from which the medieval audience could draw more personal lessons.

The evil potentates in the mysteries are all of a piece. They are formed in the image of King Herod, for whose violent rage the Gospel account of the Nativity provides the original hint, and who was pictured in the patristic tradition as an irascible tyrant. An eleventh-century Christmas play, one of the earliest Latin liturgical dramas to bring Herod on stage, accents his pomp, arrogance, and violent temper.[11] Centuries later, his character and expression had undergone only the change of exaggeration, as is evident, for example, in the Coventry pageant of the Shearmen and Taylors:

Qui statis in Jude et Rex Iseraell,
And the myghttyst conquerowre that eyuer walkid on grownd;
For I am evyn he thatt made bothe hevin and hell,
And of my myghte powar holdith vp this world rownd.[12]

---

[10] See E. K. Chambers, *English Literature at the Close of the Middle Ages*, Oxford History of English Literature, Vol. II, Part 2 (Oxford, 1947), p. 11; Karl Young, *The Drama of the Medieval Church*, rev. ed. (Oxford, 1951), I, ch. V and p. 430.

[11] Young, II, 53, 92-99.

[12] *Two Coventry Corpus Christi Plays*, p. 17.

Herod boasts that he is the cause of light and thunder, that he can annihilate any enemy with a twink of his eye, that he is a wonderful sight, resembling Mahomet and descended from Jupiter. In spite of all this, of course, the three kings escape his hostile plot, and Herod's reaction is the traditional one of violent wrath.

Herod's flamboyant boasts of godlike power, the quite unhistorical connection with Mahomet, and his ludicrous frustration are all indexes of his actual turpitude and ineffectuality. Juxtaposed with the birth of Christ as Saviour of the world, these scenes take on an additional irony that makes a mockery of everything for which Herod stands. Here, then, was the first, full-formed evil potentate in the English drama, the tyrant whose characteristics and activities were uniformly rendered throughout the mystery plays.

Not only Herod acts like Herod, however. In the Towneley cycle, the Pharao of the Moses story makes his appearance in the familiar Herodian mode, boasting of his great power, swearing by Mahomet (the god of all infidels in the mystery-cycles), and decreeing the slaughter of Jewish male infants just as Herod orders the massacre of the innocents in his play. This is not merely dramatic economy in the form of a short-cut in characterization, for the parallel between Herod and Pharao is a typological one, part of the larger analogy medieval exegetes drew between the temporal salvation of the Jews by Moses and the eternal salvation of Christians by Jesus. In each case the evil ruler who plans to execute the infant saviour is thwarted and enraged. The Towneley cycle stresses the parallel by placing the story of the child Moses immediately after the prophecies of Christ's birth and before the pageant which presents the tax-decree of Caesar Augustus at the time of the Nativity. The Roman emperor is still another Herodian; when he learns of the Jewish prophecies of a child who will cause the downfall of imperial power, his exclamation also includes the diabolical cry of defeat:

> Downe fell? dwyll! what may this be?
> Out, harow, full wo is me![13]

The Herodian image reappears in the Towneley Pilate, who is lavish in his own boasts, threats of violence, and oaths by Mahomet. But there is something else in his character which is not in the others, something which does not look back to the older liturgical drama but ahead to the morality play. Pilate boasts directly to the audience, not only of his material prowess, but of his naked evil as well:

> I am full of sotelty,
> ffalshed, gyll, and trechery;
> Therfor am I namyd by clergy
> As mali actoris.[14]

Pilate's self-revelation in its full development points to a more particular variety of evil than is characteristic of the other tyrants in the cycle; he stands for double-dealing in all its forms, especially its legal forms, for he is the self-proclaimed exemplar of the false judge. This vicious quality of double-dealing, he explains, serves as his motivation for making an apparent defense of Christ's innocence, which will be a mere cloak for his genuine malice toward Jesus:

> ffor no thyng in this warld dos me more grefe
> Then for to here of crist and of his new lawes;
>
> .   .   .   .
>
> ffor ouer all solace to me it is most lefe,
> The shedyng of cristen bloode, and that all Iury knawes.[15]

By disclosing his malicious motivation and strategy beforehand, Pilate makes possible a dimension of grim irony in the trial scene which is unique in the cycle plays; no other Pilate is so thoroughly reprehensible as this one. But what is even

---

[13] *The Towneley Plays*, eds. George England and Alfred W. Pollard, EETS, ex. ser. LXXI (London, 1897), p. 80.
[14] *ibid.*, p. 243.
[15] *ibid.*, p. 244.

more important, Pilate's sense of glory in his own wickedness, the exemplary quality of his particular brand of
evil, the joy he professes in the destruction of Christ, and the
self-revealed plot of hypocritical deceit, are all dramaturgical
elements which foreshadow the characteristic behavior of the
morality Vice as he appears in the sixteenth-century drama.
The Towneley Pilate is the most conspicuous progenitor of a
long line of English stage-villains including Marlowe's Barabas; he is the great-grandfather of the sons of Machiavelli.

The two most conventional reactions to adversity registered
by the proponents of evil in the mystery-cycles are wrath and
despair. The former is exhibited by the Herodian figures just
considered; the latter is the expression of Cain, Judas, and
the damned souls at the Last Judgment. Sometimes, as in the
Chester Herod, the two are combined. The despair of the
Chester Herod, as expressed in the speech quoted earlier in
this chapter, is registered in terms quite inappropriate in a
figure predating Christian doctrine on sin and damnation, but
fitting in view of his dramatic function as an *exemplum* for
the Christian audience. The note of desperate self-condemnation in his speech is essentially the same as that found in the
words of the Towneley Cain,

> Syn I haue done so mekill syn,
> that I may not thi mercy wyn,
> And thou thus dos me from thi grace.
> I shall hyde me fro thi face;
> And where so any man may fynd me,
> Let hym slo me hardely;
>
> .   .   .   .
>
> In hell I wote mon be my stall.
> It is no boyte mercy to craue . . .[16]

or in the laments of the damned souls in the York Judgment
play:

[16] *ibid.*, p. 19.

What schall we wrecchis do for drede,
Or whedir for ferdnes may we flee?
When we may bringe forthe no goode dede,
Before hym þat oure juge schall be.
To aske mercy vs is no nede,
For wele I wotte dampned be we,
Allas! þat we swilke liffe schulde lede,
Þat dighte vs has þis destonye.

. . . .

Allas! for drede sore may we quake,
Oure dedis beis oure dampnacioune . . .[17]

The convention here, like most of the conventions in the religious drama, is governed not by the attempt to portray human suffering and remorse with any degree of realism, but to convey symbolically a doctrinal truth: the man who despairs is the damned man. It is a convention that was still quite alive on the English stage into the seventeenth century.

The formality in the speeches of suffering throughout the mystery-cycles is due to many causes: the strength of convention, the narrative function of most of the speeches, the element of doctrine which must be expressed, the very noticeable rhyme schemes. In addition, there is hardly time to dwell very long in each of the cycle pageants on any one expression of grief; the play must move along rather quickly, covering the necessary ground without much elaboration. The cycle drama is symbolic drama, and its conventions are, at least in one respect, a kind of dramatic shorthand. In the Norwich play of the Fall of Man, for example, Adam and Eve are not given any long lamentations after the expulsion from Eden; they are merely escorted from the garden of Paradise by two symbolic figures, Dolor and Miserye. Herod's death in the Hegge cycle is represented in terms quite different from the Chester treatment: in the midst of a celebration banquet after the mas-

---

[17] *York Plays*, ed. Lucy Toulmin Smith (Oxford, 1885), pp. 500-501.

sacre of the innocents, Herod is struck down by *Mors*, who warns the audience to beware of pomp and pride, and to beware of him. But the use of abstract figures is only one measure of formality. Another is the liturgical background of some of the more familiar laments: those of Christ on the cross, of Mary at the crucifixion, of Mary Magdalene on the morning of the Resurrection, of the bereaved mothers in the Innocents play—all had their roots in the psalms, lyrics, and hymns of the Latin liturgical drama, and some had also been paralleled in English medieval lyric poetry. The strength of this tradition helped to perpetuate the formal, lyrical expression of sorrow in English drama for centuries.

The strain of lyric lament, however, is not a characteristic of the speeches given to evil figures, whose mode of suffering is wrathful or desperate, but it does characterize the innocent sufferers. Except for the traditional plaints connected with the Passion, the situations which give rise to the expression of innocent suffering all involve some kind of domestic bond. The plays of Abraham and Isaac and of the Slaughter of the Innocents are the most notable examples; some Cain plays include the sorrow of Adam and Eve over the death of Abel. This speech by one of the mothers in the Towneley Innocents play is representative of both the lyrical formality and the domestic sentiment involved:

> Alas for shame and syn / alas that I was borne!
> Of wepyng who may blyn / to se hir chylde forlorne?
> My comforth and my kyn / my son thus alto torne!
> Veniance for this syn / I cry, both euyn and morne.[18]

The parent's lament over a lost child, then, stands as one of the more important kinds of suffering displayed in the mystery-cycles, a kind of suffering which, because of its independ-

---

[18] *Towneley Plays*, p. 176. The last line is echoed by the speeches of the other mothers in what amounts to a lyric refrain.

ence from the Passion story, could easily be adapted to the developing needs of secular drama in a later age.

The mystery-cycles of the medieval stage provided a bedrock of serious meaning and enduring conventions for the development of the English theater. Built to convey a theme of highest eminence to an audience of broadest diversity, they combined symbolism, typology, realism, and homiletics. Within a dramatic context representing the providential order that governed all things and all mankind, there arose a dramaturgical method which staged evil as something comic, not only for reasons grounded in the medieval philosophy of evil but for the more practical homiletic purpose of engaging the least sophisticated of minds. Though evil in the mysteries could be laughed at, it could not lightly be dismissed; even in its most grotesque or ludicrous manifestations it remained a ubiquitous force in the earthly existence of man. Along with the comedy of evil other conventions were being firmly established: the discomfiture of the godless was consistently represented by two basic emotions—wrath and despair; the suffering of innocents, on the other hand, was dramatized in lyric lamentation, and consistently arose from established situations either as part of Christ's passion or within a domestic context. And all the elements of suffering and evil were rendered endurable and intelligible in terms of the over-ruling, benevolent, and just scheme of Christian providence. Awareness of this scheme, both in its ideological and dramaturgical dimensions, was the key to the interpretation of suffering and evil on the medieval stage.

II. THE MORALITY PLAY: THE
ALLEGORY OF EVIL

In the mystery-cycles the story of the divinely ordered destiny of humanity was given its broadest and most inclusive expression; in the morality play that same story was transposed to the minor scale of the individual Christian's career on earth. It was still a drama of the Fall and the Redemption, but in it Adam was replaced by Everyman, and Christ by the Christian legacy of repentance. The doctrine of man's salvation was the essential core of the morality play throughout its two centuries on the English stage. The terms of that doctrine were the governing forces in the dramatization of whatever elements of suffering and evil were included in the morality tradition.

The English morality play is staged homiletic allegory. Within its transparently didactic framework, the personifications of abstract vices and virtues contend for the allegiance of the central figure or figures that represent man. The characteristic plot is a contest, and its characteristic movement is from the seduction of mankind by vice to the salvation of mankind by virtue and repentance. The fundamental issue of the morality play is thus always the same, and it is by definition a highly serious one; the fundamental evil involved, sin in one or another of its particular forms, is also always the same, and just as serious. But the dramaturgical expression of the issue and the evil, drawing from the heritage of the mystery plays, combined both moral gravity and comic effect; the comedy of evil persisted along with the allegory of evil; like the allegory, it found its support and basis in the doctrinal and homiletic formulation which was responsible for the morality tradition.[19]

In the morality drama there are no villains as such, no malicious or wicked human figures who embody the evil that exists in the universe of the play. No Herods, Pharaos, or Pilates appear, and with one or two exceptions, even the Devil plays a negligible role. Instead, evil is represented in a strictly

[19] For the most comprehensive analysis of the morality play and of its influence on the Elizabethan drama, see Bernard Spivack, *Shakespeare and the Allegory of Evil: The History of a Metaphor in Relation to His Major Villains* (New York, 1958). Also helpful are Willard Farnham, *The Medieval Heritage of Elizabethan Tragedy*, corrected reprint ed. (Oxford, 1956), pp. 173-270; Hardin Craig, "Morality Plays and Elizabethan Drama," *SQ*, 1 (1950), 64-72; T. W. Craik, *The Tudor Interlude: Stage, Costume, and Acting* (Leicester, 1958); and Kesler, pp. 66-132.

allegorical dimension, in the figures of the vices, who stand for whatever immoral forces were abstracted by Christian thought from the experience of sinful man. The Vice, who usually goes under the label of some specific sin, is a dramatic metaphor for a principle that has its only real existence in the inner, moral life of man. But within the abstract world of the morality play, he takes on a dramatic reality which is irrepressible, and which will even invade the English plays which do not happen to be moralities.

In reviewing the characteristics of the Vice in morality drama, one can do no better than to summarize Bernard Spivack's expert analysis of this "homiletic showman, intriguer extraordinary, and master of dramatic ceremonies."[20] From the original conventional context of the Seven Deadly Sins, the vices became more specialized in the history of the morality in accord with the more specific homiletic aims of the plays in the sixteenth century. This selective development gave rise to the practice of having one vice stand in a position of higher dramatic importance than the others, a position defined by both his doctrinal distinction as *radix malorum* and his concomitant role as the prime mover of the moral evil in the play. Hence, the appearance of *the* Vice. Like all vices, he represented the force of moral destruction in the life of man; as *the* Vice, he became the chief antagonist of the human protagonist, the master intriguer and seducer whose aim was always the spiritual ruin of his victim. In dramatic terms, this role took shape in two directions: the alienation of the human hero from the personifications of virtue who supported and counseled him, and the association of the Vice with his victim as a friend, master, and preceptor. The universal method in this twofold stratagem was deceit, the artful dissimulation which is at once the Vice's indelible dramatic characteristic and the greatest source of his professional pride. The simplest

[20] *Shakespeare and the Allegory of Evil,* p. 151. Spivack's discussion of the Vice figure extends to p. 205.

form of such deceit was the use of a virtuous alias, sometimes accompanied by physical disguise, and often developed by specious argumentation. Such action was the dramatic symbol for a universal principle of medieval theology: that evil is chosen by man only under the aspect of an apparent good— the philosopher's observation of what Spivack calls "the devious beginning and insidious growth of every evil in our mortal nature."[21] The use of the virtuous alias reflects as well the "characteristic effort of human nature to miscall by a palatable name the evils to which it is addicted."[22]

The Vice not only had a dramatic function in relation to the human protagonist of the play; he also had a function in direct relation to the audience. This was the fundamentally homiletic one of revealing point-blank the precise nature of the sin he stood for. Envy's disclosure to the audience in *Impatient Poverty* (1560) is a characteristic example:

> Is he gone, then haue at laughynge
> I syr is not thys a ioly game
> That conscience doeth not knowe my name
> Enuy in fayth I am the same
> what nedeth me for to lye
> I hate conscience, peace loue and reste
> Debate and stryfe that loue I beste
> Accordyng to my properte
> when a man louethe well hys wyfe
> I brynge theym at debate and stryfe
> This is sene daylye
> Also betwene syster and brother
> There shall no neyghboure loue an other
> where I dwell bye

---

[21] *ibid.*, p. 155.

[22] *ibid.*, p. 156. The dramatic embodiment of this principle in English drama is not limited to the morality play; it can be traced back at least as far as the demon's prologue to the Ludus Coventriæ Passion Play: *Ludus Coventriæ or the Plaie called Corpus Christi*, ed. K. S. Block, EETS, ex. ser. CXX (London, 1922), p. 228.

And nowe I tell you playne
Of one man I haue dysdayne
Prosperyte men do hym call
He is nye of my blood
And he to haue so moche worldly good
That greueth me worste of all[23]

This histrionic intimacy with the audience was extended to greater lengths than the strictly homiletic purpose necessitated: the Vice would often become self-laudatory in his revelations, demonstrating cynical scorn for his victim and mankind generally; he would proudly reveal his plots and stratagems beforehand; in the presence of his victim he would engage in humorous asides, and sometimes even keep up a cunning game of mumbling something about his true designs to the human hero, only to cover up the line with some innocuous but comic saying that sounded like his first revelation. One of his more startling manifestations of deceit was his trick of tears and laughter: one minute he would be weeping in sympathy and concern for the protagonist, in the effort to convince him of his affection; the next minute, his laughter before the audience declared his real scorn for the frailty of human virtue that was so easily destroyed by his dissimulation. Thus, the combined functions of the Vice made him a destructive antagonist, a mocking comedian, and an instructive voice all in one.

The Vice's comic side extended at times into scenes which had no direct connection with the career of the central human figure: it took the form of slapstick, gross and obscene jests, social and religious satire, profanity and puns, songs, dances, and fustian. The vices themselves would regularly engage in quarrels and brawls over the matter of supremacy, illustrating the element of strife and discord that was inherent in vice or the passions as viewed by Christianity. Here, as elsewhere, the

[23] *A Newe Interlude of Impacyente pouerte* (1560), ed. J. S. Farmer, Tudor Facsimile Texts (1907), cᵛ-c2. Hereafter this facsimile series will be referred to as TFT.

comedy was symbolic and allegorical, no matter how realistic its dramaturgical expression may have been. Just as in the comic elements of the mystery-cycles, "the passages of farce in the morality plays have, at bottom, the purpose of making particular revelations about the nature of moral turpitude— its frivolity, its irreverence, its animalism, its destructive appetites, and its brainsick folly."[24]

For all his many dimensions, the Vice of the morality play was essentially passionless and non-human, lacking both feeling and responsibility, and never in need of motivation other than that provided by his own definition. It was part of his nature to demonstrate a certain sense of immunity to either pain or destruction. Discomfited he could be in individual cases, but always he could look forward to new inroads and new conquests in the broad field of human life. It was, after all, part of the homiletic emphasis of the morality play to stress the vices' perennial threat to human spiritual well-being. As a result, the Vice does not suffer; he has neither the moral nor human capacity to do so. In the morality tradition, suffering is reserved for the representatives of mankind.

The kind of suffering that afflicts the human heroes of the morality plays is as stereotyped as the plot and the *dramatis personae*; it is the suffering of retribution. Normally it takes either or both of two forms, physical affliction and spiritual despair. John Skelton's *Magnyfycence* (1513-1516) provides illustrations of both. Here the hero has risen to prosperity by yielding to the pressures of the vices and of Fansy, the personification of his own mental faculty. At the height of his fond delusion, he boasts of his security:

> Fortune to her lawys can not abandune me;
>> But I shall of Fortune rule the reyne.
> I fere nothynge Fortunes perplexyte.
>> All Honour to me must nedys stowpe and lene.[25]

[24] Spivack, p. 122.

[25] *Magnyfycence*, ed. Robert Lee Ramsay, EETS, ex. ser. XCVIII (London, 1906), ll. 1459-1462. Subsequent references to this edition will appear in my text.

Not long afterwards the inevitable overthrow happens; a figure called Adversity beats down Magnyfycence, takes his goods and clothes, and declares to the audience that he is the "Stroke of God" sent to humble the proud. Adversity turns the fallen hero over to Poverty, who catalogues his physical characteristics in much the same way the vices have described their moral characteristics:

> A, my bonys ake! me lymmys be sore;
> Allasse, I haue the cyatyca full euyll in my hyppe!
> Allasse, where is youth that was wont for to skyppe?
> I am lowsy and vnlykynge and full of scurffe;
> My colour is tawny, colouryd as a turffe.
> I am Pouerte, that all men doth hate.
> I am baytyd with doggys at euery mannys gate;
> I am raggyd and rent, as ye may se ...   (1955-1962)

The afflictions of Poverty are obviously to be applied to the new state of Magnyfycence, who, when he regains consciousness, breaks into one of the most formal, stilted, and extended laments of any morality hero:

> O feble Fortune, O doulfull Destyny!
> O hatefull Happe, O carefull Cruelte!
> O syghynge Sorowe, O thoughtfull Mysere!
> O rydlesse Rewthe, O paynfull Pouerte!
> O dolorous herte, O harde Aduersyte!
> O odyous Dystresse, O dedly Payne and Woo!
> For worldly Shame I wax bothe wanne and bloo.
> Where is nowe my Welth and my noble estate?
> Where is nowe my treasure, my landes, and my rent?
> Where is nowe all my seruantys that I had here a late?
> Where is nowe my golde vpon them that I spent?
> Where is nowe all my ryche abylement?
> Where is nowe my kynne, my frendys, and my noble blood?
> Where is nowe all my Pleasure and my worldly good?
> Allasse my Foly! allasse my wanton Wyll!
> I may no more speke tyll I haue wept my fyll. (2048-2063)

This is no more than a painful rendition of the familiar *ubi sunt* theme of the late medieval lyrics; it is as mechanical in expression as the staging of the hero's fall, but it is typical of the sorrow registered by those morality figures who have been punished for their sins in a material way.[26]

This sort of retributive affliction—in terms of earthly punishment rather than spiritual damnation—becomes a dominant theme of the moralities as they move from the eschatological framework of the fifteenth-century plays to the increasingly secular stresses of the sixteenth century.[27] Temporal rewards and punishments take on more and more importance, as is witnessed, for example, by Dalila's disease and Ismael's hanging in *Nice Wanton* (printed 1560), by the nature of Confusion's bequest to the unhappy hero of *The longer thou liuest the more foole thou art* (1560-1568)—reproof, derision, open shame and a bad name—and by the title of Ulpian Fulwell's moral interlude (printed in 1568 and 1587): *Like wil to like quod the Deuel to the Colier, very godly and ful of plesant mirth. Wherin is declared not onely what punishement followeth those that wil rather followe licentious liuing, then to esteem & followe good councel: and what great benefits and commodities they receiue that apply them vnto vertuous liuing and good exercises.* The eschatological emphasis of *Everyman* and *The Castle of Perseverance* had been left far in the distance.

The suffering of spiritual despair, nevertheless, was not forgotten. Shortly after his clash with Adversity, Magnyfycence is met by Despair, who tries to convince the miserable man that his sins are too great to be forgiven by God's mercy. The response of Magnyfycence is as conventional as it is brief:

[26] One of the more developed examples is Dalila's lament in *Nice Wanton* (1560), TFT (1908), B^v-B2.

[27] See Farnham, *Medieval Heritage*, pp. 204-232; and Spivack, pp. 206-226.

Alasse my wyckydnesse! That may I wyte!
But nowe I se well there is no better rede,
But sygh, and sorowe, and wysshe my selfe dede.

(2304-2306)

This is the cue for the entrance of Myschefe, who represents
the tendency to the desperate act of suicide. He brings a knife
and a halter (one of Judas' familiar props in the mysteries)
to Magnyfycence, who is saved from suicide only by the entrance of Good Hope.[28]

The desperate speech of Lusty Juventus, in a play that
appeared half a century after Skelton's, demonstrates the persistence of the medieval dramatic convention used to express
despair, and also illustrates how the homiletic purpose of the
morality play leads to the hero's moralizing of his own predicament even in the midst of grief:

Alas, alas, what haue I wrought and done?
Here in this place I wyll fall downe desperate,
To aske for mercy now I know it is to late
    (Here Iuuentus lyeth downe.
Alas, alas, that euer I was begat,
I would to God I had neuer bene borne,
All faythfull men that behold this wretched state,
May very iustly laugh me to scorne.
They may say my tyme I haue euyll spent and worne,
Thus in my first age to worke myne own destruction,
In the eternall paines is my part and portion.[29]

The grief involved in such speeches as these is clearly subsidiary to what it is chiefly meant to convey: the doctrine of
despair as an obstacle to repentance. The doctrine demanded
the convention. As a result, the grief is there whether or not

[28] An identical situation is found in the fifteenth-century morality, *Mankind*.
[29] R[ichard] Wever, *An Enterlude called lusty Iuuentus* [c. 1565], TFT
(London, 1907), E3-E3ᵛ.

it has been adequately motivated in dramatic terms, that is, in terms of the dramatic action used previously to reveal or develop the character of the human figure. Furthermore, the grief ordinarily gives way to hope in as swift and mechanical a fashion as it arose, again because this is part of the lesson that the play must convey. Indeed, the suffering of despair in the morality play was so standard and mechanical a fixture, so independent, really, of the dramatic personality of the human figure who exhibited it, that it could be thrown off or made permanent according to the wish of the author, without altering anything in the character of the sufferer or in the nature of his expression of such suffering. This is precisely what happens in the late morality play by Nathaniel Woodes, *The Conflict of Conscience* (1581), which was printed in two versions distinguished by differing reports made in the epilogue as to the outcome of the hero's despair: in one he never loses it (implying his damnation), and in the other he is finally moved to repentance.

The suffering of the human heroes of the morality plays, in either its physical or spiritual forms, is always retributive because of the homiletic nature of these plays. It functions as a warning *exemplum*, and is developed only to the degree that is necessary to convey the moral message. Since the morality hero is essentially the man who falls victim to vice, there are no suffering innocents in these plays, only suffering sinners. In the rigidly defined structure of the morality, both suffering and evil are non-problematic. Their reason for existence is supremely intelligible: it is based on the universal assumptions governing the understanding of the moral nature of man. The Vice represents the evil which is rooted in man himself, and which poses a constant temptation to his worst inclinations, as well as a constant threat to his spiritual security. For the man who falls there await the punishments of physical affliction and spiritual desperation, from which he can be extracted only by grace and trust in God. The basic framework is simple and mechanical, designed to be understood by everyone; and like most simple mechanisms, it was destined to last a surprisingly long time.

A word should be said about an interesting group of English plays that appear in the decade of the sixties, which, though not strictly morality plays, nevertheless clearly borrow the morality conventions: *Appius and Virginia,* by "R.B.," John Phillip's *Patient Grissell,* John Pikering's *Horestes,* and Thomas Preston's *Cambises.* Besides being roughly contemporaneous, these plays are also alike insofar as they are derived from narrative or historical sources. Though not at all theologically oriented, they reflect strongly the strong ethical purpose and homiletic habit of the native English dramatic tradition; no better witness of this preoccupation is needed than the full titles themselves:

A new Tragicall Comedie of Apius and Virginia, Wherein is liuely expressed a rare example of the vertue of Chastitie, by Virginias constancy in wishing rather to be slaine at her owne Fathers handes, then to be deflowered of the wicked Iudge Apius.

The Commodye of pacient and meeke Grissill, Whearin is declared, the good example, of her pacience towardes her Husband: and lykewise, the due obedience of Children, toward their Parentes.

A Newe Enterlude of Vice Conteyninge, the Historye of Horestes with the cruell reuengment of his Fathers death, vpon his one naturill Mother.

A lamentable Tragedie, mixed full of plesant mirth, containing the life of Cambises king of Percia, from the beginning of his kingdome, vnto his death, his one good deede of execution, after that many wicked deedes and tyrannous murders, committed by and through him, and last of all, his odious death by Gods Iustice appointed.

The situations and patterns of behavior illustrated by these very individualized figures of legend and history, like those of the morality tradition, were at least intended for interpretation as metaphors or symbols of universal experience. Furthermore, each play borrowed from the moralities the figure of the Vice, dressing him in completely secular costume, but employing him still as the prime mover and prompter of evil. In the play of *Horestes*, the Vice is none other than Revenge; in *Appius and Virginia*, Haphazard is his name; *Grissell* features Politic Persuasion, and *Cambises* Ambidexter. Each is symbolic of a particular kind of evil, an evil which is demonstrated not only in the main line of action, but also in subordinate scenes of broad comedy which echo the play's major theme. The comedy of evil thus persists even in plays of a non-religious character.

In *Horestes* the major action gets under way when the Vice, under the alias of "Courage," persuades Horestes, who is torn between the idea of revenge and the natural love of his kindred, to kill his father's murderers. After a scene in which Horestes is granted permission and troops to march against the powers of Egistus and Clytemnestra, two comic soldiers engage in a slapstick brawl and swear their own "revenge" against each other, demonstrating by implication the base and destructive nature of the revenge principle. The Vice himself later has a scene in which he sings joyfully of the destruction that war brings; he is still the mocking, destructive agent of the morality, but with a new field of activity: his primary object is material and social disruption within the family and the state, rather than moral disruption of individual man. He is the antithesis of the characteristic Tudor ideal of social unity and order. In the end he is ousted from the court by Amity, the effect of a diplomatic marriage between Horestes and the daughter of Menelaus, a marriage which restores peace and harmony between Horestes and his uncle, who had at first sought revenge for Clytemnestra's death. The Vice, Revenge, is still very much the metaphor for the particular evil that the play demonstrates.

In *Grissell*, *Appius and Virginia*, and *Cambises* the Vice figures are all court counselors. Politic Persuasion represents the flattering parasite who poses a constant threat to the well-being of the ruler and his state. Haphazard embodies and encourages a code of behavior that places personal pleasure above justice and duty. Ambidexter exemplifies a vicious double-dealing that is the basis of his own two-faced counsel, his comic dealings with the clownish "ruffins" of the play, and the breaches of justice committed by Sisamnes and Cambises. Unlike strictly human parasites or flatterers, these figures have no personal motivations behind their destructive impulses; Vices by definition have sufficient cause for their war against anything and everything that is just or good.[30]

All four plays rely on the traditional morality conventions to represent the source and nature of evil in their stories; in the representation of suffering they are rather more ambitious. With the dramatization of individualized figures from literary or historical legend came new emotional situations and new problems of staging such emotion. The solutions reached by the dramatists vary in their degree of originality. Pikering, in staging the mental struggle of Horestes to decide whether or not to take revenge on his own mother, fell back on an established morality technique; he rendered the inner struggle as an external argument, in which Nature, representing the natural affections every child was assumed to have for its parent, tries without success to dissuade Horestes from his vengeful mission. Something quite similar happens in *Appius and Virginia*, where the lustful judge's torment of conscience is staged with the help of two emblematic personifications who represent visually, though not in speech, the forces at strife within Appius. The stage direction for the following speech by Appius reads, "*let Consince and Iustice come out of him, and let Con-*

[30] See Spivack's detailed discussion of their activities, pp. 269-278, 286-291.

siēce hold in his hande a Lamp burning and let Iustice haue a sworde and hold it before Apius brest."

But out I am wounded, how am I deuided?
Two states of my life, from me are now glided,
For Consience he pricketh me contempned,
And Iustice saith, Iudgement wold haue me condemned:
Consience saith crueltye sure will detest me:
And Iustice saith, death in thende will molest me,
And both in one sodden me thinkes they do crie,
That fier eternall, my soule shall destroy.[31]

More characteristic of Appius than this allegorized plaint are the laments which have as their basis not a moral conflict but the torments of unsatisfied sexual desire. His first appearance shows him caught up in this passion, and a little later he begins a long speech in this way:

> The furies fell of Lymbo Lake,
>   my Princely daies doo shorte:
> All drownde in deadly woes I liue,
>   that once dyd ioy in sport,
> I liue and languish in my lyfe,
>   as doth the wounded Deare:
> I thirst, I craue, I call and crie,
>   and yet am naught the neare:
> And yet I haue that me so match,
>   within the Realme of mine:
> But *Tantalus* amids my care,
>   I hunger sterue and pine:
> As *Sissifus* I roule the stone,
>   In vaine to top of Hill . . .   (580-593)

---

[31] *A new Tragicall Comedie of Apius and Virginia* (1575), ed. R. B. McKerrow and W. W. Greg, Malone Society Reprints (London, 1911), ll. 501-508. The s.d. extends to l. 512. Subsequent references to this edition will appear in my text. Hereafter this reprint series will be referred to as MSR.

Before he is interrupted by his counselors, Appius calls on all the classical deities of heaven to grant his desires or else destroy him, and he exhorts the classical figures of hell to persecute those who will not help him. Obviously, when faced with the task of representing a grand passion, the dramatist took his cue from the plays of Seneca.

Virginia, the exemplary virgin, expresses no suffering in this play: she calmly begs her father to kill her, and adds the request that her head be borne to Appius:

> Bid him imbrue his bloudy handes, in giltles bloud of
> mee:
> I virgin dye, he leacher liues, he was my ende you see:
> No more delayes, lo kisse me first, then stretch your
> strongest arme,
> Do ryd my woe, increase my ioy, do ease your childe of
> harme.
>
> (956-959)

As Virginius is about to strike the blow that will behead her, the maid falters a bit, and asks to be blindfolded. This touch is not in the legend proper, but it had been a characteristic bit of "business" in the Abraham and Isaac plays of the mystery-cycles, where the dramatic situation is manifestly analogous. Old Virginius, of course, has great sorrow to express, both before and after he slays his daughter. Before he is met by Comfort, who finally persuades him that his grief will be abated by the just execution of Appius, the only relief he can imagine lies in suicide, a sentiment which fits the generally classical conception of the characters in this early "Roman play."

The note of domestic pathos which is struck in *Appius and Virginia* is dominant in *Patient Grissell*, a play in which another suffering innocent is used as a moral exemplar. The laments in this drama are all of a piece—provoked by the severing of some domestic bond, they describe the painful situation, make an appeal to the Muses to aid in the plaint, and are generally structured as self-contained poems, not spilling over into the ensuing dialogue. One example should suffice; here is Grissell mourning her mother's death:

> Ah Grissell now maist thou complayne, infortune
> thine (alasse)
> Thie tender dayes in deadly dole, thou now must
> learne to passe,
> For, thou haste lost a Jewell great, whose lyke is rare
> to finde,
> Whose want to waile, vnto thine eyes, a flood of
> teares is sinde:
> Thou now art motherlesse become, the graue hir
> lodge doth rest,
> Whose deth to mourne w^t sobbing shrieks, & sighs,
> y^u now art prest
> Was neuer child had greater losse, nor cause of cark-
> ing care,
> Helpe me to weepe all such (ah las) that carefull
> Children are:
> For I alacke do misse my ioye, and best instructris
> found,
> I rest aliue? but shee by death, lieth closed fast in
> ground.
> Wherfore ye Muses nine: that on *Pernasso* rest,
> *Caleiope, Thersicora,* and *Clio,* do your best:
> Strayne forth your noates of wailfull woes, weepe
> you & mourne with mee:
> That Gods and men, my inward grief, apparant now
> may see.[32]

One does not often associate *Cambises* with domestic pathos, but as a matter of fact the reliance on scenes involving such suffering is a major part of the sensational character of this

---

[32] John Phillip, *The Commodye of pacient and meeke Grissill*, MSR (London, 1909), ll. 479-492. For other such speeches see ll. 714-727 and 1195-1210.

play. The execution of Sisamnes, though just, is rendered in cruel terms by the bringing in of his son Otian to witness the beheading and flaying. Otian's grief as he expresses it before the execution is typical of the self-descriptive, narrative tone of most of the passages cited from these four plays:

> O father deer, these words to hear, that you must
>   dye by force
> Bedews my cheeks w^t stilled teares, ye King hath no
>   remorce.
> The greeuous greefes and strained sighes,
> My hart doth breake in twaine:
> And I deplore most woful childe, that I should see
>   you slaine.
> O false and fickle frowning dame, that turneth as
>   the winde:
> Is this the ioy in fathers age, thou me assignest to
>   finde?
> O dolefull day, vnhappy houre, that louing childe
>   should see:
> His Father deer before his face thus put to death
>   should be.[33]

The pathos and cruelty of this scene are completely eclipsed later in the play when the drunken Cambises, in order to demonstrate his "sobriety," shoots an arrow through the heart of Praxaspes' son. Here it is the parent's turn to lament, and both mother and father are given the opportunity. Praxaspes, left alone on stage with the corpse, has only half a dozen lines to do so; his wife, however, has twenty-seven lines. These speeches of suffering are the most fully developed in the play, and their function seems to be to accent as heavily as possible the pathetic effects of Cambises' cruelty. Neither Otian nor Praxaspes' wife makes any other appearance; they are there solely to register their doleful cries, in verse that

---

[33] Thomas Preston, *Cambises*, TFT (1910), C2^v. Subsequent references to this edition will appear in my text.

sounds as barbaric to a modern ear as the staged cruelties of Cambises.

The cruel deeds of Cambises are noteworthy in themselves, for they represent something new in the development of the popular play on the English secular stage: the direct dramatization of extreme physical suffering and of death in a more realistic mode than ever before. In the moralities proper, physical violence never went much beyond the scuffles and horseplay of the vices, or the symbolic and somewhat mechanically expressed sickness and death of "man." Now, however, the blood begins to flow in earnest: Virginius cuts off his daughter's head and brings it to Appius; in *Horestes* Egistus is hanged on stage; Cambises has Sisamnes beheaded and flayed, shoots an arrow into a small boy's heart (which is then cut out and presented to Praxaspes), and finally has his brother Smirdis stabbed by Murder and Cruelty. His own death is the earliest one known in English secular, non-academic drama to be staged as the protagonist's "tragic fall." The king enters the cleared stage with *"a swoord thrust vp into his side bleeding,"* and launches into a death speech that begins with an echo of the mystery plays' discomfited devils or thwarted tyrants, proceeds through a narrative exposition addressed directly to the audience, and concludes with a neat bit of self-moralization:

> Out alas what shal I doo? my life is finished:
> Wounded I am by sodain chaunce, my blood is
>   minished.
> Gogs hart what meanes might I make my life to
>   preserue?
> Is there nought to be my helpe? nor is there nought
>   to serue?
> Out vpon the Court and Lords that there remaine:
> to help my greefe in this my case, wil none of them
>   take paine?

Who but I in such a wise his deaths wound could
    haue got?
As I on horseback vp did leap, my sword from
    scabard shot.
And ran me thus into the side, as you right well may
    see:
A maruels chaunce vnfortunate that in this wise
    should be.
I feele my selfe a dying now, of life bereft am I:
And death hath caught me with his dart, for want
    of blood I spy.
Thus gasping heer on ground I lye, for nothing I
    doo care:
A iust reward for my misdeeds, my death doth plaine
    declare.
        Heere let him quake and stir.   (F3ᵛ-F4)

That Cambises' death is really no "maruels chaunce" is as-
serted by his last words, then confirmed by the presence and
the mocking words of Ambidexter, as he comes on to watch
the last death throes, and by the final judgment of one of the
lords who discover the corpse:

A iust reward for his misdeeds, the God aboue hath
    wrought:
For certainly the life he led was to be counted
    nought.   (F4)

The suffering and death of Cambises is thoroughly retributive in nature, but at the same time the retribution is totally of
this world. The spiritual issue of despair and of the destiny
of Cambises' soul is never raised. Death itself has become the
major instrument of punishment for a wicked life; the contrast with such plays as *Everyman* and *The Castle of Perseverance* is total: in them death is dramatized as the universal
destiny for good and bad, the occasion and the gateway for
the more significant conflicts and issues. *Cambises* is illustrative

of the general trend of the English morality tradition: from the generalized human figure to the historical or legendary individual, from religious to secular allegory, from spiritual to material deterioration and destruction, from the comic outcome of final salvation to a tragic end in physical death, from a basic moral concern with doctrine and exhortation to a growing dramatic concern with sensational effects. It is illustrative, too, of what "tragedy" meant to the Elizabethan world. "The tragicall history of this wicked king" (F4ᵛ), as the epilogue calls it, is a concrete example of a basic pattern of Elizabethan tragedy: a thoroughly cruel and evil protagonist, after wreaking suffering and destruction on a series of victims, meets at last his own barbarous and "deserved" death.

III. *DE CASIBUS* TRAGEDY: THE
NON-DRAMATIC TRADITION

The retributive fall of King Cambises is a dramatic example of a kind of tragedy that had its deepest roots in a certain tradition of non-dramatic literature: the prose or poetical narrative of the declines of great men from prosperity to misery. The great medieval source of the tradition was Boccaccio's celebrated and influential Latin work, *De Casibus Virorum Illustrium*. In England, the tradition was represented by the work of Chaucer and Lydgate in the medieval period, and by the *Mirror for Magistrates* and its imitators in the Renaissance.[34] *De Casibus* tragedy, as it was developed in Renaissance England, dealt chiefly with the fall of princes and kings, notably wicked ones, with the intent to admonish rulers and men in general to avoid the crimes and vices that had brought destruction and misery to the exemplars in the tales. The full title of the 1559 *Mirror* is self-explanatory: *A Myrrovre For Magistrates. Wherein may be seen by example of other, with howe greuous plages vices are punished: and howe frayle and*

[34] See Farnham, *Medieval Heritage*, chs. iii, iv, vii, viii; and Lily B. Campbell, *Shakespeare's Tragic Heroes: Slaves of Passion* (New York, 1952), pp. 3-24.

vnstable worldly prosperitie is founde, euen of those, whom Fortune seemeth most highly to fauour. William Baldwin's dedication leaves no doubt as to the mundane character of the suffering that punishes the vicious, nor of the moral purpose of each tale; God, he writes, plagues those who abuse justice in any way "with shamefull death, diseases, or infamy. Howe he hath plaged euill rulers from time to time, in other nacions, you may see gathered in Boccas booke intituled the fall of Princes, translated into Englishe by Lydgate: Howe he hath delt with sum of our countreymen your auncestors, for sundrye vices not yet left, this booke named *A Myrrour for Magistrates*, can shewe. . . . For here as in a loking glas, you shall see (if any vice be in you) howe the like hath bene punished in other heretofore, whereby admonished, I trust it will be a good occasion to move you to the soner amendment. This is the chiefest ende, whye it is set furth, which God graunt it may attayne."[35] The function of suffering in these tragedies is clearly outlined: "For the onlye thynge which is purposed herin, is by example of others miseries, to diswade all men from all sinnes and vices" (p. 267).

The theme of mutability and transience, the fragile nature of worldly prosperity evoked in the *Mirror* title, had always been a strong element in *De Casibus* narrative, but, as Professor Farnham has demonstrated, it yields in the English Renaissance to a more and more explicit emphasis on the responsibility of the individual for the fate that befalls him. The conventional reference to the inevitable movement of Fortune's wheel again and again brings forth the assertion that the cause of evil lies not in Fortune's fickleness, but in the free will of man.[36] Jack Cade, in his tragedy, addresses himself directly to the problem:

[35] *The Mirror for Magistrates*, ed. Lily B. Campbell (Cambridge, 1938), pp. 65-66. Subsequent references to this edition will appear in my text.

[36] To Farnham's documentation of this point (*Medieval Heritage*, pp. 281-290, 295-298) may be added the following comments by figures in the 1563 additions to the *Mirror*: "The abuse and skornyng of gods ordynaunces," says Anthony, Lord Rivers, "Is chefest cause of care & wofull chaunces"

> Shal I cal it Fortune or my froward folly
> That lifted me, and layed me downe below?
>
> . . . .
>
> What euer it were this one poynt sure I know,
> Which shal be mete for euery man to marke:
> Our lust and wils our euils chefely warke.
>
> . . . .
>
> Now if this happe wherby we yelde our mynde
> To lust and wyll, be fortune, as we name her,
> Than is she iustly called false and blynde,
> And no reproche can be to much to blame her:
> Yet is the shame our owne when so we shame her,
> For sure this hap if it be rightly knowen,
> Cummeth of our selues, and so the blame our owne.
>
> . . . .
>
> For Fortune is the folly and plage of those
> Which to the worlde their wretched willes dispose.
>
> (pp. 171-172)

The identical sentiment is expressed in John Higgins' *The
First parte of the Mirour for Magistrates* of 1574, where Iren-
glas sums up the dominant Elizabethan attitude:

> No Fortune is so bad, our selues ne frame:
> There is no chaunce at all hath vs preseru'de:
> There is no fate, whom we haue nede to blame:
> There is no destinie, but is deseru'de:
> No lucke that leaues vs safe, or vnpreseru'de:
> Let vs not then complayne of Fortunes skill:
> For all our good, descendes from goddes good will,
> And of our lewdnes, springeth all our ill.[37]

(p. 248); Lord Hastings adds that "A heathen god they hold, whoe fortune keepe,/ To deal them happs, whyle god they ween a sleepe" (p. 288);
Richard III cries out, "Ah cursed caytiue why did I clymbe so hye,/ Which
was the cause of this my balefull thrall" (p. 370). "I was th' only author,
of myne owne woe," laments James IV in the 1587 addition (p. 485).

[37] *Parts Added to The Mirror for Magistrates by John Higgins & Thomas
Blenerhasset*, ed. Lily B. Campbell (Cambridge, 1946), pp. 212-213.

The misery that fell upon the tragic figures in *Mirror* literature was most often attributed to the particular vice of ambition. In his dedicatory essay Higgins restates the prevailing
stress when he singles out intemperance as the major cause of
evil and ruin: "For to couet without consideration: to passe
the measure of his degree: and to lette will runne at randon, is
the onely destruction of all estates."[38]

This purely retributive view of affliction leaves unanswered
the problem of the virtuous or innocent sufferer—a problem,
it must be admitted, that apparently was not a serious concern
to the poets and dramatists of early Elizabethan tragedy. It
was not completely slighted, however, in the *Mirror*. The 1559
edition included the tale of King Henry VI, who was acknowledged as a manifestly virtuous man, and in it Henry himself
brings up the problem of the causes of suffering. There are
two causes, he claims: God's will and man's sin; the bad man
suffers as punishment for sin, while the good man suffers as a
test from God. He admits his own virtue and his own suffering, and says that only God knows why he has been afflicted,
adding the suggestion, nevertheless, that perhaps God has
used him as a pattern to show to others the brittle nature of
worldly honor (pp. 214-215). Where there is no vice, there
still remains mutability.

In the world of Elizabethan *De Casibus* tragedy, then, the
cause of suffering and evil is primarily seen in man's sin; the
form that evil takes is crime or vice; the form that suffering
takes is physical affliction and death. Except for Sackville's
Induction to the *Mirror*, which sets the scene in the classical
underworld, there is no emphasis at all on damnation as the
outcome of sin—the worst suffering seems to be regarded as
the loss of material glory, prosperity, or position. Insofar as
this type of literature is directed primarily at readers who enjoy such benefits, the emphasis is perhaps appropriate after all.

The individual *De Casibus* lament as it appears in the *Mir-*

[38] *ibid.*, p. 31.

ror for Magistrates is, characteristically, a first-person narrative in verse recited by the "ghost" of the historical figure in question. In it he rehearses the details of his career on earth, convicts himself of the crimes he has committed, and points to himself as an example to be avoided. Surprisingly enough, there is little direct expression of suffering; most of the tales deal almost entirely with narrative matter and moral admonition. When personal anguish is expressed, it is ordinarily in terms which contrast the shameful outcome of the fallen prince with his lost splendor, as witness this stanza from the tragedy of King Richard II:

> Beholde my hap, see how the sely route
> Do gase vpon me, and eche to other saye:
> Se where he lieth for whome none late might route,
> Loe howe the power, the pride, and riche aray
> Of myghty rulers lightly fade away.
> The Kyng whych erst kept all the realme in doute,
> The veryest rascall now dare checke and lowte:
> What moulde be Kynges made of, but carayn clay?
> Beholde his woundes, howe blew they be about,
> Whych whyle he lived, thought neuer to decay.
>
> (p. 112)

In the 1559 edition of the *Mirror*, this theme of lost glory is most developed in the lament of King Edward the Fourth, which concludes the book. Edward's plaint is medieval in its conventions of expression, embodying the familiar *ubi sunt* pattern, and even retaining a Latin refrain:

> Where is now my conquest and victory?
> Where is my ritches, and royall array?
> Where be my coursers and my horses hye?
> Where is my mirth, my solas, and playe?
> As vanity to nought all is wyddred away:
> O Lady Bes, long for me may you call,
> For I am departed vntill doomes day:
> But love you that lord that is soveraine of all.

Where be my castels and buyldinges royall?
But Windsore alone now have I no moe.
And of Eton the prayers perpetuall,
Et ecce nunc in pulvere dormio.   (p. 238)

In the 1563 *Mirror*, one finds in Sackville's tragedy of
Henry, Duke of Buckingham, another variety of suffering:
the torments of mind and conscience that were commonly
thought to afflict the tyrant and murderer. Henry records the
suspicion, fear, bad dreams, and agonies of conscience that
followed atrocious killings:

The gylteles bloud which we vniustly shed,
The royall babes deuested from theyr trone,
And we like traytours raygning in theyr sted,
These heauy burdens pressed vs vpon,
Tormenting vs so by our selues alone,
Much like the felon that pursued by night,
Startes at eche bushe as his foe were in sight.

Nowe doubting state, nowe dreading losse of life,
In feare of wrecke at euery blast of wynde,
Now start in dreames through dread of murdrers knyfe,
As though euen then revengement were assynde.
With restles thought so is the guylty minde
Turmoyled, and never feeleth ease or stay,
But lives in feare of that which folowes aye. (pp. 324-325)

This theme is developed for six more stanzas, and represents
a convention of moral thought which in literature was often
associated with the careers of Buckingham and Gloucester,
and which probably reached its highest poetic and dramatic
expression in Shakespeare's *Macbeth*. Fundamentally, it is yet
another form of retributive suffering, the suffering that grows
out of viciousness itself.[39]

[39] For texts of moral philosophy describing this psychological punishment
of sinners, see Campbell, *Shakespeare's Tragic Heroes*, pp. 16-22.

Before another generation had passed, the tragic figures of English *De Casibus* literature were to become the *dramatis personae* of the Elizabethan history plays. It was only natural to expect that the influence of the themes of suffering and evil as well as of the mode of handling these themes in this popular non-dramatic form of tragedy would be felt in the theater when the histories were dramatized.[40] Indeed, the moral vision of English *De Casibus* tragedy informed not only the practice of playwrights, but the critical theory of dramatic tragedy as well. We have only to recall the familiar dicta of Sir Philip Sidney and of the author of *The Arte of English Poesie* (1589) to see the substantial uniformity of this outlook. Sidney stoutly defended the "right vse" of "high and excellent Tragedy, that openeth the greatest wounds, and sheweth forth the Vlcers that are couered with Tissue; that maketh Kinges feare to be Tyrants, and Tyrants manifest their tirannicall humors; that, with sturring the affects of admiration and commiseration, teacheth the vncertainety of this world, and vpon how weake foundations guilden roofes are builded."[41] *The Arte of English Poesie* revealed a similar purpose in the origins of tragedy: "But after that some men among the moe became mighty and famous in the world, soueraignetie and dominion hauing learned them all manner of lusts and licentiousnes of life, by which occasions also their high estates and felicities fell many times into most lowe and lamentable fortunes: whereas before in their great prosperities they were both feared and reuerenced in the highest degree, after their deathes, when the posteritie stood no more in dread of them, their infamous life and tyrannies were layd open to all the world, their wickednes reproched, their follies and extreme insolencies derided, and their miserable ends painted out in playes and pageants, to shew the mutabilitie of fertune, and

---

[40] See Farnham, *Medieval Heritage*, chs. ix and x.

[41] *An Apologie for Poetrie* (1595, written c. 1583), in *Elizabethan Critical Essays*, ed. G. Gregory Smith (Oxford, 1904), I, 177.

the iust punishment of God in reuenge of a vicious and euill life."[42]

IV. SENECAN TRAGEDY AND THE ELIZABETHANS:
THE UNLEASHING OF PASSIONS

"No author exercised a wider or deeper influence upon the Elizabethan mind or upon the English form of tragedy than did Seneca," writes T. S. Eliot, with the weight of scholarship firmly behind the assertion.[43] There can be no doubt that Seneca, so esteemed both for style and moral "sentence" that his works formed an essential part of every cultured Elizabethan's formal education, and whose plays were imitated by academic authors both in England and on the Continent, held an eminent, if not the eminent, position among antique tragedians in the eyes of Marlowe's contemporaries. The conventions and characteristics of Senecan tragedy, with their parallels in the Elizabethan drama, have been tabulated more than once. The obvious themes of fate and fortune, revenge, madness, intense misery and abominable crime, as well as the equally obvious exaggerations of rhetoric and expression, of sensational description and mythological allusion, have been noted and traced again and again. It is clear, of course, that all these characteristics of content and form appear to some degree in early Elizabethan tragedy, including the plays of Marlowe;

[42] *Elizabethan Critical Essays*, II, 35. Other related passages from criticism of the sixteenth and seventeenth centuries are cited by Campbell, *Shakespeare's Tragic Heroes*, pp. 25-38.

[43] Eliot's statement opens his introductory essay to The Tudor Translations' ed. of *Seneca His Tenne Tragedies: Translated into English: Edited by Thomas Newton, Anno 1581*, 2 vols. (London and New York, 1927), I, v. Seneca's impact on the Elizabethans has been examined by John W. Cunliffe in *The Influence of Seneca on Elizabethan Tragedy* (London, 1893), and in his introduction to *Early English Classical Tragedies* (Oxford, 1912); F. L. Lucas, *Seneca and Elizabethan Tragedy* (Cambridge, 1922); Farnham, *Medieval Heritage*, ch. ix. Howard Baker has argued for medieval rather than Senecan influence in *Induction to Tragedy: A Study in a Development of Form in "Gorboduc," "The Spanish Tragedy," and "Titus Andronicus"* (University, La., 1939).

but a closer look at the central concerns of Seneca's suffering characters will clarify, I think, the nature of the Elizabethan indebtedness to the Senecan treatment of suffering and evil.

Much of the gore and sensationalism that one immediately associates with Senecan tragedy is conveyed by language alone rather than by dramatic action. The reason, classical scholars tell us, is that the Senecan plays were probably written not to be staged but to be publicly recited—hence, the overbearing emphasis on rhetoric and epigram, on lurid description and prolix allusion, all manifestations of verbal ingenuity and highly-wrought public declamation. As Eliot puts it, "the drama is all in the word, and the word has no further reality behind it. His characters all seem to speak with the same voice, and at the top of it; they recite in turn."[44] Most of the physical suffering and violence is "off stage," reported at length and with grotesque detail in an attitude of high-pitched hysteria. When violent action appears to be taking place directly, such as Hercules' slaying of his children, it is often described simultaneously by another actor or by the Chorus. At other times, as with the suicides of Phaedra and of Jocasta, the dialogue is self-descriptive. The image is carried to the audience not by sight, but by words.[45]

Since most violent acts are reported, there is little opportunity for the Senecan sufferer to express physical anguish directly. The great exception is the agony of Hercules in *Hercules Oetaeus*, where the hero's body is literally disintegrating under the burning force of Nessus' poison. The dismayed Hercules catalogues the physiological process in lurid detail, yet is driven to sorrow not so much by the physi-

[44] *op.cit.*, p. ix.

[45] The Elizabethans, however, were themselves unaware of this non-theatrical nature of Senecan tragedy; they staged the plays, and translations of them, at their academies, and wrote others like them for similar acting. Original plays modeled most closely after Seneca retained the reporting of violence and physical destruction; but it was not long before the directly staged violence of the popular, non-academic plays had its impact on such "classical" tragedy.

cal pain as by the psychological realization that his great
strength is being corrupted. In a despairing elegiac passage he
chronicles the past achievements of his hands, arms, shoulders,
and so forth, and then launches into his greatest expression of
torment. As the Chorus notes, *pudet auctoris, non morte dolet*
—he grieves not at death, but is ashamed of its cause.[46] The
ingloriousness of his doom, the hidden character of his enemy,
the female instigator he sees behind it all, are what shame and
enrage him. Hercules concludes his lament with frenzied beseeching of Jove, Juno, and the elemental forces of the world
to destroy him at once, not so much because the bodily pain
is unendurable, but because the manner of his defeat is so base,
and because the world sees now what it never saw before, the
spectacle of Hercules weeping. Indeed, when Hercules learns
at last that Nessus, his old enemy, is ultimately responsible
for the calamity, he immediately finds the calm courage to bear
all things without wincing, and goes to meet an unsuffering
death in the flames of his great funeral pyre. At his death
Hercules shows himself victor over all mortal pain.

Most characteristic of Senecan tragedy is not physical suffering, but the suffering of mental anguish, brought about
either by a consuming passion or by intense feelings of guilt.
The jealous fury of Medea, or of Deianira in *Hercules Oetaeus*, are examples of the former cause, in which the passion has
its root in personal character. The passion can also be a result
of the curse of the gods, and such is the case in the raving
ambition and revenge of Alcides in *Hercules Furens*, where
Juno is the divine afflicter, and in the overpowering incestuous
desire of Phaedra in *Hippolytus*, which is the work of Venus.
In each of these situations except that of Hercules, who is the
victim of insanity, the characters realize the criminal nature
of their desires, but are either unable or unwilling to control

[46] *Seneca's Tragedies*, Loeb Classical Library ed. (London, 1953), II,
l. 1209. Hereafter Loeb editions will be referred to as LCL.

themselves. And in all cases such suffering serves as the frenzied prelude to horrific catastrophe.

The mental anguish of guilt-feelings, on the other hand, always follows catastrophe. It should be emphasized that, in Seneca's plays, such torment is nearly always the fate of one who has unknowingly been the cause of destruction he would never have willed had he been familiar with all circumstances. Oedipus is of course the classic example, whether in Greek or Senecan tragedy. But Seneca seizes time and again on this kind of predicament, revealing his Stoic obsession with pessimistic fatalism. And each time he will cast it in the same mold, counterpointing the extravagant guilt-suffering of the character who has unwittingly committed the tragic deed with the unheeded urgings of his companions that unintentional error bears no guilt—*haut est nocens quicumque non sponte est nocens*—and that reason should therefore mitigate such suffering.[47] Jocasta tries to reason thus with the self-blinded king in *Oedipus*, just as Antigone does with him in the fragment *Phoenissae*.[48] In *Hercules Oetaeus*, Hyllus is unable to persuade Deianira that she is not culpable for the destruction of Hercules; Deianira commits suicide, as many of the others in such situations would like to do. In *Hippolytus*, Theseus cannot imagine a punishment gruesome enough to fit what he feels is his crime in slaying his innocent son; he indulges in the conventional frenzied prayer that all the torments of the hell of classical mythology will be his. Iole in *Hercules Oetaeus* suffers intensely from the feeling that her beauty indirectly

[47] *Hercules Oetaeus*, l. 886.

[48] It is curious to see how the distinction between fatal error and responsible guilt, which is brought out by Seneca in many of his plays, seems to be overlooked, not only by his Elizabethan interpreters, but even by the Senecan Chorus. Alexander Nevile, for example, in the preface to his translation of *Oedipus*, cites the protagonist as "a dreadfull Example of Gods horrible vengeaunce for sinne" profitable for the vice-ridden age in England (*Seneca His Tenne Tragedies*, I, 190). In the play itself, the moral drawn by the Chorus after the recognition scene is the characteristic but inappropriate one of "stay with the middle course and avoid destruction"—including an allusion to Icarus (*Oedipus*, ll. 892 ff.).

caused the destruction of her family and country. But perhaps the best example of all is the guilt-suffering of Hercules in *Hercules Furens*, after he learns that he has slaughtered his wife and children. Neither Amphitryon nor Theseus can at first persuade him that his insanity has precluded guilt. Hercules rages against himself, beseeching Jove for all kinds of torture, asking for a hell below the known hell, threatening to kill himself. His companions refuse to return his weapons to him lest he now commit the voluntary crime of suicide. Hercules, however, regains his weapons by threat, and is checked from self-slaughter only by his stepfather Amphitryon's assertion that he too will die by his own hand if Hercules should do so. This relenting of Hercules, together with the determination to live on with the burden of his tragic past, constitutes the greatest of all his labors. It represents the Stoic ideal of fortitude summed up by Antigone in *Phoenissae*:

> . . . non est, ut putas, virtus, pater
> timere vitam, sed malis ingentibus
> obstare nec se vertere ac retro dare.   (190-192)

There are other kinds of suffering, to be sure, in the plays of Seneca. The sorrow of parents for the death of children takes memorable form in the figures of Andromache and Hecuba in *Troades*, of Alcmena in *Hercules Oetaeus*, and of Thyestes in the play of that name. *Troades* lays stress, too, upon the sorrows of captivity. But all in all, it is the mark of Senecan tragedy to emphasize the pre-catastrophic torment of overwhelming passion and the post-catastrophic agony of guilt-feeling where there has been no voluntary crime.

Whatever the motivation for psychological suffering in Seneca, the form of its expression is disturbingly uniform: it is difficult indeed to distinguish the speeches of Medea from those of Deianira, or to differentiate the way that Deianira at a later time invokes the sufferings of a classical hell from the way of Theseus in *Hippolytus*. So conventional are the emotional posturings of these characters that when an Elizabethan translator of Seneca such as Jasper Heywood came to "round out" the play of *Thyestes* by the addition of some final outburst by the distraught father who has unknowingly banqueted on his children, all that was necessary was to have Thyestes run through the catalogue of the tortures of the classical underworld like other Senecan sufferers.[49] With the single exception of the dying Hercules in *Hercules Oetaeus*, there is no way to distinguish Senecan characters in their expression of suffering. As A. Kent Hieatt has remarked, one of the causes of this wooden uniformity is that "there is no outer limit to any emotion which is felt by Senecan characters," no element of precision in the imagery that will particularize and illuminate the motive or significance of the suffering. The similes Seneca employs, he continues, give an *affective* force to what is being said, but little else—the persistent use of general hyperbole represents a goal and an achievement of "consistent and absolute sensationalism."[50] The Senecan expression of suffering, in other words, ignores the dramatic function of using suffering as a revelation of meaning in character and action.

The formal character of the set speech typifying Senecan suffering extends as well to the basic pattern of the Senecan play, which tends to be, as Lucas puts it, "an alternation of melancholy monologues and epigrammatic duologues with musical interludes by the chorus between the now established five acts."[51] The duologues are rendered by ingenious stichomythia, more often than not in situations that pit the passionate urges of the protagonist against the rational counsel of a companion or associate. And the chorus characteristically interprets the action and points the Senecan morals. The interplay

[49] *Seneca His Tenne Tragedies*, I, 93-95.

[50] "Medieval Symbolism and the Dramatic Imagery of the English Renaissance," unpublished Ph.D. dissertation (Columbia University, 1954), pp. 137-138.

[51] *Seneca and Elizabethan Tragedy*, p. 56.

of the three—monologue or "passion," stichomythic debate, and choral comment—provides the structure for the Senecan conflict of good and evil. In the Stoic scheme of things, the unruly emotions are the sources of danger and destruction; the Senecan plays provide extreme illustrations of what horrible things happen when jealousy, revenge, and lust dominate a human being. The evil Seneca portrays is further complicated by the inimical character of fate, and the woe that is inherent in high places. The passions of his protagonists and the plots of his plays represent the expression of evil in the world. The voices of rational admonition, the characteristic instructions to keep to the moderate and humble path and to face affliction without flinching, are represented in the actors who try to calm the protagonist, and in the interpretations of the chorus; these counterforces raise the ethical issues and proclaim the Stoic solutions.

It should be obvious that such a formal structure would have its appeal to the Elizabethan who looked upon tragedy as the example of mutability and of retribution for vicious living. Thomas Newton, in his dedicatory preface to the 1581 translations of the Senecan plays, doubted "whether there bee any amonge all the Catalogue of Heathen wryters, that with more grauity of Philosophicall sentences, more waightynes of sappy words, or greater authority of soũd matter beateth down sinne, loose lyfe, dissolute dealinge, and unbrydled sensuality: or that more sensibly, pithily, and bytingly layeth doune the guedon of filthy lust, cloaked dissimulation and odius treachery: which is the dryft, whereunto he leueleth the whole yssue of ech one of his Tragedies."[52] Whether or not "the whole yssue" of Senecan tragedy lay in the direction indicated by Newton, the Elizabethans tended to think that it did, and their tendency was confirmed in practice when writers of the universities and the Inns of Court adapted the Senecan tragic

[52] *ed. cit.*, I, 5.

form to the language and the moral prepossessions of the English.

The most notable thing about early English classical tragedy, insofar as the treatment of suffering and evil is concerned, is its combination of Senecan formality with Elizabethan morality. In the highly developed rhetorical fits of passionate utterance by Seneca's suffering characters, with all their superabundance of classical allusion and elaborate simile, the Elizabethan dramatist found a sanction and a model for the extended verbal expression of human suffering upon the stage; in language as well as in plot, the passions were unleashed. But in "clyming to the height of *Seneca* his style," as Sidney phrased it,[53] the tragedian did not neglect the "notable moralitie" of his ancient model: in the Stoic exhortations of rational self-control and contempt for Fortune's fickleness he found the analogues for the ascetic urgings of Christianity; in the Senecan stress on the inevitable adversities of the great and on the fragile condition of human contentment, he found the parallel to the *De Casibus* theme of mutability. These affinities of moral outlook were given whole-hearted development, but their dramatic shaping was conducted from the standpoint of characteristic Elizabethan moral concerns and definitions of evil.

Thomas Legge's *Richardus Tertius* (acted at Cambridge in March 1579/1580), though by no means the earliest "Senecan" play by an Englishman, is one of the closest to the Senecan model, for it is written in Latin verse which often echoes, line for line, some of the more notable set pieces in the Senecan canon.[54] At the same time, it shows the English habit of

---

[53] *An Apologie for Poetrie, ed. cit.*, p. 197.

[54] Elizabeth's anxiety over the loss of her son to Richard, for example, is based on Andromache's lament over Astyanax in *Troades*, and Shaw's remorse for his part in the conspiracy is expressed in the same terms as that of Oedipus in the *Phoenissae*. A full list of such parallels and borrowings will be found in the analysis of the play by George B. Churchill, *Richard the Third up to Shakespeare*, Palaestra, x (Berlin, 1900), pp. 280-375.

borrowing the Senecan conventions for a native theme, the tyrannical rise and fall of Richard of Gloucester, which had been fully exploited earlier in the *Mirror for Magistrates* tragedies. The play (or plays—there are three full sections of five acts each) is filled with monologues of misery, with lurid and seemingly interminable messengers' reports, with sticho-mythic debates and sententious maxims, and with classical allusions and similes often bordering on absurdity. It may be doubtful whether the Elizabethans chafed at figures from the Christian era of history addressing rhetorical prayers to a god consistently invoked as the hurler of lightning and thunder-bolts, but the incongruity does become inescapable when the Archbishop himself renders a prayer to the "Rector potens Olimpi." And just as in Seneca, there is no attempt to distin-guish characters by the manner of their speech; young Prince Edward speaks with as great a catalogue of learned allusion and imagery as the most sophisticated of his elders. So strong is the imitative character of Legge's play that it even includes speeches that describe in detail action immediately observable to the audience, such as this comment by Hastings on Glou-cester's entrance:

> sed ecce retro dux venit dubia gradu
> quassans caput, torvo supercilio furit
> duro labellum dente comprimit ferox
> et pectore irato tegit dirum malum.[55]

Despite the violent nature of the happenings involved in this episode of English history, none of the physical suffering is staged. But there are exhibitions of grief in great abundance.

[55] Robert Joseph Lordi, "Thomas Legge's *Richardus Tertius*: A Critical Edition with a Translation," unpublished Ph.D. dissertation (University of Illinois, 1958), p. 187. Lordi's translation (p. 188) is as follows: "But behold, the Duke returns with a hesitating step. Shaking his head, he rages with a knitted brow. Savagely he presses his lip with a harsh tooth and he hides dire evil in his angered heart." A more extreme example of this kind of speech is Howard's description of the Queen's sorrow at the parting with her son (p. 139).

Many stress the mutability theme, but even more accent the anxiety, fear, and remorse attendant upon evil careers of ambition. Emphasis on this evil *in its political context* establishes the play, for all its Senecanisms, as a characteristically Tudor "tragedy." The protagonist's villainy is defined by his political crimes, and his fall comes not from an inimical Senecan fate, but as just retribution for his wickedness. Richmond's oration to his soldiers leaves no doubt of that. In the Elizabethan transposition of Senecan tragedy to the English academic stage, political evil above all else emerges as the characteristic cause of suffering and destruction.

This statement holds true for three of the four extant classical tragedies in English produced at the Inns of Court in the latter part of the sixteenth century: *Gorboduc* (1561/1562), *Jocasta* (1566), *Gismond of Salerne* (1567/1568), and *The Misfortunes of Arthur* (1588). All but *Gismond* deal with calamities of state. Willard Farnham has demonstrated clearly how the Senecan techniques in these three plays have been put to the service of characteristic Tudor political concerns and a moral philosophy that insists on individual responsibility and retributive suffering for evil acts.[56] In *Gorboduc* the chain of bloody (but off stage) events is set off by the king's authoritative action against good counsel; in the wake of this wrong decision follow murderous ambition, flattery, disloyalty, rebellion, and a gloomy prospect of continuing civil disruption. Eubulus, the good counselor, in summing up the chaotic situation at the end of the play, points the unequivocal moral:

> Hereto it commes when kinges will not consent
> To graue aduise, but followe wilfull will.[57]

The Misfortunes of Arthur, based, like *Gorboduc*, on the legendary history of Britain, develops such familiar themes as mutability, the sorrows of kingship, the folly of aspiration,

[56] *Medieval Heritage*, pp. 352-363.
[57] *Early English Classical Tragedies*, pp. 62-63.

and the self-perpetuating nature of revenge, but accentuates most of all the horrors of civil war and rebellion. The evil is political, the suffering is of the kingdom as much as of individuals, and results from personal and responsible sins which have cried out for retribution. Such is the judgment of Arthur as he looks upon the corpse of Mordred:

> I see (alas) I see (hide, hide againe:
> O spare mine eye) a witnesse of my crimes:
> A fearefull vision of my former guilte.
>
> .   .   .   .
>
> Alas, how happie should we both haue been,
> If no ambitious thought had vext thy head.
> Nor thou thus striu'de to reaue thy Fathers rule . . .[58]

Even *Jocasta*, which is a line-by-line translation of Dolce's Italian play based on a Latin version of Euripides' *Phoenissae*, emphasizes the Elizabethan sense of morality by presenting before each act emblematic dumb shows which portray the dire effects of ambition, revenge, and Fortune, by including in the printed version of the play marginal glosses which interpret Oedipus' suffering and fall as "A mirrour for Magistrates,"[59] and by the addition of an original epilogue condemning the "high-aspiring minde."[60]

The retributive urgency which pervades these plays of political destruction is felt as well in the more personal tragedy of *Gismond of Salerne*. This transforms Boccaccio's *Decameron* story of the young widow whose secret love meets with violent revenge at the hands of her possessive father into a dramatic object lesson in the destructive effects of lust.[61] The malevolent Cupid who introduces the play as a tragic spectacle of his domination, the fury Megæra who inspires Gismond's father to revenge, and the moralizing Chorus all insist that

---

[58] *ibid.*, p. 287.
[59] *ibid.*, p. 157.   [60] *ibid.*, p. 158.
[61] See Farnham, *Medieval Heritage*, pp. 360-362.

fickleness and lust have brought suffering and death to the young lovers.

Aside from the mechanical insistence on the moral evil involved in the story, *Gismond* displays a typically Senecan elaboration of suffering and grief. The entire first act is devoted to the lament of Gismond for her dead husband; the mutability theme is accentuated heavily, and the lament is developed by the characteristic Senecan situation of a stichomythic debate between the impassioned sufferer and the rational confidante attempting to calm her. Most of the fourth act is given over to Tancred's furious wrath after his discovery of the lovers. Like any raving figure out of Seneca, he calls on Jove to send down fire from heaven to end his cruel torments, then beseeches the earth and the underworld to receive him; he prays that the gods will destroy both the lovers and himself in one holocaust, but finally fixes on the plan of killing his daughter's lover and sending his heart to Gismond. The lover's execution is narrated by a messenger; its sensationalism is eclipsed by the scene in which Gismond weeps over her lover's heart, sent to her in a cup, and poisons herself. Her speech follows Boccaccio's original closely, but her death has an effect not included in the *Decameron*: it spurs Tancred to a very rhetorical resolution to slay himself.[62]

Gismond's death is the only one to take place on stage in all of the academic tragedies under discussion. Physical violence and destruction are more typically rendered indirectly by lurid report, a practice stemming from imitation of the general Senecan method. It should be obvious that the representation of psychological suffering is also generally imitative

[62] Robert Wilmot's revision of this play, printed in 1591 under the title *Tancred and Gismund*, is notable for its tailoring to fit the tastes newly formed by developments on the popular stage: it is redone in blank verse, accentuates the revenge theme, portrays the execution of Palurine in dumb show, and elaborates wildly on the last act, in which Tancred puts out his eyes in self-punishment and commits suicide on stage.

of Seneca. There are some exceptions in *Gorboduc*, however, which may be the result of an attempt to differentiate the expression of mental anguish to fit the character involved. The king, for example, consistently reacts to tragic news with the wish for his own death, although it is not quite clear whether this reaction represents merely escapism or a sense of personal expiation for the crimes of others. In any case, in view of what his counselors tell him, it is certainly intended as an index of the king's weakness and lack of courageous resilience or initiative. Gorboduc's style of suffering bears some relation to the death-wish of Seneca's remorseful characters, but with the crucial distinction that he shows no sense of personal guilt. If anything, his suffering is closer to the suffering of despair in the morality tradition, albeit a completely secularized version. Porrex, when brought to account before the court for his fratricide, asserts in calm and dispassionate terms that he is deeply grieved inwardly to have done the crime, and that he has no other desire but to see justice enacted upon himself. His grief and remorse remain surprisingly unhistrionic without losing the quality of sincerity—and there is little precedent in Seneca for such expression. Marcella, the maid who reports the slaying of Porrex by Videna, shares with Gorboduc and the Queen (whose one long speech of sorrow and revenge is thoroughly Senecan) the burden of "passionate" expression of grief. Her elegiac lament includes a coloring of romance which is completely foreign to the Senecan plays, and which represents a poetic sophistication of the *De Casibus* theme:

> Ah noble prince, how oft haue I behelde
> Thee mounted on thy fierce and traumpling stede,
> Shining in armour bright before the tilt,
> And with thy mistresse sleue tied on thy helme,
> And charge thy staffe to please thy ladies eye,
> That bowed the head peece of thy frendly foe?

How oft in armes on horse to bend the mace?
How oft in armes on foote to breake the sworde,
Which neuer now these eyes may see againe.[63]

Although this passage retains the quality of the set piece its sentiment would not fit just any "Senecan messenger" at all; it is somehow appropriate to a Queen's maid.

Despite such important departures from the conventions of Senecan drama, early English classical tragedy remains heavily indebted to its Latin prototype in the representation of suffering and evil. Senecan precedent helped immeasurably to establish the destructive passions generated by ambition, revenge, and wicked love as the focal points of the vision of evil in the academic plays. Hence, it is no surprise, in the ensuing generation, to find the same passions dominating the tragic drama of the popular stage as well. The products of the academic stage, in holding relatively fast to the patterns of Senecan expression, also strengthened the precedent for the elaborate and lengthy speech of human tribulation. Under the aegis of Seneca, the language of suffering took the stage in earnest. But more than language was needed to make human suffering both tragic and truly dramatic, more than "*Seneca let blood line by line and page by page*," as Nashe had phrased it.[64] The completion of the task was the work of the popular dramatists, the writers for the public theaters that came to prominence in the last decades of the sixteenth century, writers like Thomas Kyd, Christopher Marlowe, and William Shakespeare.

V. *THE SPANISH TRAGEDY*

Marlowe's *Tamburlaine* and *The Spanish Tragedy* of Thomas Kyd have long been considered the major heralds of

[63] *Early English Classical Tragedies*, p. 49. The *De Casibus* tone is not surprising, since the act in which this speech appears has been assigned to Sackville, the contributor to the *Mirror for Magistrates*.

[64] Preface to Greene's *Menaphon*, *The Works of Thomas Nashe*, ed. Ronald B. McKerrow, corrected reprint ed. F. P. Wilson (Oxford, 1958), III, 316.

serious drama on the popular Elizabethan stage. These plays are generally considered to have appeared about simultaneously, but scholars have argued for dating *The Spanish Tragedy* as early as 1582, which would place it ahead of Marlowe's earliest dramatic work and therefore warrant a consideration of Kyd as one of Marlowe's predecessors.[65] In any case, Kyd's impact on the Elizabethan theater was certainly felt in the earliest years of Marlowe's dramatic career, and must be regarded as a major element in the development of English tragedy.

It is almost an understatement to say that with *The Spanish Tragedy* suffering takes the center of the stage, whether it be physical, in the hangings and stabbings of murderers and suicides, or mental, in the lamentations and actions of Hieronimo, Bel-Imperia, the Portuguese Viceroy, Isabella, and the ghost of Andrea. Death and revenge for death are the focal themes of the play, and Kyd's genius embodies them in theatrically sensational situations which were to provide a favorite pattern for future Elizabethan tragedy. The "Chorus" itself operates as a concrete symbol of the focal themes, made up as it is of the ghost of Andrea and the allegorical figure of Revenge. They take no part in the action of the play, yet they represent in visual terms what all the action is about. And it is certainly above all in visual terms that Kyd chooses to represent the suffering and death of his characters.

Compared with earlier English plays, *The Spanish Tragedy* is remarkable for the quantity and variety of its staged physical violence: Horatio is hung in an arbor and stabbed to death, Serberine is shot down, Pedringano hanged, Isabella runs lunatic and stabs herself; Balthazar stabs Lorenzo in the play-within-the-play, to be stabbed in turn by Bel-Imperia before she slays herself; Hieronimo stabs the Duke and himself after

---

[65] See especially T. W. Baldwin, *On the Literary Genetics of Shakespere's Plays 1592-1594* (Urbana, 1959), pp. 177-199; and Philip Edwards' edition of *The Spanish Tragedy* (London, 1959), pp. xxi-xxvii.

biting out his own tongue, and the play ends with at least half-a-dozen corpses littering the stage. But these are only the more obvious sensational effects of the play, effects which could be multiplied as easily as they could be imitated. More important is the mode in which Kyd presents them, a mode which is peculiarly dramatic in its use of conventions and ironies.

As an initial illustration of this mode, let us consider the first scene which represents human suffering directly rather than by report, the scene in the first act which shows the effect of the Spanish-Portuguese war on the Viceroy of Portugal.[66] The Viceroy has a speech lamenting his fall from fortune, a speech which has obvious affiliations both with the Senecan theme of the mutability of fortune and with the *De Casibus* tradition of literary tragedy. But Kyd sets the theme into action, and turns the familiar allusion into concrete stage business:

> But wherefore sit I in a Regall throne,
> This better fits a wretches endles moane.
> Yet this is higher then my fortuues reach,
> And therefore better then my state deserues.
>   Falles to the ground.
> I, I, this earth, Image of mellancholly,
> Seeks him whome fates adiudge to miserie:
> Heere let me lye, now am I at the lowest.
> *Qvi iacet in terra non habet vnde cadat,*
> *In me consumpsit vires fortuna nocendo,*
> *Nil superest vt iam possit obesse magis.*   (314-324)

The Viceroy has thrown himself from his throne to a step or some lower seat, and then finally to the ground. The formal, emblematic aspect of his action is given additional emphasis by the Latin tercet, and by the succeeding action. He removes his crown and offers it up to "Fortune," who is not present

---

[66] *The Spanish Tragedie* (1592), MSR (Oxford, 1948 [1949]), ll. 306 ff. Subsequent references to this edition will appear in my text.

physically but only in the Viceroy's imagination; he pictures her as blind, deaf, and "wilfull mad" in her lack of pity for her victims. The total effect is hardly one of psychological realism, but it nevertheless succeeds in conveying the quality and significance of this suffering through representation of the familiar literary conventions of *De Casibus* tragedy in visual dramatic terms.

The *De Casibus* convention of the fall from Fortune's wheel is employed ironically in what is probably the most memorable scene in the play, the slaying of Horatio in the garden. The murderers, in swift attack, hang Horatio in the arbor and stab him to death; Lorenzo adds an ironic caption to the picture of the dangling corpse:

> Although his life were still ambituous proud,
> Yet is he at the highest now he is dead.   (931-932)

But the previous part of the murder scene reflects an even subtler employment of literary conventions adapted to the purposes of dramatic irony. Horatio and Bel-Imperia conduct their love dialogue under the metaphor of battle, a common enough convention of Elizabethan love poetry; but the terms of battle and death, which have for them only pleasant and witty connotations, have for the audience a sinister and ironic impact, since the forces which plot the evil destruction of Horatio are lurking behind the scenes while the love-talk goes on.[67] In the bower, Horatio and Bel-Imperia match their word play with physical endearments, which reach a climax in the following exchange:

> *Bel.* O let me goe, for in my troubled eyes,
> Now maist thou read that life in passion dies.
> *Hor.* O stay a while and I will dye with thee,
> So shalt thou yeeld, and yet haue conquerd me.
>   (913-916)

[67] Moody E. Prior has discussed this ironic use of the love-war imagery in *The Language of Tragedy* (New York, 1947), pp. 52-53.

The sexual pun on death is swiftly and suddenly followed by the real death which strikes Horatio at this point, and the imagery of love and war finds its dramatic fusion and culmination in the spectacle of Horatio strung in the arbor, receiving the stabs which Lorenzo glosses: "I thus, and thus, these are the fruits of loue" (925). The poetic convention has once again been transmuted into dramatic and theatrical terms, the stage-picture providing a visual emblem of the ironic significance of the imagery: the metaphor of death yields to the actuality.

The death of Horatio brings into prominence the suffering of his father Hieronimo, who now becomes the central figure of the play. His anguish begins in the darkness of the garden, and does not end till his own suicide in the last lines of the play. Howard Baker has pointed out the general devices by which Kyd gives articulate poetic expression to Hieronimo's sorrow: the use of image and metaphor to convey a precise emotional state; the use of concretely represented "images"—stage images rather than verbal ones—to reflect Hieronimo's grief; and the linking of the Virgilian descent into hell, already used by Sackville in his *Induction* to the *Mirror for Magistrates*, with the old man's suffering.[68] The last of these might be considered as an extension of the first, the use of poetic image or metaphor; the second we may call the use of dramatic image. The interesting thing about Kyd's dramaturgy is that he continually tries to convert the poetic into the dramatic image, making the metaphor actual. This was his method with the Viceroy's fall from fortune and with Horatio's murder; it continues to be his method with the suffering of Hieronimo.

A characteristic illustration is the following speech, uttered by Hieronimo before he learns the identity of his son's killers:

[68] *Induction to Tragedy*, pp. 98-105.

Yet still tormented is my tortured soule,
With broken sighes and restles passions,
That winged mount, and houering in the aire,
Beat at the windowes of the brightest heauens,
Solliciting for iustice and reuenge:
But they are plac't in those imperiall heights,
Where countermurde with walles of diamond,
I finde the place impregnable, and they
Resist my woes, and giue my words no way.

(1588-1596)

Here is the poetic articulation of suffering with no outlet, and of frustrated desire for justice, the two points which plot precisely the curve of Hieronimo's emotion. In the context of this scene the image is purely poetic, but in the larger context of the play's developing action it becomes dramatic when, some scenes later, Hieronimo actually does sue for justice and revenge, attempting to gain the hearing of the King. But the King is "countermurde with walles of diamond"—in this case Lorenzo, who succeeds in keeping Hieronimo away from the ruler, thus driving him to deep distraction.

Kyd exploits the dramatic or stage image to reflect Hieronimo's grief in the scene, late in the third act, where Hieronimo as Marshall is called upon for judgment in the cases of some poor pleaders who seek justice of the King. One of the suitors is a "double" of Hieronimo, that is, he is an old man supplicating for his murdered son. The obvious analogy is more than enough to resurrect Hieronimo's own sorrow:

Heere, take my hand-kercher and wipe thine eies,
Whiles wretched I, in thy mishaps may see,
The liuely portraict of my dying selfe.

(2068-2070)

But the handkerchief he draws out is the one he had dipped in Horatio's blood as a pledge of revenge, and the sight of it prompts him to plunge deeper into his own motive and cue for passion. It is at this point that he indulges in the fantasy of a passage to hell to further his revenge, asking the old man to be his Orpheus:

> Though on this earth iustice will not be found:
> Ile downe to hell and in this passion,
> Knock at the dismall gates of *Plutos* Court,
> Getting by force as once *Alcides* did,
> A troupe of furies and tormenting hagges,
> To torture *Don Lorenzo* and the rest.[69]
>
> (2094-2099)

Kyd capitalizes on this moment of distraction, making Hieronimo tear the papers of the suitors, thinking at the time of how he shall rend the limbs of his enemies: again, a kind of translation of metaphor into action. Hieronimo rushes out for a moment, and returns, thinking first that the old man is Horatio, and then a fury, finally seeing the reflection that he saw at the start of the scene:

> Thou art the liuely image of my griefe,
> Within thy face, my sorrowes I may see.
>
> (2154-2155)

Hieronimo's thoughts have come full circle after his momentary fit of illusion and distraction; he regains his sanity with the recognition of the old man's identity and analogous significance.

Such treatment of Hieronimo's suffering and desire for revenge does not further the plot in any way, nor does it tell us anything new about the character of Hieronimo; but it

[69] Professor Prior has shown that from the moment of discovering Horatio's death, Hieronimo's speech is characterized by images of darkness, night, and the classical underworld. These dark, infernal images stop with his discovery of an ally in Bel-Imperia. *Language of Tragedy*, pp. 53-57.

does provide an intense realization of that suffering and desire in terms of visual dramatic action which, sensational as it may be, is effective in prompting both sympathy and terror at Hieronimo's plight.

Hieronimo's suffering finds still another analogue in the grief of his wife Isabella, whose reactions to the loss of Horatio differ from his in degree rather than in kind. Just after Hieronimo learns without doubt the identity of the murderers, Kyd juxtaposes two scenes which show the pathetic effects of the murder on two innocent victims, Isabella and Bel-Imperia, thereby gaining emotional support for the motive of justice by revenge. Isabella runs lunatic and has an illusory vision of Horatio in heaven dancing with the fiery Cherubins; Bel-Imperia is shown in prison, lamenting over her unmerited maltreatment. Isabella appears only once more, in the fourth act, where she wreaks revenge on the inanimate objects she insanely holds responsible for Horatio's destruction, the tree on which he was hung and the garden in which he was killed. This done, she stabs herself. Immediately following this scene Hieronimo takes his own revenge by killing the human agents responsible for the deed, and he too ends in suicide. The garden of evil has been cut down, first literally, and then figuratively, with the destruction of all the human agents of evil and death in the play.

Although the great scenes of suffering and death in *The Spanish Tragedy* are linked by the unity of analogy, it is true that Kyd also introduced some entirely gratuitous bits of pain and cruelty. The most striking case in point is the entirely unmotivated and confusing action at the end of the catastrophe, in which Hieronimo bites out his tongue rather than tell the King and Duke what he has apparently just disclosed—the nature of his revenge scheme and the accomplices involved. This, together with the assassination of the Duke, are incidents which bear no logical or analogical relation to anything that has gone before. Nevertheless, such gratuitous suffering is the exception rather than the rule.[70]

Kyd's tragedy, although it deals out death to all the guilty characters, focuses primarily on the suffering of innocents: Hieronimo, Bel-Imperia, and Isabella. That they are innocent in fact is the judgment we are given in the play itself; the final Chorus looks forward to the heavenly reward of each of them, as well as of Horatio, just as it portends classical infernal punishments for the guilty.[71] This final statement of poetic justice also indicates a relationship of primary importance to the conception of evil and the cause of suffering in the play: the innocents suffer, not because of any tragic destiny or any element of hostility in the universe, but because of the deliberate crimes of villainous characters; the guilty suffer because their injustice in the long run brings about their destruction. The responsibility for evil, then, resides in the human agent. When the human agent chooses to act in an evil way, he contributes not only to the suffering of his victims, but also to his own inevitable destruction. The "universe" of the play remains in the last analysis one that is ultimately ordered, patterned, and just. The order, the pattern, and the justice are defined by the norm of retribution which is the familiar mark of the Elizabethan conception of tragedy.

[70] The wholesale slaughter and destruction that mark *Solyman and Perseda* (at least eighteen people, representing the bulk of the cast, are killed on stage) is of an entirely gratuitous and mechanical nature; deaths occur at the slightest provocation and without any preparation. The play has been attributed to Kyd on the slightest of hints, and many scholars, such as T. W. Baldwin, deny Kyd's authorship. The poetic style is not really like that of *The Spanish Tragedy* at all, nor is there discernible anything like the dramatic technique of converting metaphor into action that marks the earlier play.

[71] The judgment given in the play itself defends Hieronimo's revenge, a fact which Fredson Bowers overlooks in his discussion of the play, which claims that the Elizabethan audience would immediately lose sympathy with Hieronimo once he starts employing the tactics of guile and deception: *Elizabethan Revenge Tragedy: 1587-1642* (Princeton, 1940), pp. 65-85.

ह∾

When Christopher Marlowe left Cambridge in 1587 to take up a new way of life in the theater-world of London, the medieval mystery-cycles had been banned for less than a decade, the morality tradition had entered its last stage of vitality before its practical dissolution in the 1590's, new editions of the *Mirror for Magistrates* were still being published to meet the enduring Elizabethan taste for this kind of literary tragedy, the spirit of Seneca had been given rhetorical but passionate voice in English blank verse on the academic stage, and (perhaps) the dramatic genius of Kyd had already exploded into popular favor in the public theaters. The materials for English tragedy were indeed spread out in great abundance and diversity: possibilities and precedents for staging the tragic elements of suffering and evil were manifold. What Marlowe did with these resources will be considered in the following chapters.

CHAPTER II · LOVE
AND VIOLENCE: SUFFERING IN *DIDO*
AND *TAMBURLAINE*

Ride golden loue in chariots richly builded.
Vnlesse I erre, full many shalt thou burne,
And giue wounds infinite at euery turne.

—Marlowe's translation
of Ovid, ELEGIES I.2

What bloudie sturres doth glut of honor breede?

—Epilogue to JOCASTA

CHAPTER II · LOVE
AND VIOLENCE: SUFFERING IN *DIDO*
AND *TAMBURLAINE*

F ew forces are more elemental in the make-up of man than love and violence, few divinities of the ancients more familiar than Venus and Mars. And in the reactions to these forces in human experience, few men have been able to avoid suffering. Love and violence, together with the suffering they inevitably entail, have always provided fruitful themes for tragedy; it is no wonder that they form the central core of the earliest tragic dramas of Christopher Marlowe, translator of both Ovid and Lucan. In *The Tragedie of Dido Queene of Carthage* Marlowe presented the suffering victims of love, in *Tamburlaine the Great* the victims of martial violence. The representation of human suffering in these plays is so markedly simple and clear-cut that it can be reduced to these root principles without destroying its thematic significance. In both cases the mode in which Marlowe represents suffering is particularly effective in dramatic characterization. Even more important, Marlowe has imbued his scenes of suffering with an unusually strong sense of irony; his dramaturgy insists on the ironic implications of destruction or sorrow, hidden to the characters but revealed to the audience, and it exploits the ironic contradictions and ambivalences in human behavior motivated by love or by violence.

I. *DIDO QUEEN OF CARTHAGE*

The concern for adapting the representation of suffering to the purposes of dramatic characterization is notable even in what may well be the earliest of Marlowe's plays, *The Tragedie of Dido Queene of Carthage.*[1] The sorrows of Aeneas

[1] There is general critical agreement that *Dido*, despite the title-page reference to both Marlowe and Nashe, is predominantly, if not totally, the

and Dido, already set forth by Virgil in Books I, II, and IV of the *Aeneid*, undergo a degree of variation in Marlowe's play which adds considerably to their specifically dramatic effectiveness. A striking instance is the development of the situation in which Aeneas weeps when he sees the war of Troy depicted

---

work of Marlowe. See E. K. Chambers, *The Elizabethan Stage* (Oxford, 1923), III, 426; C. F. Tucker Brooke's ed. of *The Works of Christopher Marlowe* (Oxford, 1910), pp. 388-389; John Bakeless, *The Tragicall History of Christopher Marlowe* (Cambridge, Mass., 1942), II, 41-46; F. S. Boas, *Christopher Marlowe*, rev. ed. (Oxford, 1953), p. 50. The problem of date, however, is more uncertain; as Chambers notes, the play has affinities both to early and to late work by Marlowe and therefore cannot be dated by internal evidence (III, 426). General opinion leans heavily toward an early date, basing this judgment on the verse style, which most resembles that of *Tamburlaine*, on the numerous lines which seem to have been refashioned to fit other plays, and on the academic nature of the subject and source. See e.g., Brooke's ed. of *Works*, pp. 387-388, and his *The Life of Marlowe and The Tragedy of Dido Queen of Carthage* (London, 1930), pp. 115-117; Bakeless, II, 54-58; T. W. Baldwin, *On the Literary Genetics of Shakespeare's Plays 1592-1594* (Urbana, 1959), pp. 163-165. The major spokesman for a later date is T. M. Pearce, who argues for a date in Marlowe's mid-career about 1591, on the grounds that the play displays an experienced knowledge of stagecraft, and appears to have been written with conscious attention to details of production in a private playhouse, as is evidenced by many lines indicating particular stage properties, setting, costume, and action: "Evidence for Dating Marlowe's *Tragedy of Dido*," *Studies in the English Renaissance Drama*, ed. Josephine W. Bennett *et al.* (New York, 1959), pp. 231-247. Bakeless asserts that such characteristics could well have been the product of a later revision, and sides with Brooke in the conjecture that the play as we have it is a revision of the earliest of Marlowe's plays. *Dido* is indeed unique among Marlowe's plays in that it was performed by a boys' acting company and exhibits the staging effects characteristic of private productions. Chambers discusses these in his chapter on the staging of court plays (III, 35-36). Moreover, the nature of the subject matter and general presentation is also characteristic of either academic or court performances; with the exception of a *Dido and Aeneas* in the Admiral's Company repertory in 1598, all recorded Dido plays in sixteenth-century England were so designed. I would therefore disagree with Bakeless in attributing the details noticed by Pearce to later revision, and conjecture that the play was originally conceived with an eye to private production. On the other hand, I see no necessity for assigning such a composition to Marlowe's later career; for the differences between *Dido* and *Tamburlaine* in staging technique can be attributed to the differences between private productions by child actors and public productions by adult companies rather than to the differences between inexperience and maturity.

at Juno's temple.[2] Virgil records his sorrow, his amazement, his tears; Marlowe, in the first scene of the second act, adds some characteristic features. When Achates asks Aeneas why he stands suddenly in amazement, the hero answers first with a hyperbolic classical allusion:

> O my *Achates*, Theban *Niobe*,
> Who for her sonnes death wept out life and breath,
> And drie with griefe was turnd into a stone,
> Had not such passions in her head as I.[3]

The allusion is chosen with singular appropriateness: not only does it reinforce the visual picture of Aeneas standing in frozen amazement and express the quality of his mental anguish, but it has also been prompted by another feature of Marlowe's stage-picture at this point: the stone statue of Priam which is used in the play instead of Virgil's series of paintings. The material stone image, Aeneas' static posture, and the verbal figure that expresses his grief are functionally united in giving dramatic expression to stunned sorrow. The situation is further developed without any precedent in Virgil: the sorrow that has been given life by the stone figure now seeks to give life to stone. Aeneas' grief carries with it the illusion that the statue of Priam is actually alive and that Troy has not been overcome. The pitiful irony of this illusion is reinforced by the fact that his companions do not share it, but remind him of the objective facts:

> *Ach.* Thy mind *Æneas* that would haue it so
> Deludes thy eye sight, *Priamus* is dead.
> *Æn.* Ah *Troy* is sackt, and *Priamus* is dead,
> And why should poore *Æneas* be aliue?   (B2ᵛ)

An additional pathetic touch is added by Marlowe's bringing into the dialogue the naïve comment of Aeneas' small son:

---

[2] *Aeneid*, I, 456-496. Line references are to the LCL ed.
[3] *The Tragedie of Dido Queene of Carthage*, TFT (Oxford, 1914), B2. Subsequent references to this edition will appear in my text.

> *Asca.* Sweete father leaue to weepe, this is not he:
> For were it *Priam* he would smile on me.   (B2ᵛ)

The intensity of Aeneas' suffering has been developed through action, imagery, and dramatic irony, while at the same time the deepest loyalties of "pious Aeneas" have been revealed.

Marlowe continues to reinforce the impression of those loyalties in the following scenes where Aeneas meets Dido and is entertained at her feast. The first words of Aeneas to Dido, in response to her asking who he is, are not to be found in Virgil:

> Sometime I was a Troian mightie Queene:
> But *Troy* is not, what shall I say I am?   (B3)

In the banquet scene, Marlowe—again without precedent in Virgil—has pictured Aeneas as sad and silent, a man who responds to Dido's assurance that he cannot be miserable, since she is able to make him "blest," with the cry, "O *Priamus*, O *Troy*, oh *Hecuba!*" (B3ᵛ) Aeneas' suffering, then, reveals his deepest concerns and ties, and makes it all the more inevitable that he should later be able to break the personal tie of love for Dido, in response to his higher duty.

In the farewell scene Marlowe again makes significant changes, which center the focus of pity on Dido and soften any signs of struggle in the mind of Aeneas. It is Dido, not Aeneas, who is the tragic figure, a victim of her burning love and of the gods' concern for Aeneas. Her intense yearning for Aeneas, as well as the epic hero's easy willingness to disregard his vows to her, have already been demonstrated in the fourth act, when Aeneas, prompted by a dream, made an initial attempt to sail away (another innovation by Marlowe). Now, in the climactic central scene of the fifth act, Dido pleads desperately for him to stay, invoking their past oaths of fidelity. Marlowe uses the basic phases of her emotion and argument as given in Virgil,[4] but expands Dido's lines and cuts down

---

[4] *Aeneid*, IV, 296-392.

Aeneas' replies by about two-thirds. More important, he has introduced and concluded the scene in his own way—a way which in both instances heightens the dramatic irony. Virgil's version of this last meeting opens with Dido bursting in upon Aeneas in a fury, after having raved wildly through the streets of the city; she is already completely aware of what Aeneas intends to do, and proceeds to load him with incriminations. In Marlowe's adaptation, Dido enters with only a hint of what is going on, and learns to her unbelieving dismay from the lips of Aeneas himself that he is leaving. As the full impact of the news strikes her, the emotional pitch of her speech and of the scene rises to intensity. Marlowe has reworked the encounter into a dramatic "recognition" scene. Furthermore, instead of following Virgil in having Dido break away from the scene in revengeful wrath and anguish, Marlowe has Aeneas leave without saying a word, at a crucial moment in Dido's speech, after which Dido falls prey to the illusory effects of deep grief:

> Why star'st thou in my face? If thou wilt stay,
> Leape in mine armes, mine armes are open wide:
> If not, turne from me, and Ile turne from thee:
> For though thou hast the heart to say farewell,
> I haue not power to stay thee: is he gone?
>   [Aeneas has obviously just gone out.]
> I but heele come againe, he cannot goe,
> He loues me to too well to serue me so:
> Yet he that in my sight would not relent,
> Will, being absent, be abdurate still.
> By this is he got to the water side,
> And, see the Sailers take him by the hand,
> But he shrinkes backe, and now remembring me,
> Returnes amaine: welcome, welcome my loue:
> But wheres *Æneas?* ah hees gone hees gone!

(F4ᵛ)

The illusion again is a means by which to reveal the deepest yearnings of the suffering character, and of itself is effective dramatic irony increasing the impact and pathos of the scene.

Throughout these last scenes of the play, Marlowe makes Dido's suffering less mad, less vengeful, and more human and pitiable than in Virgil.[5] He accents the yearning that will inevitably be frustrated, and even repeats the device of illusion once more:

> *Dido.* O *Anna, Anna,* I will follow him.
>
> *Anna.* How can ye goe when he hath all your fleete?
>
> *Dido.* Ile frame me wings of waxe like *Icarus,*
> And ore his ships will soare vnto the Sunne,
> That they may melt and I fall in his armes:
> Or els Ile make a prayer vnto the waues,
> That I may swim to him like *Tritons* neece:
> O *Anna,* fetch *Orions* Harpe,
> That I may tice a Dolphin to the shoare,
> And ride vpon his backe vnto my loue:
> Looke sister, looke louely *Æneas* ships,
> See see, the billowes heaue him vp to heauen,
> And now downe falles the keeles into the deepe:
> O sister, sister, take away the Rockes,
> Theile breake his ships, O *Proteus, Neptune, Ioue,*
> Saue, saue *Æneas, Didos* leefest loue!
> Now is he come on shoare safe without hurt:

---

[5] Boas is disappointed with Marlowe's attempt at what he feels is the dramatist's hardest task in the farewell scene—"to reproduce the agony of a woman scorned. . . ." He fails to find the "Bacchic frenzy" in the queen's words that is so evident in Virgil (*Christopher Marlowe,* p. 63). This is to ask Marlowe to be more Virgilian, which is to miss the point. Marlowe's *Dido* is much more akin to the warm and sympathetic Dido of Ovid's *Heroides* (Letter VII), whose love and concern for Aeneas' well-being rule out all rancor and revenge. The contrast is even more evident in Dido's talk with Anna after Aeneas has gone: Virgil has Dido call him traitor and foe ("perfidus ille" and "hostem superbem"—*Aen.* IV, 421, 424); when Anna calls Aeneas "Wicked" in Marlowe's play, Dido reprimands her: "Call him not wicked, sister speake him faire. . ." (G).

> But see, *Achates* wils him put to sea,
> And all the Sailers merrie make for ioy,
> But he remembring me shrinkes backe againe:
> See where he comes, welcome, welcome my loue. (G⁷)

Dido's anguish over the loss of Aeneas has worked her into a state of desperate frenzy. The fantastic appeals she makes at the start of this speech are one indication of her hysteria; the illusory vision of Aeneas' ships tossed by the sea, followed without logical order by his "refusal" to put out to sea again, are another. Yet neither the images evoked nor the hallucinations are merely haphazard. The extravagance of the former serves to underline the actual, ironic helplessness of her situation; while the latter are reflections of actual happenings of the past—Aeneas *was* once cast upon her shore, and he *did* return after one attempt to leave. The pattern of the play's past action is repeated, but this time in a context where a happy resolution is impossible. Marlowe's prosody here also contributes to the representation of hysterical mental anguish. The frequent, urgent repetitions at the start of a line ("Looke sister, looke . . . See see, the billowes . . . Saue, saue *Æneas* . . .") are metrically emphasized by the suppression of the customary unaccented first syllable in the iambic line; the repeated, stressed monosyllable calls for a stronger emphasis the second time it is uttered, resulting in a crescendo movement within the line that reinforces the crescendo of emotion expressed in the speech as a whole. The passage succeeds in presenting Dido's state of mental suffering with vivid, dramatic irony. The irony is further developed immediately afterwards, when Anna calls Dido back to her senses, and the Queen sees how she herself has been partly responsible for her present tragic plight:

> Must I make ships for him to saile away?
> Nothing can beare me to him but a ship,
> And he hath all my fleete . . . (G2)

Interestingly enough, the devices used here by Marlowe—
the fantastic appeals arising from a helpless situation, the
false hopes and illusions echoing past patterns in the play,
the prosodic structure reinforcing the emotional urgency of
the situation, and the final ironic awareness of the sufferer's
own responsibility in bringing about this doom—are much
akin to those in the final monologue of *Doctor Faustus*.

The loss of Aeneas constitutes Dido's greatest agony and
the emotional climax of the play; her death comes as the inevitable and anticlimactic result. Virgil devoted more than
two hundred lines to Dido's preparations for death and her
final suicide;[6] Marlowe compresses this into less than fifty
lines,[7] adding to the catastrophe the suicides of both Iarbas
and Anna. The sudden, final spectacle of the triple suicide at
Dido's funeral pyre is emblematic of the fiery destruction
wrought in this play by overbearing, passionate love. Its impact is neither relieved nor tempered by any further action or
speech: the bodies of the three dead lovers are all that remain
on the stage; there is no choral comment, no epilogue, only
the dead—the dead who have destroyed themselves at the loss
of their loves.

Marlowe has not piled up the two extra corpses merely for
sensation's sake. His catastrophe represents the culmination
and resolution of both the main action involving Dido's tragic
love and the subordinate, analogous action involving the loves

[6] *Aeneid*, IV, 450-553, 584-705.

[7] No other extant Renaissance play about Dido's tragedy confines the
length of the catastrophe to such a degree. Each of them—Alessandro Pazzi
de Medici's *Dido in Cartagine*, Giambattista Giraldi-Cinthio's *Didone*,
Lodovico Dolce's *Didone*, Estienne Jodelle's *Didon se sacrifiant*, William
Gager's *Dido* (in Latin)—devotes at least the entire fifth act to her death.
In addition, they all display Senecan sententiousness and stichomythia—
elements noticeably absent from Marlowe's play. See Robert Turner, *Didon
dans la Tragédie de la Renaissance Italienne et Française* (Paris, 1926);
and, for a discussion of Gager's play, Frederick S. Boas, *University Drama
in the Tudor Age* (Oxford, 1914), pp. 183-191. Sections of Gager's play
are printed as an appendix to Volume III of Alexander Dyce's edition of
Marlowe's *Works* (London, 1850), pp. 316-338.

of Anna and Iarbas. Each of the three is a victim of unre-
quited love, of a desire that promises no fulfillment, for the
object of desire has allegiance elsewhere. Dido prefers Aeneas
to Iarbas, Iarbas prefers the unattainable Dido to Anna. Moreover, both Dido and Iarbas help to bring about the loss that
leads each to despair and self-destruction. Dido has provided
Aeneas with the ships that enable him to leave her, and her
awareness of this fact deepens her suffering. After Aeneas' first
attempt to leave, she had confiscated the sails and tackle to in-
sure his staying, and Aeneas' final escape is made possible only
by the willing assistance of Iarbas. He thinks that by getting
rid of Aeneas, he will at last attain Dido; he thus assists unwittingly in the indirect cause of Dido's death. Furthermore,
motivated again by the desire to gain Dido's favor, Iarbas helps
her build the pyre on which she will later be burnt: a particularly effective bit of stage irony. The lover helps to destroy
his beloved, and then destroys himself.

Marlowe's sense of irony reveals itself not only in his plotting, but also in his strategic placing of imagery in speech.
The inevitable disaster that will be Dido's is known, of course,
before the play begins, and affords the dramatist the context
for the use of ironic imagery. Marlowe has carefully placed
one such image at the high point of Dido's fortunes, indeed,
at the high point of the main action: the meeting of Dido and
Aeneas in the cave, where she confesses her love and exchanges
marriage vows with the hero. Her initial confession of love is
veiled in an allusion that has a meaning, not only for Aeneas
(who does not at first see it), but also for the audience:

> *Prometheus* hath put on *Cupids* shape,
> And I must perish in his burning armes:
> *Æneas*, O *Æneas*, quench these flames. (D4ᵛ)

Prometheus, the bringer of fire, has inflamed her with a love
that will end in her destruction in flames that are more than
figurative. The catastrophe is ironically evoked at the height
of her passion.

That Dido should see Aeneas as the means to her salvation is also ironic, and the theme is reasserted at another high point in her fortunes, just after Aeneas has renewed his vows of loyalty to her following his first effort to leave. Dido, having surrendered her crown to him, and having heard the protestations of his love once more, resolves to do nothing that will ever displease him (especially never to burn his ships):

> It is *Æneas* frowne that ends my daies:
> If he forsake me not, I neuer dye,
> For in his lookes I see eternitie,
> And heele make me immortall with a kisse.   (F)

Again the catastrophe is evoked, and again Marlowe's poetry carries with it dramatic irony as well as hyperbolic beauty. "Make me immortall with a kisse" will reappear in *Doctor Faustus*, with the same beauty but with an even deeper irony.

Carefully developed as is the theme of ironic loss, its counterpoint in the overall composition, the sense of ironic play, must not be neglected. Despite the threefold tragedy of lost love and destroyed lovers, the Virgilian tone of *sunt lacrimae rerum* is not the tone of Marlowe's drama. As Professor Boas has noted, "Nothing could be farther from the decorous gravity of Virgilian epic than the opening scene of *Dido*,"[8] which presents Jupiter "*dandling* Ganimed *vpon his knee, and* Mercury *lying asleepe*" (A2). There was, of course, ample precedent in classical literature for depicting the Olympian residents with levity, but it was another thing to introduce such treatment into the Virgilian legend. The sporting gods, just as in the *Iliad*, seem to lack the stature and worth of the human characters whose destinies they so unperturbedly control. The playfulness of these gods is, of course, shown in the play by the actions of Cupid, who, disguised as Aeneas' little son Ascanius, manages to wound Dido with his fatal arrow. The mechanism of the disguise, included in the Virgilian source,

[8] *Christopher Marlowe*, p. 53.

is developed with an eye to dramatic exploitation. Marlowe has the boy-Cupid inflict his wound during an exchange between Dido and Iarbas, at a moment when Dido is almost inclined to accept Iarbas' proposal of marriage. The wound of love leads her to encourage and discourage him in swift alternation, until he leaves in despair. The conflicts that Dido expresses in such confusion provide what is really comic interest, and emphasize her helplessness as well. Precisely the same kind of comedy is exploited in the following scenes with Aeneas, where Dido tries to fight her sudden, overbearing affection for him with attempts at restraint and modest decorum. Here she is presented as the comic victim of her passion, just as in the end she will be the tragic victim. Marlowe reinforces this comic aspect of his theme, again by analogous action, at the end of the fourth act, where the disguised Cupid touches with his arrow Dido's eighty-year-old nurse, who suddenly feels the incongruous urge to love and tries to argue herself out of it. *Dido*, then, treats both the tragedy and the comedy of love, in which the ironic sense plays an essential and central role; though the matter is Virgilian, the spirit is Ovid's: the dwellers on earth as well as the dwellers on Olympus are motivated and victimized by the power of love.

It would be an over-simplification, though one not far from the truth, to say that the human suffering and destruction in this play, the evil that befalls the characters, can all be traced to passionate love. Even the fall of Troy, as related in lurid detail by Aeneas in the second act,[9] is linked as usual with its root cause: that "ticing strumpet" Helen. The theme, of course, is a common one. Dolce's *Didone* had been set in motion by a long speech of Cupid, glorying in his cruel triumphs over men and gods, and promising a new tragic spectacle of

---

[9] The lurid detail of Marlowe's handling of this account, which goes far beyond Virgil's more restrained treatment, has been linked recently with romance sources by Ethel Seaton, "Marlowe's Light Reading," *Elizabethan and Jacobean Studies: Presented to Frank Percy Wilson in Honour of his Seventieth Birthday* (Oxford, 1959), pp. 27-33.

his power. The earliest extant English love-tragedy, *Gismond of Salerne* (acted 1567/1568, revised and printed, 1591), borrows Dolce's speech and theme for its own story,[10] which develops the idea of destructive lust far beyond the story's source in Boccaccio's *Decameron*. The moralizing Chorus at the end of the fourth act, for example, emphasizing the destructive fruits of lust, allude first to Helen of Troy, and then cite Medea, Dido, Leander, and Phyllis, all of whom "do shew the end of wicked loue is blood" (iv. *Chor.* 12). In *The Rare Triumphes of Loue and Fortune* (acted 1582)[11] the ghost of Dido is paraded as a victim of Venus. Marlowe extends the theme by adding two tragic victims of love and one comic victim to the Dido story. In so doing, he emphasizes human responsibility involved in destruction by love, as well as victimization at the hands of the sporting gods. For neither Iarbas nor Anna has been wounded by Cupid's arrow in the literal way that Dido has been: their love is their own, their suicide their own. Similarly, Dido's suicide is not a necessary effect of Cupid's wound, but springs from her character and will; the Nurse, too, had been wounded by Cupid, but without the same catastrophic results. All three suicides, and the suffering that prompts them, stem from an agonizing and unbearable sense of loss, a loss that the sufferer refuses longer to endure.

II. *TAMBURLAINE THE GREAT:*
PART I

It is not the central figure, as in *Dido*, who undergoes the greatest human suffering in the first part of *Tamburlaine*. If, as seems reasonable, we ought to consider Part I as a play in itself,[12] it is immediately obvious that there is nothing tragic

[10] See J. W. Cunliffe, ed., *Early English Classical Tragedies* (Oxford, 1912), p. 315.

[11] MSR (Oxford, 1930), p. vi.

[12] The prologue to Part II states that the second play was written in response to the general popularity of the first; furthermore, Part I not only

about Tamburlaine: there is no defeat or destruction that he must undergo, no physical or mental anguish that he displays. The major burden of the play, as most critics have remarked, is the sensational revelation of Tamburlaine's superhuman character and ability. To that end all the tools of the dramatist are directed: the action consists of a series of Tamburlainian victories, each greater than the last; the rhetoric of what the 1590 title page so aptly called a tragical *discourse* consistently magnifies the importance of the hero and all his adventures;[13] the imagery intensifies the impression of magnitude and awe-inspiring achievement, surrounding Tamburlaine and his deeds with enhancing figures of speech drawn from the divinities of classical mythology, from jewels, treasure, precious stones and metals, stars, planets and other heavenly bodies.[14] And to help reveal the superhumanity of his hero, Marlowe has put to striking use the spectacle of suffering. Those who oppose Tamburlaine are those who must suffer, and the violent terms in which they do it underline in dramatic action and language the superhuman power and feeling of the "Scourge of God."

The function of suffering in this play is to demonstrate the terrible truth in Menaphon's description of Tamburlaine at the start of Act Two:

> Thirsting with souerainty with loue of armes,
> His lofty browes in foldes, do figure death,
> And in their smoothnesse, amitie and life . . .[15]

---

comes to a resolution without foreshadowing or hinting at a sequel, but it also includes most of the historical material available to Marlowe in his sources. See Paul H. Kocher, *Christopher Marlowe: A Study of his Thought, Learning and Character* (Chapel Hill, 1946), pp. 69-70; and Clifford Leech, "The Two-Part Play: Marlowe and the Early Shakespeare," *Shakespeare Jahrbuch*, XCIV (1958), 90-92.

[13] The manipulation of formal rhetorical principles in *Tamburlaine* has been analyzed by Donald Peet, "The Rhetoric of *Tamburlaine*," *ELH*, XXVI (1959), 137-155.

[14] Moody Prior's analysis of the imagery of Part 1 reveals the constant exploitation of these sources and categories: *The Language of Tragedy* (New York, 1947), pp. 33-46.

[15] *Tamburlaine the Great* (London, 1590), B2ᵛ-B3. Readex Microprint

For not only does Tamburlaine claim to be master of Fortune,[16] but lord over life and death as well. As he says to the suppliant virgins of Damascus:

> Behold my sword, what see you at the point?
> *Virg.* Nothing but feare and fatall steele my Lord.
> *Tam.* Your fearfull minds are thicke and mistie then,
> For there sits Death, there sits imperious Death,
> Keeping his circuit by the slicing edge.
> But I'am pleasde you shall not see him there,
> He now is seated on my horsmens speares:
> And on their points his fleshlesse bodie feedes.
> *Techelles*, straight goe charge a few of them
> To chardge these Dames, and shew my seruant death,
> Sitting in scarlet on their armed speares.   (E3)

The slaughter of these pathetic victims is not shown upon the stage, but there are others whose fall at the hands of Tamburlaine is displayed directly: Cosroe, Agydas, Bajazeth, Zabina, and Arabia. All the latter are of noble rank, and their destruction constitutes what is "tragical" in Part 1 of *Tamburlaine*.

If one focuses solely on the figure of its central hero, *Tamburlaine* represents indeed what Willard Farnham calls "a rebellious violation of all that *De Casibus* tragedy had set out to convey,"[17] for the great conqueror-hero whose watchwords are ambition and power, whose highest ideal is the "sweet fruition of an earthly crowne," is master of Fortune till the very end of the play, where he makes truce with all the world. But the procession of his victims, as one by one they meet their downfall, is as dramatic a catalogue of *De Casibus* tragedies

---

of the Huntington Library copy in *Three Centuries of Drama: English, 1512-1641*, ed. Henry W. Wells (New York, 1953). Subsequent references to this edition will appear in my text.

[16] A rather dangerous boast which he shares with such earlier dramatic figures as Seneca's Medea (LCL ed., l. 520) and Skelton's Magnyfycence (see p. 28 above).

[17] *The Medieval Heritage of Elizabethan Tragedy*, corrected reprint ed. (Oxford, 1956), p. 369.

as one could expect. What could be a more explicit example
of the mutability of Fortune in the life of rulers than the
spectacle of the dying Cosroe, lamenting the fall that has
followed so swiftly upon his rise to kingship:

> Barbarous and bloody *Tamburlaine*,
> Thus to depriue me of my crowne and life.
> Treacherous and false *theridamas*,
> Euen at the morning of my happy state,
> Scarce being seated in my royall throne,
> To worke my downfall and vntimely end.
>
> (c-cᵛ)

The sentiment is conventional enough, but the ultimate context is less so: the rise and fall of this prince is the immediate
result not of an abstract Fortune's fickleness, but of the whims
and ambitions of Tamburlaine.

Cosroe's dying words are notable in another way. His speech
is couched in objective, physiological terms for the most part,
a device which calls attention to his suffering and yet does not
attract very much sympathy or pity:

> My bloodlesse body waxeth chill and colde,
> And with my blood my life slides through my wound.
> My soule begins to take her flight to hell.
> And sommons all my sences to depart:
> The heat and moisture which did feed each other,
> For want of nourishment to feed them both.
> Is drie and cold, and now dooth gastly death
> With greedy tallents gripe my bleeding hart,
> And like a Harpye tires on my life.   (c2)

There is a blending here of physiological description with
figurative speech; the modern reader, unfamiliar with the
theory involved, is apt to confuse the two. Up to the last
three lines, the process is described in literal terms; as Una
Ellis-Fermor notes in her edition of the play, the idea is that

when blood, the element combining moisture and heat, leaves the body, the balance of the four elements constituting the human body is destroyed, leaving only the properties of cold and dryness, which alone cannot support life.[18] The heart, considered as the principal member of man's body, is the last thing that dies;[19] its death is simultaneous with the departure of the soul, the spiritual life-principle whose properties include the senses. These details of physiology, as Ellis-Fermor has also noted, are drawn by Marlowe from a theoretical system "purely medieval and Aristotelian, untouched by the more advanced thought of his time. . . ."[20] It was the system taught at Cambridge University well into the seventeenth century as part of the standard curriculum,[21] and Marlowe undoubtedly studied it there.

Such objective, physiological rendering of the details of suffering and death is characteristic of *Tamburlaine*. In Part I, for example, the captive Bajazeth describes his hunger pains in such terms; in Part II the Captain explains his dying sensations to his wife Olympia in the same way, and the diagnosis of Tamburlaine's malady is a classic example of this use of "scientific" explanation. But what is especially noteworthy is that Marlowe's attempt at the dramatization of physical suffering by such means is a completely original phenomenon; as far as I have been able to find, no English play before *Tamburlaine* relies on these physiological details to express the process of death, pain, or hunger. The physiological effects of *emotional* states had been reported both in early plays and in the popular romances of the 1560's,[22] but the representation

[18] *Tamburlaine the Great: In Two Parts*, revised ed. (London, 1951), p. 114.

[19] See Carroll Camden, Jr., "Marlowe and Elizabethan Psychology," *PQ*, VIII (1929), 75.

[20] *ed. cit.*, p. 89.

[21] William T. Costello, S.J., *The Scholastic Curriculum at Early Seventeenth-Century Cambridge* (Cambridge, Mass., 1958), pp. 83-102.

[22] Albert L. Walker, "Convention in Shakespeare's Description of Emotion," *PQ*, XVII (1938), 35, 38.

of physical suffering itself through such details is apparently original with Marlowe in the English drama. The closest parallel to which one can point is Seneca's rendering of the suffering of Hercules in *Hercules Oetaeus*, where, under the dominating introductory image of Hercules' wasting affliction as a devouring scorpion or crab, the effects on his decaying anatomy are catalogued:

> ... sanguinis quondam capax
> tumidi igne cor pulmonis arentes fibras
> distendit, ardet felle siccato iecur
> totumque lentus sanguinem avexit vapor.
> primam cutem consumpsit, hinc aditum nefas
> in membra fecit, abstulit pestis latus,
> exedit artus penitus et costas malum,
> hausit medullas. ossibus vacuis sedet;
> nec ossa durant ipsa, sed compagibus
> discussa ruptis mole conlapsa fluunt.[23]

The Elizabethan translation by "J.S." in Thomas Newton's 1581 edition of Seneca exploits the crude, intense sensationalism of the passage:

> And hoat within my boyling bones the seathing
> Marowe burnes.
> My River whilom ranke of bloude my rotting
> Lunges it tawes,
> And teareth them in shattred gubs, and filthy
> withered flawes.
> And now my Gall is dryed up, my burning Lyver
> glowes,

[23] *Hercules Oetaeus*, ll. 1220-1229. The LCL translation by Frank Justus Miller is as follows: "My heart, once filled with pulsing streams of blood, hotly distends the parched fibres of my lungs; my liver glows, its bile dried quite away, and a slow fire has exhausted all my blood. First did the dread plague feed upon my skin, next to my limbs it passed, devoured my sides, then deep in my joints and ribs the pest ate its way, and drank my very marrow. In my hollow bones it lurks; nor do my bones themselves retain their hardness, but, shattered with broken structure, fall in a crumbling mass."

The stewing heate hath stillde away the bloude, and
    Jove hee knowes
My upper skin is scorcht away and thus the Canker
    stronge
Doth eate an hole that get it may my wretched
    Limmes amonge,
And from my frying Ribs (alas) my Lyver quite is
    rent.
It gnawes my flesh, devowers all, my Carkas quite
    is spent,
It soakes into the empty bones, and out the juyce it
    suckes
The bones by lumps drop of while it the joyntes
    a sunder pluckes.[24]

The figurative aspect of this speech swamps the physical details in a deluge of horror, yet the physical details are there.
The overwhelming effect is apparently sordid by intent. In
this respect Marlowe's use of physical detail is very different:
it seems rather to reflect a characteristic tendency to employ
his formal knowledge with particular precision.[25]

The knowledge, however, does not seem to be included for
show, but to enhance the drama; Marlowe's poetic and dramatic skill makes more of the physiological details than the
details themselves, simply set down for their own sake, could
possibly do. The death speech of Cosroe is a good case in
point. The physical fact that the death of the heart is the death
of the man lies beneath the poetic image that closes the speech:

> . . . and now dooth gastly death
> With greedy tallents gripe my bleeding hart,
> And like a Harpye tires on my life.

[24] *Seneca His Tenne Tragedies*, The Tudor Translations ed. (London and
New York, 1927), II, 234.

[25] Other reflections of this tendency in *Tamburlaine* are the use of details gathered from many historical sources, the employment of astronomical
learning, the geographical plotting of Tamburlaine's conquests according

Marlowe, like Kyd, is not satisfied with the merely poetic image; he translates it at once into dramatic action. The moment Cosroe falls dead, Tamburlaine takes the crown from the corpse's head and puts it on his own. That this juxtaposition is not merely a coincidence is confirmed by the Harpy allusion: the Harpies of later mythology were winged monsters sent to torment Phineus by seizing upon his food and bearing it off before he could eat it.[26] This is analogous to the dramatic situation: Tamburlaine has seized and borne off the newly won crown of Cosroe before he has had opportunity to enjoy it; indeed, the allusion makes more sense with regard to the crown than with regard to Cosroe's life, since the crown has been the recent point of attraction.

The transition from physiological detail to poetic image to dramatic image is complete in this instance, but not in others. It may well be that Marlowe found the effects of physiological detail in the description of suffering unsuccessful in the long run, for after *Tamburlaine*, with the exception of a few brief lines in *The Massacre at Paris*, there is no further attempt to render suffering dramatic in this way.[27]

Even within *Tamburlaine* Marlowe employs a considerable variety of ways to depict the suffering of his protagonist's victims. After Cosroe, the next prince to fall is Agydas, the Median lord whose attempts to dissuade Zenocrate from loving Tamburlaine are overheard by the hero and greeted with a silent, wrathful frown that strikes terror into Agydas' heart. Again, the emphasis is on Tamburlaine's frown as the herald of death. Agydas realizes this to such a degree that he commits suicide rather than face the horrors Tamburlaine may offer him. There is something incongruous about the way in

to the map of Ortelius, and of course the constant manipulation of classical mythology.

[26] Ellis-Fermor, *ed. cit.*, p. 114.

[27] Carroll Camden's article on "Marlowe and Elizabethan Psychology" cites 28 passages from the plays which seem to reflect a precise use of scientific terminology; 20 of these are drawn from the two parts of *Tamburlaine*.

which Agydas expresses his initial fear and astonishment—
in an involved epic simile of a dozen lines; equally incongruous is the mixture of plain fear and Stoic honor that motivates
his suicide. If there is no cynical irony intended here, the
scene suffers decidedly from dramatic immaturity. But in any
case its function is clear: to emphasize the fearfulness of even
the silent wrath of Tamburlaine.

The most memorable "tragedy" of Part 1 of *Tamburlaine*
is the fall of Bajazeth. He meets military defeat at the end
of the third act; in the fourth, he is humiliated by being carried about in a cage, used as a living footstool for Tamburlaine, and fed scraps from the banquet table as though he
were a dog. Bajazeth's reaction to this treatment is expressed
in consistent terms throughout: in his furious indignation he
flings curse after curse at Tamburlaine, most of them framed
in the imagery of hell, darkness, and the underworld. But
even such dire threats are converted to the enhancement of
Tamburlaine's superhuman stature; as the conqueror says:

> I glorie in the curses of my foes.
> Hauing the power frõ the Emperiall heauen,
> To turne them al vpon their proper heades. (D7)

Marlowe has dramatized the details of Bajazeth's captivity
that were found in the historical sources of his day, details
which themselves speak eloquently of the character of Tamburlaine.[28] He has brought upon the stage, in a spectacular
and sensational way, the fall of an emperor; and he has integrated that fall with the main line of action, the indomitable
rise of Tamburlaine. The *De Casibus* image is at work here,
insofar as Bajazeth is concerned, and it is exploited dramatically—to further action as well as characterization—in a way
that far surpasses Kyd's toying with the theme in *The Spanish
Tragedy*, the representation of the conquered Viceroy of Por-

---

[28] The appendices to the Ellis-Fermor edition contain the relevant ex-
tracts from these sources.

tugal. One of Marlowe's probable sources, Thomas Fortescue's *The Foreste*, draws the conventional *De Casibus* moral after having described the lowly treatment of Bajazeth: ". . . whence assuredly we may learne not so much to affie in riches, or in the pompe of this worlde: for as muche as he that yesterdaie was Prince and Lorde, of all the worlde almost, is this daie fallen into suche extreame miserie, that he liuith worse then a dogge, fellowe to theim in companie."[29] Marlowe, to be sure, does not explicate the moral in this way at this stage; but he does insert it later in the reaction of Zenocrate to the deaths of Bajazeth and his wife.

The final sufferings and suicides of Bajazeth and Zabina constitute the catastrophe of the last act, and take place on stage during the time that Tamburlaine reaches the height of military achievement in this play by defeating the Soldan of Egypt and the Arabian king. As Tamburlaine leaves for the battle, Bajazeth and Zabina hurl curses upon him and his fortunes; but left alone, they are forced to admit the inevitability of his victory, feeling that his invincibility is written in the stars. Such a realization prompts Zabina to despair, and her words at this point reflect the hell-like quality of their suffering, and set the scene for the suicides to follow:

> Then is there left no *Mahomet*, no God,
> No Feend, no Fortune, nor no hope of end?
> To our infamous monstrous slaueries:
> Gape earth, and let the Feends infernall view,
> As hell, as hoplesse and as full of feare
> As are the blasted banks of *Erebus*:
> Where shaking ghosts with euer howling grones,
> Houer about the vgly Ferriman, to get a passage to *Elisiã*
> why should we liue, O wretches, beggars slaues
> Why liue we *Baiazeth*, and build vp neasts,
> So high within the region of the aire,

---

[29] Ellis-Fermor, p. 293. Whetstone's *English Myrror* repeats the sentiment, p. 300.

By liuing long in this oppression,
That all the world will see and laugh to scorne.
The former triumphes of our mightines,
In this obscure infernall seruitude?   (E5-E5ᵛ)

The linking of great sorrow with the tortures of classical hell
is a familiar enough device both in poetry and drama before
Marlowe, but the opening lines of this speech reflect a mingling of concepts connected with the Christian hell: chiefly,
the privation of God and the eternity of a hopeless existence.
The closing lines of the speech accent another privation suf-
fered by the emperor and his wife: the loss of their mightiness.
The contrast between their present misery and former greatness is a theme that Bajazeth seizes upon in the next speech;
it is once again the conventional *De Casibus* theme:

O dreary Engines of my loathed sight,
That sees my crowne, my honor and my name,
Thrust vnder yoke and thraldom of a thiefe.
Why feed ye still on daies accursed beams,
And sink not quite into my tortur'd soule?
You see my wife, my Queene and Emperesse,
Brought vp and propped by the hand of fame,
Queen of fifteene contributory Queens,
Now throwen to roomes of blacke abiection,
Smear'd with blots of basest drudgery:
And Villanesse to shame, disdaine, and misery . . .
                                                        (E5ᵛ)

While Zabina is temporarily absent from the scene, Bajazeth
brains himself against the cage after a final, vengeful curse on
Tamburlaine couched in the imagery of storm and darkness.
Zabina, returning to find her husband dead, goes mad; Marlowe emphasizes the total incoherency and agitation of her
delirious state by abandoning the rhythms of blank verse and
throwing her disconnected phrases into prose form (E6ᵛ). This
very effective technique is not original with Marlowe; *The*

Rare Triumphs of Love and Fortune, played before the Queen in 1582, includes the prose ravings of Bomelio set within a verse play. But Marlowe may be the first to use it in the tragic drama. At the end of the passage, with its deeply ironic phrase "make ready my Coch, my chaire, my iewels, I come, I come, I come," Zabina hurls herself against the cage and meets her death as did her husband. Her suffering and death, unlike Bajazeth's, have no parallel in the historical sources. Marlowe's addition not only increases the pathos and terror of the catastrophe; it also represents a rendering of suffering more human than the scene otherwise displays. For part of the effect of presentation according to the *De Casibus* theme is to shift the focus from the humanity of the suffering victims to their fallen state. Situation rather than character is emphasized: the greatest kings of earth, so proud and confident at one time, can suffer depths of degradation and despair.

The orthodox moral significance is drawn from this situation by the sorrowing Zenocrate. She comes upon the bloody spectacle already lamenting the fall of Damascus, the massacre of her countrymen, and the slaughter of the suppliant virgins, and discovery of the corpses intensifies her grief:

> Earth cast vp fountaines from thy entralles!
> And wet thy cheeks for their vntimely deathes:
> Shake with their waight in signe of feare & griefe:
> Blush heauen, that gaue them honor at their birth,
> And let them die a death so barbarous.
> Those that are proud of fickle Empery,
> And place their chiefest good in earthly pompe:
> Behold the Turke and his great Emperesse.   (E7)

"Behold the Turke and his great Emperesse" becomes the refrain for the remainder of her speech, in which she applies the warning to her beloved Tamburlaine "That fights for Scepters and for slippery crownes"; she beseeches Jove to pardon his pitilessness and not to allow misfortune to fall upon him. Her own nature, with its deep feeling for the suffering of others, is revealed by her lament; it functions in direct contrast to the unwavering ruthlessness of Tamburlaine's character.

Tamburlaine himself is far above the need for such warnings as Zenocrate may express; his reaction to the corpses (including by this time the dead lover of Zenocrate, Arabia) is thoroughly in keeping with the dominating thrust of the play:

> Al sights of power to grace my victory:
> And such are obiects fit for *Tamburlaine*,
> Wherein as in a mirrour may be seene,
> His honor, that consists in sheading blood,
> When men presume to manage armes with him.
>
> (F)

Though the images reflected in them may be identical, Tamburlaine's mirror is absolutely unlike the *Mirror for Magistrates*.

The presence of these two contrasting attitudes side-by-side has been the cause of much confusing and conflicting criticism of the play. On the one hand there is Una Ellis-Fermor's interpretation, which focuses primarily on the romantic aspirations of the hero and which finds, naturally enough, something incongruous about the *De Casibus* theme; on the other hand there is Roy W. Battenhouse's severely moral interpretation which demands that Tamburlaine be recognized and condemned as a sinful exemplar of pride and ambition.[30] Both interpretations are equally extreme, tending to accent one attitude at the expense of the other. Moody Prior, who approaches the work by way of its dominant imagery, is troubled by the presence and structural placement of the "dark" images —those which allude to the underworld and the powers of darkness in connection with Tamburlaine's acts of cruelty.

[30] *Marlowe's "Tamburlaine": A Study in Renaissance Moral Philosophy* (Nashville, 1941).

They dominate the central portion of the play and the section just preceding the conclusion, and seem to detract from the extravagant and lofty imagery with which Tamburlaine himself endows all his acts. Prior concludes that the lack of integration is a symptom of Marlowe's failure, and that it complicates any attempt at interpretation of Tamburlaine's career.[31]

That the two contrasting themes were as noticeable to the Elizabethans as to the modern audience is shown by two divergent contemporary imitations of Part 1 of *Tamburlaine*, *The Comicall Historie of Alphonsus, King of Aragon*, and *The First part of the Tragicall raigne of Selimus*.[32] *Alphonsus*, generally attributed to Robert Greene and assigned a date immediately following the success of *Tamburlaine*, is an obvious copy of the major features of Marlowe's play: its conqueror-hero is introduced at the very start as "that man of *Ioue* his seed,/ Sprung from the loines of the immortal Gods,"[33] and his characteristic rant includes a familiar boast:

> I clap vp Fortune in a cage of gold,
> To make her turne her wheele as I thinke best.
>
> (1614-1615)

His career involves greater and greater victories, the crowning of his three associates, and a climactic encounter with a Turkish lord whose daughter he marries in triumph at the end: all obvious parallels with *Tamburlaine*. There is no hint of criticism of his actions: he is the admirable hero to the end. But what is especially revealing in the perspective of our own investigation is that the play is noticeably free from the violent slaughter that marks *Tamburlaine*. Alphonsus himself kills his first antagonist in battle; his father stabs an escaping Duke of Milan (whose post-battle speech in the *De Casibus* vein is

---

[31] *Language of Tragedy*, pp. 44-46.
[32] See Leech, "The Two-Part Play," pp. 92-97.
[33] *Alphonsus, King of Aragon*, MSR (Oxford, 1926), ll. 24-25.

the sole vocal expression of suffering in the play);[34] and the Turk Amurack stabs a servant whose message from Mahomet has proved false—these three acts sum up the suffering in *Alphonsus*. It is neither exceptionally spectacular nor integrated with any theme or characterization.

Selimus, on the contrary, is a sordid spectacle of one unnatural atrocity after another, all of which are committed by two ambitious sons of Bajazet, Selimus and Acomat. Selimus, the principal conqueror-villain, dominates the opening and closing sections. After professing himself an absolute atheist, Machiavellian, and tyrant, he proceeds to poison his father, strangle his two brothers, a sister, and a handful of others, in his triumphant march to the throne. The blatancy of his viciousness is self-condemnatory; yet he is not without his magniloquent excuses:

> But we, whose minde in heauenly thoughts is clad,
> Whose bodie doth a glorious spirit beare,
> That hath no bounds, but flieth euery where.
> Why should we seeke to make that soul a slaue,
> To which dame Nature so large freedome gaue.[35]

Acomat, before his own ambition is thwarted by Selimus, murders his innocent young niece and nephew, and greets his father's peace-seeking emissary by pulling out his eyes and cutting off his hands. The gross physical horrors perpetrated by the ambitious brothers are balanced by the mental sorrows of the Emperor Bajazet, who opens the play with a long monologue lamenting the fears, cares, and suspicions attendant upon the mutable office of kingship—a theme he repeats until the moment of his death. Here in *Selimus*, then, the elements that make up the "dark side" of *Tamburlaine* are exaggerated with obvious moral overtones.

In dealing with the problem of ambivalence in *Tambur-*

[34] Ll. 1388-1405.
[35] *The Tragical Reign of Selimus*, MSR (Oxford, 1908), ll. 349-353.

laine one should also keep in mind that the historical sources
Marlowe appears to have used contain the very same contrasting attitudes found here. Thomas Fortescue, immediately after
moralizing on the fall of Bajazeth, is able to return to the
triumphant climb of Tamburlaine with a tone of admiration;[36]
in his main account of the conqueror's history there is no indication that Tamburlaine's career should be judged as an
evil one, or interpreted according to the moral of mutability
which Bajazeth exemplifies. On the other hand, as Battenhouse has pointed out,[37] Fortescue in another chapter lists
Tamburlaine among those cruel kings and bloody tyrants who
may be called "Ministers of God" because they persecute the
wicked, but who nonetheless are themselves "not hence held
for iust, ne shall they escape the heuy iudgement of God."[38]
This chapter attempts to demonstrate that God finally sends
wretched and miserable torments to such ministers; the examples offered to prove this point, however, do not include Tamburlaine. Indeed, as Fortescue notes in his conclusion to the
main account, all historians agree that Tamburlaine "neuer
sawe the backe, or frounyng face of fortune, that he neuer
was vanquished, or put to flighte by any, that he neuer tooke
matter in hande, that he brought not to the wished effect, and
that his corage, and industrie neuer failed hym to bryng it to
good ende."[39]

[36] Ellis-Fermor ed., p. 293.
[37] *Marlowe's "Tamburlaine,"* p. 13.
[38] *The Forest* (London, 1576), 13^v.
[39] Ellis-Fermor ed., pp. 297-298. An examination of the historical accounts of Tamburlaine in Marlowe's day, including the moral attitude of
the historians toward Tamburlaine, serves as a corrective to elements in the
interpretations of both Battenhouse and Ellis-Fermor. Battenhouse's treatment of Marlowe's sources (pp. 129-149) ignores the note of admiration
that characterizes many of the accounts. Outside of Fortescue's adverse comment mentioned above, an openly condemnatory attitude seems evident in
only one other account, that of Perondinus; but Perondinus also included
details of Tamburlaine's treachery and of his maltreatment of Bajazeth's
wife which Marlowe chose to ignore. The strongly biographical interpretation of Tamburlaine, on the other hand, such as Ellis-Fermor's, tends to
overlook the fact that most of Tamburlaine's qualities (which Ellis-Fermor

What, finally, are we to make of the play *Tamburlaine*, with its ambivalent themes? What do the suffering and violence—which are the direct or indirect result of Tamburlaine's ambitious deeds—imply about the hero's character and ethic? One thing that should be noticed is that nowhere in Part I is the audience allowed to *see* Tamburlaine kill or physically injure anyone, not even at second-hand through an underling. He disdains to punish the coward-king Mycetes; Cosroe and Arabia die of wounds inflicted by no specified person; Agydas, Bajazeth, and Zabina all kill themselves. Marlowe thus avoids the possibility of Tamburlaine's figure being tarnished by direct, observed engagement in personal slaughter. He is always at least one remove from his victims; Death, his servant, does the work for him. Tamburlaine himself, for all his thirst for war and blood, remains somehow "above" suffering and death. Nevertheless, three corpses, concrete emblems of the destructiveness inherent in his rise to power, litter the stage at the conclusion of the play,[40] and Zenocrate's speech recording the off stage massacres puts them in even wider context. Yet Zenocrate loves Tamburlaine still, and her father the Soldan respects him almost as much as do his faithful soldiers. In spite of the suffering he has brought about, the hero retains the admiration of all the other living characters. And so the ambivalence remains, perhaps even emphasized by Marlowe's dramaturgy: the ambitious rebel, a figure consistently vilified in the academic tragedies and other orthodox sources, is here brought to a final exaltation— but his feet are planted in blood. One cannot ignore the ironic contrast between the magniloquent words in which Tamburlaine expresses his achievement and the macabre sight which defines

---

identifies with Marlowe's) are already stressed in the histories, and are not due to Marlowe's invention. See Leslie Spence, "Tamburlaine and Marlowe," *PMLA*, XLII (1927), 604-622.

[40] Clifford Leech has called attention to this in "Marlowe's 'Edward II': Power and Suffering," *The Critical Quarterly*, I (1959), 183.

it in visual terms: Bajazeth dead in his cage, Zabina lifeless beneath it, Arabia's bleeding corpse. Marlowe's last scene thus accents the paradox of the inhuman effects of Tamburlaine's superhuman ambitions, a paradox which is more of a problem than a resolution. The victorious and Titanic figure of Tamburlaine cannot be separated from the dark shadow of human suffering that he himself casts; in Part I he alone represents the source of all the violence and destruction in the universe of the play. Not until Part II does the shadow of suffering begin to fall on Tamburlaine himself.

III. *TAMBURLAINE THE GREAT:* PART II

The change in tenor that marks the second part of *Tamburlaine* is noted in the prologue. Death, designated by Tamburlaine as his slave in Part I, now

> ... *cuts off the progres of his pomp.*
> *And murdrous Fates throwes al his triumphs down.*
>
> (F3)

For although the "bloody Conquests" and military victories of the hero continue, the limitations of mortality begin to encroach persistently on "the pompe of proud audacious deeds." Zenocrate dies; one of Tamburlaine's sons is revealed as a somewhat comic coward; the other two are quite obviously no match for their father; finally, sickness and death put an abrupt stop to Tamburlaine's campaign to conquer the world. All these events call for some reaction on Tamburlaine's part —and that reaction is consistently one of fiery rage.

The wrathful brow of the conqueror was introduced as a theme in Part I, but with one exception the Tamburlaine of that play hardly had any occasion to become angry, so assured was he at all times of overcoming all obstacles. The exception was his wrathful look at Agydas, who had attempted to dissuade Zenocrate from her attraction to Tamburlaine; and that look alone—without a single accompanying word—was sufficient to terrify Agydas into suicide. Tamburlaine in Part I, for all his grandiloquence, had no occasion to raise his voice in fury; in Part II his wrath becomes extravagantly voluble.

The central example, heralded by the title of Part II, is his "impassionate fury, for the death of *his Lady and loue, faire Zenocrate.*" Tamburlaine's long speech preceding her death is not one of personal sorrow, but a poetic and rhetorical vision of supercosmic preparations of the gods to "entertaine diuine *Zenocrate.*" Zenocrate herself faces the prospect of death with rational calm and resignation; for her it is a "necessary change" for "this fraile and transitory flesh"—an attitude thoroughly in keeping with her awareness of mutability in Part I. She is upset much more to hear Tamburlaine's threat to end his own life after her death; she persuades him rather plaintively to "let" her die and to go on living himself:

> But let me die my Loue, yet let me die,
> With loue and patience let your true loue die . . .
>
> (G7ᵛ)

While the music plays, and Zenocrate is dying, Tamburlaine utters a second long speech in praise of her great beauty. Suddenly, when she is finally dead, he shifts from his lyric mood to the violence of mad fury:

> What, is she dead? *Techelles*, draw thy sword,
> And wound the earth, that it may cleaue in twaine,
> And we discend into th'infernall vaults,
> To haile the fatall Sisters by the haire,
> And throw them in the triple mote of Hell,
> For taking hence my faire *zenocrate*.
> *Casane* and *theridamas* to armes,
> Raise Caualieros higher than the cloudes:
> And with the cannon breake the frame of heauen,
> Batter the shining pallace of the Sun,
> And shiuer all the starry firmament:

. . . .
Behold me here diuine *zenocrate*,
Rauing, impatient, desperate and mad,
Breaking my steeled lance, with which I burst
The rusty beames of *Ianus* Temple doores,
Letting out death and tyrannising war:
To martch with me vnder this bloody flag,
And if thou pitiest *Tamburlain* the great,
Come downe from heauen and liue with me againe.

(G8)

There is something of the Herodian spirit in this explosion of frenzied wrath, especially in the violent but fruitless action that obviously accompanies the speech. But neither the expression nor the context holds Tamburlaine's behavior up to ridicule, and there is much more involved here than out-Heroding Herod. The reaction is entirely in keeping with Tamburlaine's character, framed as it is in terms of physical violence and military attack; it reveals a new stress which is in full play in Part II—the demand for the impossible, that demand which keeps pace with the ever-increasing growth of Tamburlaine's aspirations and audacities. It is a stress which the repetitive structure of the play necessarily calls forth: if each aspiration and each conquest is to be greater than the last, the limits of human possibility must be strained to the breaking point. The totally fantastic nature of Tamburlaine's commands are somewhat akin to the illusory wishes of Dido— they are intensely desired, but impossible, even for such a person as Tamburlaine, and hence they underline his inevitable ironic helplessness in the face of death. His companions, realizing the impotency of such protests and threats, urge patience:

Ah good my Lord be patient, she is dead,
And all this raging cannot make her liue,

. . . .
Nothing preuailes, for she is dead my Lord.

(G8)

The Tamburlaine who has never been wounded in body except by himself now confesses to a deeply wounded spirit,
whose smart he hopes to salve with willful persistence in illusion:

> For she is dead? thy words doo pierce my soule
> Ah sweet *theridamas*, say so no more,
> Though she be dead, yet let me think she liues,
> And feed my mind that dies for want of her . . .

(G8-G8ᵛ)

Tamburlaine, as would be expected, meets this obstacle with
action to fit his words. He has Zenocrate's body embalmed and
preserved in a sheet of gold, to carry with him for the rest
of his days; as a sign of mourning he burns to the ground the
town where she died. Yet once his grief has been vented in
such violent terms, it ceases abruptly. Though his sons express their lasting sorrow as they march away from the burning
town, Tamburlaine is able to turn immediately to business,
and lectures them on the "rudiments of war." There is no
room in his make-up for lingering pain; his extravagant action
attends to everything and is sufficient for him. Human emotion shall not impede his love of war.

The identical pattern-reaction to personal grief or frustration—voluble rage accompanied by violent action—is repeated
by Tamburlaine when, discovering that his son Calyphas has
refused to enter battle, he stabs him to death, in spite of his
companions' urgings for forgiveness. The horror of this action is accentuated by the fact that this is the first time in
the course of both plays that Tamburlaine is actually shown
killing anyone; that his first directly represented act of destruction should be inflicted on his own progeny is deeply

ironic, and bloodies the image of his honor considerably.[41]
Ironic, too, is the placing of the actual stabbing: it comes as
a concluding gesture to the most aspiring speech that Tamburlaine has yet uttered:

> Here *Ioue*, receiue his fainting soule againe,
> A Forme not meet to giue that subiect essence,
> Whose matter is the flesh of *Tamburlain*,
> Wherin an incorporeall spirit mooues,
> Made of the mould whereof thy selfe consists.
> Which makes me valiant, proud, ambitious,
> Ready to leuie power against thy throne,
> That I might mooue the turning Spheares of heauē,
> For earth and al this aery region
> Cannot containe the state of *Tamburlaine*.
>
> 　　　　　　　[Stabs Calyphas.]　　(J4-J4ᵛ)

Tamburlaine's god is the image of himself—valiant, proud,
ambitious—while Tamburlaine's son is the obverse of that
image and must be dispatched as an insult to the father who
aspires to the power of Jove. Tamburlaine follows the execution with words proclaiming his enmity to Jove for sending
him such issue, and then immediately turns to the job of
demonstrating his supremacy over the captured Turkish kings.
As Professor Boas has remarked, the Tamburlaine of Part II
is a "coarser and more incredible figure than in Part I . . .
more and more the primitive barbarian."[42] But this coarsening
is no more than an accentuation and further development of

[41] Paul Kocher seems to me to have missed the dramatic point of this
event completely in stressing that Tamburlaine's stabbing of Calyphas is
"merely heroic" from the Elizabethan point of view, since contemporary
military code considered willful absence from battle deserving of death
(*Christopher Marlowe*, p. 263). Tamburlaine's fellow-soldiers are aware
of that law, yet they are also aware of the unnatural quality of killing
one's son, and plead for clemency. Tamburlaine's speech during this execution plainly illustrates that the chief motive for it is not military justice,
but the intolerable ignominy of having a son who prefers not to engage
in battle.

[42] *Christopher Marlowe*, p. 99.

the first part's essentially ambivalent theme of "honor" defined and achieved by bloody destruction. For here, as elsewhere, Tamburlaine persists in cloaking the cruelest of deeds in the most glowing accounts of his superhuman aspiration. The ironies implicit in such aspiration are brought out by the concrete stage-picture of the execution itself—the glowing words do not match the deed; the visual action undercuts the nature of the speech. If the irony of such juxtaposition is not intended, it represents a serious dramatic error.

The increasingly barbaric side of Tamburlaine's nature is further accentuated by the two other instances in the play where he himself is shown inflicting punishment on those he has conquered: having his chariot drawn by captive kings, and having the Governor of Babylon hung on the city walls and shot to death. Both scenes demonstrate Marlowe's quite obvious bent for sensationalism; nevertheless it is sensationalism that defines the character of Tamburlaine. The spectacle of an ambitious king drawn in his chariot by human captives was not unknown to the English stage before *Tamburlaine*. The 1566 Gray's Inn production of *Jocasta* by George Gascoigne and Francis Kinwelmersh began with a dumb show symbolizing the moral theme of the tragedy: "Firste, before the beginning of the first Acte, did sounde a dolefull & straunge noyse of violles, Cythren, Bandurion, and such like, during the whiche, there came in vppon the Stage a king with an Imperial crown vppon his head, very richely apparelled: a Scepter in his righte hande, a Mounde with a Crosse in his left hande, sitting in a Chariote very richely furnished, drawne in by foure Kinges in their Dublettes and Hosen, with Crownes also vpon their heades. Representing vnto vs Ambition, by the hystorie of *Sesostres* king of *Egypt*, who beeing in his time and reigne a mightie Conquerour, yet not content to haue subdued many princes, and taken from them their kingdomes and dominions, did in like maner cause those Kinges whome he had so ouercome, to draw in his Chariote

like Beastes and Oxen, thereby to content his vnbrideled ambitious desire."[43]

It is likely that Marlowe took his hint from this play, which
had been reprinted in 1587 for the second time since the original publication.[44] He has activated the stage-emblem of ambition by making it a literal incident in Tamburlaine's career,
adapting even the details to the Scythian conqueror's nature:
instead of a scepter and ball, Tamburlaine holds the reins of
his "pampered jades" in one hand and scourges them with
a whip he holds in the other.

The execution of the Governor of Babylon is only one of
the sensational deeds that fill the scene following the collapse
of Babylon (v. i). Tamburlaine, in the space of less than one
hundred lines, has the Governor hung in chains from the city
wall, scornfully watches him plead for his life, and orders
his men to shoot him to death; the two exhausted kings who
have drawn his chariot he sends off to be hanged, replacing
them with two others; he gives the command to drown all
men, women, and children of Babylon in the lake; finally,
he burns the holy books of Mahomet, daring the prophet to
stop his action by a miracle. Certainly, the cumulative effect
of these actions is to impress the audience with the untold
audacity of the man, which here reaches its height in physically
observable terms. It is precisely at this point that Marlowe
chooses to introduce the shadow of Tamburlaine's final undoing: at the end of the scene which brings both his physical
barbarism and spiritual audacity to a climax, he is struck with
a sudden distemper.

Tamburlaine's increasingly frenzied defiance of mortal limi-

[43] *Early English Classical Tragedies*, p. 69.

[44] It is also possible that the idea was prompted by some historical account of Sesostres. Hallett Smith points out that this incident in Sesostres'
career is mentioned along with Tamburlaine's treatment of Bajazeth in
Loys Le Roy's *De la Vicissitude ou Variété des Choses en l'Univers* (Paris,
1577): "Tamburlaine and the Renaissance," *Elizabethan Studies and Other
Essays in Honor of George F. Reynolds* (Boulder, Colo., 1945), p. 129.

tations reaches its height when sickness and death begin to threaten him. His initial reaction to the sudden illness, as might be expected, is: "Sicknes or death can neuer conquer me" (κ5ᵛ). When the malady becomes so great that he can no longer deny it, he strikes out in rage against the gods:

> Shall sicknesse prooue me now to be a man,
> That haue bene tearm'd the terrour of the world?
> *Techelles* and the rest, come take your swords,
> And threaten him whose hand afflicts my soul,
> Come let vs march against the powers of heauen,
> And set blacke streamers in the firmament,
> To signifie the slaughter of the Gods,
> Ah friends, what shal I doe I cannot stand ...   (κ7ᵛ)

Never in all of English drama had anyone reacted to suffering in this way, for never had a figure of such dimensions been portrayed on the English stage. Quite conventional, however, are Tamburlaine's companions, who, just as at the death of Zenocrate, urge moderation; they are related to the Senecan line of rational confidantes who try to calm an impassioned sufferer. Tamburlaine himself, half-paralyzed in his king-drawn chariot, is in this scene closer to Seneca's Hercules than to the furiously stamping Herod of the mystery plays.[45] The shame of defeat by disease is Alcides' great torture in *Hercules Oetaeus*, while the threat to storm the gods is voiced by the insane hero of *Hercules Furens* (ll. 955-973) and also by the frenzied Medea (*Medea*, ll. 424-425). Marlowe's characteristic irony asserts itself in the juxtaposition of the fantastic order to march against heaven with the realistic confession of helplessness: "I cannot stand."

That helplessness is further emphasized in the following lines, where again the dramatist develops his scene of suffering by the device of ironic illusion. Tamburlaine imagines

---

[45] Battenhouse lists several parallels between Tamburlaine and the Senecan Hercules pointed out by himself and others, pp. 196-202.

he sees his "slaue, the vglie monster death," cowardly aiming the fatal dart at him, but in vain does the self-professed master of death command him to leave (κ7ᵛ). Just as in Dido's final suffering, this illusion is worked out in terms of the play's past action and theme; as such it establishes a dramatic irony that becomes integral to the structure of the play.

Tamburlaine nevertheless manages to take the sting out of death's dart—characteristically, in terms of action. At this nadir of his physical capacity he still succeeds in bringing about the greatest military victory of his career—with a single glance at the opposition forces led by Callapine. Undoubtedly Marlowe has here strained to the breaking point the limits of even dramatic plausibility, but the subsequent action tends to remove attention from the military victory. Tamburlaine calls for a world map to trace out his past achievements and to show his remaining two sons, in whom he sees himself immortalized, what they have left to conquer in the known world. Placing the grief-stricken Amyras in his king-drawn chariot, and crowning him as successor, Tamburlaine, the Scourge of God, dies as he first appeared—in a soaring and triumphant flight of rhetoric. He alone among Marlowe's protagonists finally meets his death in a spirit of calm dignity, exemplifying in his last words and actions "that magnanimitie,/ That nobly must admit necessity" (L2). Marlowe in the final scene has shown Tamburlaine to be above all ordinary human suffering—not untouched by it, as he was in Part I, but always, by the extravagancies of his action or imagination, able to rise above it. The response to Tamburlaine's "suffering" is neither sympathy nor pity, but predominantly awe.

That awe is not unqualified by certain ironies, however, which distinguish Part II from Part I. The suffering and destruction in the first play become intelligible in terms of Tamburlaine himself, Tamburlaine the afflicter who presides over the cosmos of that drama. In Part II the universe of the play is more expansive; the vision of the source of suffering and death becomes broader, and Tamburlaine himself becomes a victim. For the first time the protagonist meets physical destruction not willed by himself. In reacting to such experience Tamburlaine enters into "an affair with the gods," challenging the higher powers for taking away Zenocrate, for sending him such progeny as Calyphas, for afflicting him with sickness, the mark of mere humanity. He retaliates as best he can, but a gold-covered corpse, a murdered son, and a weeping boy for a successor are ironic testaments of the limitations of even his power.

Tamburlaine's most delirious ravings are caused by two painfully felt losses: first, his loss of Zenocrate; second and more pervasive, the loss of his conception of himself as superhuman. His worst sufferings are thus a result of the combination of his character and the assertion of a universal order greater than himself. Faced at last with the problem of human suffering as a personal experience, he explains it away in a thoroughly characteristic manner:

> In vaine I striue and raile against those powers,
> That meane t'inuest me in a higher throane,
> As much too high for this disdainfull earth. (K8^v)

The mad Titan who gave such wild, profane orders to war against the gods now decides that they wish to reward him. He resurrects the godlike concept of himself, and dies. His imagination, in refusing to admit loss, may convince himself that he remains supreme in spite of death; but it cannot convince the audience, which is able to perceive the rationalization.

Obviously Tamburlaine's death is not to be explained by the warrior's own interpretation; but what are we to make of it? The circumstances of his fatal affliction remain exasperatingly ambiguous: although Marlowe takes pains to present a strictly physiological explanation of the disease, Tamburlaine himself sees it first as an act of the gods—but as an *envious* act rather than retribution for any kind of vice or wickedness. He is afflicted, however, moments after he has reached the height of his inhuman cruelties in the sack of Babylon, and just after his defiant burning of the Koran. The conventional scheme of the wheel of Fortune seems to be hovering in the background, along with some sense of a supernatural nemesis. But the conventional moral explications of retributive punishment, such as one finds in *Cambises* or *The Misfortunes of Arthur*, are altogether absent in *Tamburlaine*.

One cannot overlook, however, the arbitrary cruelties, the undisguisedly bloody aspirations, and the persistent stance of rebellious profanity which characterize Tamburlaine's behavior in Part ii. Together with the stress on the ironic illusions and assertions of mortal limitation in Tamburlaine's career, they indicate something about the moral nature of man and the nature of the universe without need of explicit moral commentary. As Jean Jacquot has remarked, Marlowe's superman turns out to be something of a beast, so that we finally turn from him in horror, despite his powers of seduction, and without the author's explicit use of the convention that vice is necessarily punished. And this, Jacquot adds, is the better proof of the play's moral significance.[46]

Tamburlaine, in his dynamic but futile attempt to be more than man, reveals that the drive for superhumanity through martial conquest leads inevitably to inhumanity. The law of strife, not harmony, is the foundation of his aspiration, and it can only be fulfilled in terms of destructive physical violence. Indeed, it is strife within his own being, the strife of the elements upon which he rationalizes his thirst for sovereignty in Part i, which finally and ironically brings about his death: the fiery choler aggravated by his wrathful outbursts consumes his own blood.[47] Thus, in one sense, Tamburlaine

---

[46] "La Pensée de Marlowe dans *Tamburlaine the Great*," *Études Anglaises*, vi (1953), 344.

[47] See Battenhouse's chapter, "Tamburlaine's Humour," pp. 217-225.

destroys himself indirectly by his own excesses. Marlowe's curious insistence on the malady's physiological details, which are expressed by Tamburlaine's physicians but also foreshadowed by the curse of the defeated Soria, is best explained perhaps in terms of this irony. Other aspects of his dramaturgy, however, clearly stress the "affair with the gods" as well, and point to powers in the universe more mighty than Tamburlaine the Great.

This last is apparently the function of the representation of suffering in the play which has no direct connection with Tamburlaine. This is displayed in two sub-actions drawn from sources not even remotely connected with the historical Tamburlaine: the Sigismond-Orcanes episode, taken with little alteration from the historical accounts of Bonfinius and Callimachus, and the Olympia story, derived from Cantos XXVIII and XXIX of *Orlando Furioso*.[48]

The Sigismond-Orcanes action opens the play. In it, the Christian forces led by Sigismond of Hungary and the Turks under Orcanes swear by Christ and Mahomet, respectively, to a truce which is then treacherously broken by the Christians. Orcanes, after being attacked, calls on Christ to revenge the desecration of the oath in his name, gains the victory, and proceeds to march against Tamburlaine. Why did Marlowe include this action? Ellis-Fermor suggests it is irrelevant padding hastily thrown in to fill out a sequel to the successful Part 1; Kocher and Boas interpret it as intentional anti-Christian sniping.[49] The first suggestion begs the question of dramatic relevance; the second is based on two presumptions which minimize the objective validity of the action's inclusion, namely, that Marlowe's ulterior purpose in playwriting is to project his subjective feelings against the Christian religion, and that any example of Christians not living up to their faith

[48] Ellis-Fermor, *ed. cit.*, pp. 42-44.
[49] Ellis-Fermor, *ed. cit.*, pp. 41-43; Kocher, p. 95; Boas, *Christopher Marlowe*, p. 97.

necessarily reveals an anti-Christian sentiment.[50] A more satisfactory suggestion can be found, I think, in terms of the play itself: by opening with this episode, Marlowe establishes at the very start a broad vision of the universe which looks beyond mere human agency for the source of suffering. The dramatic effect of the action is to put the responsibility for the outcome of the battle on a power that transcends the human contestants, in this case, the power of Christ. Orcanes' challenge to Christ to vindicate his power and divinity by punishing the Christians concludes with the battle cry:

> To armes my Lords, on Christ still let vs crie,
> If there be Christ, we shall haue victorie.[51]   (G5ᵛ)

The battle rages off stage; and next we see Sigismond, wounded, and giving witness in his dying speech to his own guilt and the just revenge of God:

> Discomfited is all the Christian hoste,
> And God hath thundered vengeance from on high,
> For my accurst and hatefull periurie.
> O iust and dreadfull punisher of sinne,
> Let the dishonor of the paines I feele,
> In this my mortall well deserued wound,
> End all my penance in my sodaine death,
> And let this death wherein to sinne I die,
> Conceiue a second life in endlesse mercie.   (G5ᵛ)

---

[50] The first presumption operates as the central assumption (rather than a conclusion from demonstrated facts) in Kocher's study of Marlowe, which tends to force his criticism, for all its grounding in scholarly research, into preconceived channels which often confuse rather than illuminate the dramatic issues in the plays. The second presumption, a common fallacy, would not only subvert any attempt at Christian moral satire, but, carried to its "logical" extreme, must judge much of the content of Christian sermons as anti-Christian in this respect.

[51] Kocher's interpretation of this line and the succeeding action is indicative of the blind spot his thesis produces. He asserts that "If there be Christ" is Marlowe's personal agnostic innuendo (p. 96), and ignores the dramatic fact that the whole sentence sets up a challenge which is immediately answered in the affirmative by the ensuing action. Kocher neither mentions

The idea of retribution is reasserted in the speech of Orcanes following Sigismond's death, in which the Turk attributes his victory to the justice of Christ. Despite the skeptical assertion of Gazellus that it was merely "the fortune of the wars" (G6), Orcanes continues to honor Christ for the outcome.[52]

Besides its function of setting the stage in a supernatural framework, this episode operates as an analogous action with the other great "challenge" scene—Tamburlaine's daring Mahomet to work a miracle and stop the burning of the sacred books. Unlike the challenge to Christ, this challenge goes unanswered, with the obvious implication that Mahomet is powerless.[53] Marlowe, in putting together his play from diverse sources, has again fallen back on the principle of analogy as a unifying structural force, a tendency also evident in *Dido* and *Doctor Faustus*, and firmly implanted in the English dramatic tradition of his time.

---

nor quotes the dying speech of Sigismond which comes as the first indication of that answer.

[52] Both Kocher (pp. 97-101) and Battenhouse (pp. 160-161) document the orthodoxy of Orcanes' conception of the deity. Orcanes' religious sincerity, implicit orthodoxy, and respect for Christ would no doubt establish him for Marlowe's audience as one of the more respectable Turkish characters. That he should be bridled as one of Tamburlaine's "jades" in the midst of the Babylon scene is a further indication of that scene's function, namely, to exhibit the climax of Tamburlaine's cruelty.

[53] Kocher clearly demonstrates that the Koran-burning scene contains nothing that would be unacceptable to the religious feelings of the contemporary Christian audience (pp. 87-88). Battenhouse's reading of the scene as clear blasphemy (pp. 173-174) does not adequately account for the last lines of Tamburlaine's speech which point to the God that sits in heaven as the only God worthy of worship. At the same time, this deed must be numbered among Tamburlaine's several extreme gestures of spiritual audacity, in Part II, which reveal the urge to push his mastery beyond human bounds by challenging the higher powers. Given the terms of *this* challenge, however, it would be unreasonable to expect lightning to strike at this precise point, for that would "prove" Mahomet a deity. By introducing the first traces of Tamburlaine's affliction some lines later at the very end of the Babylon scene, Marlowe has perhaps solved the problem of showing some kind of retribution for Tamburlaine's over-reaching pride and inhumanity, while avoiding the implication that Mahomet is responsible for it.

It should be noted that Sigismond is the only Christian character to meet suffering and death in either part of *Tamburlaine*. His dying speech is unique, therefore, in that it represents a completely Christian attitude toward suffering. Sigismond looks upon his afflictions not only as a punishment, but as a way of spiritual purgation; his prayer is that the physical pains of his wounds and death will be accepted by God, along with his personal contrition, as satisfaction for his sin of perjury. In accepting physical death as a penance, he makes of it a spiritual "death to sin" as well, hoping thereby to earn God's mercy and eternal life.

Marlowe's theological knowledge is employed with some precision here, in that he expresses the repentance of this fifteenth-century king of Hungary in terms of Catholic rather than Protestant doctrine. It is the notion of accepting suffering as satisfaction for sin which in this respect distinguishes the two. The Catholic formulation of penance involved three parts: contrition, confession, and satisfaction. According to the formulation of the scholastic theologians, every sin merits both eternal and temporal punishment; the former is remitted at absolution by virtue of Christ's atonement for the sins of all men (and absolution can be granted either in the Sacrament of Penance or by the desire for that Sacrament in emergency); but the latter could only be paid by some sacrifice involving inconvenience or suffering.[54] One way to make such satisfaction was through the kind of acceptance of pain made by Sigismond in the play; as the *Summa Theologica* of Thomas Aquinas states, ". . . if the scourges, which are inflicted by God on account of sin, become in some way the act of the sufferer they acquire a satisfactory character. Now they become the act of the sufferer in so far as he accepts them for the cleansing of his sins, by taking advantage of them patiently. If, however, he refuse to submit to them patiently, then they do not be-

[54] See e.g., Thomas Aquinas, *Summa Theologica*, III, lxxxvi, 4.

come his personal act in any way, and are not of a satisfactory, but merely of a vindictive character."[55]

The Protestant position, on the contrary, grounded in the doctrine of justification by faith alone, denied that satisfaction for sin could be made by works or sufferings, asserting that Christ alone satisfies for sin.[56] Indeed, as Tyndale wrote, "No bodily pain can be a satisfaction to God, save Christ's passion,"[57] and anyone who would make satisfaction to God for his sins is by Protestant standards faithless.[58] That the distinction in Sigismond's speech would have been noticed in actual dramatic presentation is dubious; the chief importance of the observation is the reassertion of Marlowe's characteristic use of his formal learning in an intellectually precise way. But the doctrine is not intended to be noticed for its own sake; it is used in a responsible way to give form to the last thoughts of the suffering King of Hungary.

The principle of analogy which links the Orcanes-Sigismond story with the main action of Tamburlaine is also operative in the other sub-action, Theridamas' capture and wooing of Olympia. Before Theridamas and Techelles come upon her, Olympia has witnessed the death of her Captain-husband, and has also slain her young son in the hope of saving him from the barbaric tortures of their conquerors. She herself longs for death and spiritual reunion with both husband and son, but her intended suicide is stopped by her captors. A note of heroic Stoicism pervades this scene, entering into the motivation and

[55] III Supp., xv, 2. Trans. Fathers of the English Dominican Province, vol. III (New York, 1948), p. 2622. The third part of the *Summa* was one of the printed books in the Corpus Christi College Library while Marlowe was studying there: Corpus Christi College MS. 575, p. 10.

[56] See Henry Bullinger, *The Decades*, ed. Thomas Harding, Parker Society (Cambridge, 1851), III, 90; Thomas Becon, *The Early Works*, ed. John Ayre, Parker Society (Cambridge, 1843), p. 102; William Tyndale, *Doctrinal Treatises*, ed. Henry Walter, Parker Society (Cambridge, 1848), pp. 228, 267.

[57] *Expositions and Notes*, ed. Henry Walter, Parker Society (Cambridge, 1849), p. 29.

[58] *Doctrinal Treatises*, p. 228.

speech of both mother and son; the admiring comments of Tamburlaine's generals when they discover what has happened emphasize the woman's resolute courage. Two scenes later another son is stabbed by another parent when Tamburlaine executes Calyphas—an ironic contrast with the first slaying. Bravery in the son and love in the parent have been converted to cowardice in the son and hate in the parent; heroism gives way to grotesque cruelty.

The further development of the Olympia story involves the vain attempts of Theridamas to win the love of his beautiful captive, whom he courts with the identical imagery and enticing visions that Tamburlaine once used with Zenocrate, though in a lower key. When Olympia remains faithful to her loved ones, and manages by a ruse to have Theridamas kill her, the thwarted warrior again echoes the language and imagery of his master at the death of Zenocrate. As Helen Gardner has suggested, it is evident that this part of the Olympia story is an analogical reflection of the relations between Tamburlaine and Zenocrate in both parts of the play, and it serves further to emphasize the major theme of Part II, the inevitable limitations of even a conquering human power.[59] One can add that it also reinforces the sense of personal loss that characterizes much of the suffering in Part II. Olympia's unendurable pain is to be cut off from her husband and son, in whom her love and life had been centered; Theridamas' sorrow over the loss of Olympia is aggravated by his own ironic cooperation in her death; Tamburlaine rages at the loss of Zenocrate, but he is left with his still greater love, the love of war and violence which magnifies his superhuman image of himself. Tamburlaine's last expressed emotion is pity for those who must now live on without him, and the play closes on the grief of the warlord's sons and companions, who

[59] "The Second Part of 'Tamburlaine the Great,'" *MLR*, XXXVII (1942), 22-23. Battenhouse sees Olympia as an exemplar of virtue intended to contrast with the moral frailties of Zenocrate (pp. 167-168).

are indeed lost without their leader. Death, and the universe which deals it out, reign supreme.

ह❧

The treatment of suffering in both *Dido* and *Tamburlaine* exposes the root causes of human anguish in love and violence. It brings to the fore the painful ironies implicit in the aspirations of the human mind to overleap the bounds of mortal limitation, to fly in the face of fact. On the technical side, it reflects Marlowe's wide-ranging attempts to suit the expression of suffering to the character of his figures, indeed, to create character through the individual response to suffering. It draws on both conventional forms and themes, such as the *De Casibus* tradition, and unconventional sources of knowledge, such as physiology and theology, to give shape to the representation of human response to pain. It reflects Marlowe's tendency to exploit the illusory effects of grief, and in so doing to accent the deep ironies involved in man's attempts to escape from pain through imagination. At the same time, however, the suffering of any individual character tends to be represented in fairly simple terms. That Marlowe was capable of more complex, ironic, and paradoxical effects is demonstrated in *Edward II* and *Doctor Faustus*; that he was also capable of even simpler and cruder things is evident in his two plays centering on a villain-protagonist, *The Massacre at Paris* and *The Jew of Malta*.

CHAPTER III · INCARNATIONS
OF EVIL: BARABAS THE JEW AND
THE DUKE OF GUISE

Sit downe and see what hainous stratagems
These damned wits contriue.

—THE BATTELL OF ALCAZAR

CHAPTER III · INCARNATIONS
OF EVIL: BARABAS THE JEW AND
THE DUKE OF GUISE

I. *THE JEW OF MALTA*

O N T H E annals of the English drama Marlowe's *Jew of Malta* has been consistently labeled a spectacle of monstrous villainy. Efforts to interpret the career of Barabas in the light of any of the classical theories of tragedy have been awkward failures, and with good reason, for the central figure of the play is not in the least heroic or admirable—nor was he meant to be. Into the character of Barabas Marlowe has poured all the vilest ingredients from the bugbears of contemporary popular imagination, fusing the infidel Jew with the ruthless Machiavellian, and animating the mixture with the spirit of the morality Vice. The result is a figure more grotesquely inhuman than Tamburlaine at his cruelest moments, a figure incarnating the inverse of orthodox Elizabethan virtues and values, a figure, ironically enough, whose closest kinship with humanity is registered in terms of avarice and egoism. Barabas is human, too, to the extent that he can feel suffering; but it is the suffering that he inflicts on others that provides the focal interest. *The Jew of Malta* is a spectacle of personified evil at work, rather than a spectacle of tragic suffering. The nature of that evil, as well as the nature of the personification, must be carefully examined; and one way to begin is to see how Marlowe's treatment of suffering in this play contributes to the greater picture.

The handling of suffering in *The Jew of Malta* reveals a basic similarity to that in *Tamburlaine*; both the physical suffering perpetrated on others by the ingenious Jew and the mental suffering he himself must undergo reflect his deepest motivations, the nature of his character, and the essential quality of his career. Furthermore, the pattern of his reaction to obstacles that cause him suffering, or at least discomfiture—whether it be the confiscation of his wealth, the conversion of his daughter, or the blackmail of his servant—is heated rage and coldly calculated revenge. The revenge takes the shape of extravagant physical destruction; the rage indicates the depth to which his pain affects him.

Barabas' most violent reaction is at the loss of his wealth to the Governor of Cyprus. After the government has confiscated his goods, Barabas, left with three other Jews, his "comforters," curses his Christian persecutors for their "policy":

> The plagues of *Egypt*, and the curse of heauen,
> Earths barrennesse, and all mens hatred
> Inflict vpon them, thou great *Primas Motor*.
> And here vpon my knees, striking the earth,
> I banne their soules to everlasting paines
> And extreme tortures of the fiery deepe,
> That thus haue dealt with me in my distresse.[1]

The other Jews urge patience, recalling the example of Job; but Barabas belittles the sufferings of Job, who, he says, lost but the merest fraction of Barabas' own wealth. It is significant that Barabas reckons only the material losses of Job, and makes no mention of the loss of his children, or of the physical afflictions that beset Job's body; it is only material wealth that Barabas deems important.

The contrast between Job and Barabas, brought out so clearly by the afflicted Jew in the presence of his three comforters, and by the direct allusion, has even further connotations. The contrast in wealth may be one of degree only, but the contrast of attitudes toward wealth and of reactions to suffering is one of kind. The patience of Job is the extreme opposite of the violence of Barabas, as are all the elements of Job's character.

[1] *The Famous Tragedy of The Rich Ievv of Malta* (London, 1633), C2ᵛ. Readex Microprint of the Huntington Library copy in *Three Centuries of Drama: English, 1512-1641*, ed. Henry W. Wells (New York, 1953). Subsequent references to this edition will appear in my text.

In his protestation of innocence, for example, Job lists those sins which would have merited such punishment as his own, but of which he is not guilty:

> If I made golde mine hope, or haue said to the
>   wedge of golde, *Thou* art my confidence,
> If I reioyced because my substance was great,
>   or because mine hand had gotten muche . . .
> If I reioyced at his destruction that hated me,
>   or was moued to *ioye* when euil came vpon him,
> Nether haue I suffred my mouth to sinne,
>   by wishing a cursse vnto his soule.[2]

Barabas is the incarnation of these very offenses. The first scene of the play presents him doting over his piles of gold, rejoicing in the extent of his treasures. "The comfort of mine age" is one of the phrases he applies to his wealth, when speaking before the Governor (c2). His self-avowed egoism in the first scene establishes the contempt he feels for all people other than his daughter and himself, even to the malevolent extent of wishing that the Turks will take over the town. And the focal point of his speech of "suffering" is to curse his offenders. It does not really matter that this point-for-point contrast may not be dramatically evident to the audience; it reveals, most importantly, the dramatist's *conception* behind the presentation of the character, which is grounded on the complete and consistent inversion of accepted values and virtues.

The depth and sincerity of Barabas' violently expressed suffering is undercut almost immediately. The "comforters," finally realizing that neither their presence nor advice will assuage Barabas' fury, leave him "in his irefull mood" (c3),

---

[2] Job xxxi. 24-30. The quotation is from the Geneva Bible (Geneva, 1560), the English translation most in use in Marlowe's lifetime. The marginal gloss to the above passage includes yet another contrast to the career of Barabas: "My seruants moued me to be reuēged of mine enemie, yet did I neuer wish him hurt."

and the Jew's whole manner swiftly changes. His hot passion is replaced by calm, collected calculation; he begins to plan his retaliation with cold precision. The sudden shift of mood is akin to the dissimulation of manner already made evident in his earlier meeting with the three other Jews; only the audience is allowed to witness the cunning of Barabas. In this instance, the effect is to cast back upon Barabas' violent rage the tempering quality of surface-show. The effect is strengthened in the subsequent encounter with Abigail, in which Barabas reveals that he had suspected some such confiscation would take place, and had hidden a good store of gold and precious jewels from his potential enemies. Abigail's sorrow offers another contrast to her father's pain, since she mourns not the loss of wealth, as Barabas first presumes, but the grief that such loss will bring to her father. Barabas reveals his true nature even more when he counsels his daughter to cease her sorrow, urging her to the same patience he himself so peremptorily refused to admit:

> No, *Abigail*, things past recouery
> Are hardly cur'd with exclamations.
> Be silent, Daughter, sufferance breeds ease . . .   (c3ᵛ)

Like the Vice of the morality plays, Barabas is eminently capable of inverting his professed sentiments to suit the person with whom he talks.

Barabas suffers two great losses in the course of his career: the confiscation of his wealth (at least that part which is not hidden), and the conversion of his daughter to Christianity. We have already seen his reaction to the first. Although it is a loss that admits of recovery, and indeed is recovered swiftly enough, the confiscation produces the fiercest emotional impact on the Jew. The rage he demonstrates at that point far outstrips in intensity and length his reaction to the "loss" of his daughter to Christianity. After learning of the matter from

Abigail's letter and from the report of Ithamore, Barabas takes only a moment to formulate his curse:

> Oh vnhappy day,
> False, credulous, inconstant *Abigall*!
> But let 'em goe: And *Ithimore*, from hence
> Ne're shall she grieue me more with her disgrace;
> Ne're shall she liue to inherit ought of mine,
> Be blest of me, nor come within my gates,
> But perish vnderneath my bitter curse
> Like *Cain* by *Adam*, for his brother's death. (F3ᵛ)

This short speech is compacted of the essential elements of the Jew's character: the Jew's loyalty to himself comes before all; hence, his daughter will be eliminated lest her life in Christianity disgrace him; the worst curse he can formulate against her is the one that is greatest in his own scheme of values but actually inconsequential to her—disinheriting her; finally, as in the comparison he once made between his loss and Job's, he distorts Scripture to justify his own action, for Cain never perished under any curse of his father Adam. The Jew takes no time to dwell upon his sorrow; he begins at once to prepare for the poisoning of the entire nunnery which harbors his daughter. He has no qualms about making the loss of his daughter a permanent one.

That the Jew should register so much less grief at the loss of his daughter than at the loss of his gold comes as no real surprise. Even though Barabas' world is admittedly bounded by three considerations only—himself, his wealth, and his daughter—the hierarchy of the three is never in question. The first allusion he makes to Abigail is weighted with irony:

> I haue no charge, nor many children,
> But one sole Daughter, whom I hold as deare
> As *Agamemnon* did his *Iphigen* . . . (B3ᵛ)

The most notable aspect of the relationship of Agamemnon to his daughter was never his affection for her but his willingness to sacrifice her for his own ends. And Barabas, whose quintessential motto is *Ego mihimet sum semper proximas* (B4), is not in the least hesitant in sacrificing, first the man his daughter loves, and second the daughter herself, to satisfy his own extravagant desire for revenge. That wealth is dearer to Barabas than his daughter is brilliantly exhibited in the famous speech which Shakespeare's Jew was to echo later:

> Oh my girle.
> My gold, my fortune, my felicity;
> Strength to my soule, death to mine enemy;
> Welcome the first beginner of my blisse:
> Oh A[b]igal, *Abigal*, that I had thee here too,
> Then my desires were fully satisfied,
> But I will practise thy enlargement thence:
> Oh girle, oh gold, oh beauty, oh my blisse!
>
> *hugs his bags.* (D2ᵛ)

Iniquity is as dear to Barabas as Mammon; his delight in his own ingenious stratagems of revenge is everywhere evident, especially in the words uttered with his last breath. The main impact of his death speech, screamed forth while he is boiling in the caldron he had prepared for his enemies, is to reveal how much he glories in his crimes and revels in his curses:

> And villaines, know you cannot helpe me now.
> Then *Barabas* breath forth thy latest fate,
> And in the fury of thy torments, striue
> To end thy life with resolution:
> Know Gouernor, 'twas I that slew thy sonne;
> I fram'd the challenge that did make them meet:
> Know, *Calymath*, I aym'd thy ouerthrow,
> And had I but eicap'd [*sic*] this stratagem,
> I would haue brought confusion on you all,

Damn'd Christians, dogges, and Turkish Infidels;
But now begins the extremity of heat
To pinch me with intolerable pangs:
Dye life, flye soule, tongue curse thy fill and dye!   (k2)

Obviously no pity or sympathy is evoked by this death scene,
nor does the manner of the Jew's destruction seem out of pro-
portion to the nature of his crimes. On the contrary, it is but
fitting that the Jew should stew in his own hideous pot.

The pot itself is fitting in more ways than one. Literally and
objectively, it is the trap that ironically catches the trapper,
but its conventional symbolic and emblematic significance
makes it even more appropriate. From medieval times the
caldron as an instrument of torture was a very common *motif*
in the iconography of hell;[3] and as Harry Levin has pointed
out,[4] it appears in Geoffrey Whitney's *A Choice of Emblemes*
(1586) as an emblem for the text from the Gospel of Luke
(xviii.14), *Qui se exaltat, humiliabitur*.[5] Furthermore, in de-
tailing the criminal punishments of sixteenth-century England,
William Harrison in his "Description" notes that "such as
kill by poyson are eyther skalded to death in lead or seething
water."[6] Marlowe has chosen for his Jew a mode of suffering
and death which goes beyond mere dramatic shock-value and
carries with it appropriate retribution for the specific evils
which make up the character of Barabas.

That character is thrown into relief in still another way
by contrast with the character of Abigail, whose suffering and
reactions to suffering fall into a classical pattern of deepened
wisdom and calm resignation. Her very name recalls the Biblical Abigail of 1 Kings xxv whose soft words appeased David's

---

[3] Donald Clive Stuart, "The Stage Setting of Hell and the Iconography
of the Middle Ages," *Romanic Review*, IV (1913), 336-337.
[4] *The Overreacher: A Study of Christopher Marlowe* (Cambridge, Mass.,
1952), p. 77.
[5] (Leyden, 1586), d4ᵛ.
[6] In Raphael Holinshed, *The Firste volume of the Chronicles of England,
Scotlande, and Irelande* (London, 1577), 03ᵛ.

wrath and dissuaded him from revenge. In Marlowe's play she stands apart from all other characters as the only fully sympathetic person. Her first appearance reveals her sorrowing over the grief her dispossessed father must endure at the loss of his estate. Her dutiful compliance with his plans demonstrates her trust and obedience, at the same time that it reveals the Jew's callousness toward his daughter's feelings. From the lips of the gloating Ithamore she learns of her father's responsibility for the death of her lover, and this shock calls forth her new awareness of the evil that surrounds her:

> But I perceiue there is no loue on earth,
> Pitty in Iewes, nor piety in Turkes. (F2ᵛ)

This bitter insight prompts her conversion to Christianity, but it does not destroy her loyalty to her father, in spite of the treachery he has displayed. It is especially noteworthy that she ultimately blames not her father, nor even his henchman Ithamore, but the principle of infidelity that underlies the lives of Jews and Turks in general, a principle which she sees as a spiritual condition. As she explains to the Friar in a later scene:

> But now experience, purchased with griefe,
> Has made me see the difference of things.
> My sinfull soule, alas, hath pac'd too long
> The fatall Labyrinth of misbeleefe,
> Farre from the Sonne that giues eternall life. (F3)

Abigail has found wisdom through suffering, a wisdom which enables her to die without fear, and without thoughts of her own welfare:

> Death seizeth on my heart, ah gentle Fryar
> Conuert my father that he may be sau'd,
> And witnesse that I dye a Christian. (Gᵛ-G2)

The complete and utter contrast of her attitude toward Barabas with his attitude toward her is stressed at this point by juxtaposing Abigail's death scene with the picture of Barabas rejoicing at the death-knell of the nuns. Even the conscience-less Ithamore is surprised at Barabas' glee; he asks the Jew if he does not feel some sorrow at Abigail's death, and hears in reply: "No, but I grieue because she liu'd so long" (G2ᵛ). The Jew's make-up admits no love, no compassion, no consideration for anything or anyone other than himself. Disdainfully he proclaims while busily preparing the trap into which he himself eventually falls: "For so I liue, perish may all the world" (κ).

Viewed from the perspective of a broadly naturalistic drama, a drama that makes some efforts at psychological realism or, at least, adequately motivated characterization, the Jew of Malta will always appear an inhuman and incredible creature. From the same point of view the vision of evil underlying the play must be judged as basically a simplistic one: suffering and evil are not problems, but the result of sheer villainy on the part of totally selfish characters. Justice triumphs and evil is destroyed when the cunning traitor is cunningly betrayed. But there is a danger here that such a perspective and its consequent judgments are altogether too conditioned by presuppositions of the modern theater, and do not take into account the nature of the Elizabethan stage, which had firm roots in medieval traditions and modes of thought that long outlived Marlowe himself. The morality tradition, in which characters are not really persons but moral principles, or dramatic metaphors for moral principles, is particularly relevant in the case of *The Jew of Malta*; the character of Barabas begins to make more sense when the demand for psychological realism is relaxed and examination of the dramaturgical and moral principles which underlie his character is intensified. Such an examination must include the ideas involved in the labels affixed to the protagonist by Marlowe—Barabas as Jew, Barabas as Machiavel—as well as the characteristic dramaturgical qualities Barabas shares with the morality Vice.

Abigail's reaction to her father's treachery provides a convenient starting point: it is not Barabas himself that is evil but his "Jewishness"—Jewishness understood partly in the literal or racial sense, but more pervasively in the figurative sense, the sense that evokes a spiritual condition characterized by lack of faith and love. For the Christian of the Elizabethan age, as for the Christian of centuries previous, "Jew" and "Turk" were familiar epithets applied not only to opponents of Christianity but also to those Christians who acted as the non-Christian was imagined to behave, especially in manifestations of infidelity, usury, and greed.

Both literal and figurative representations of Jewishness were embodied in the dramatic tradition of England. The crucifixion plays of the medieval mystery-cycles emphasized the perfidy of the Jews who put Christ to death, but chief stress lay on the character of Judas, who, in his close relation to Jesus and the Apostles, became the popular symbol for all those who betray Christ for self-gain. In Elizabethan times Biblical plays treating Old Testament figures could not escape portraying Jewish characters, but more often than not these were treated with the religious respect warranted by Scriptural sources and by the Divine favor that accrued to such people as Abraham, David, and others. "Jewishness" as such is clearly not an issue in these plays; it is, however, in Lewis Wager's Biblical morality play, *The Life and Repentance of Mary Magdalene* (printed 1567), which has as its Vice a character called Infidelity. The evil he represents is, essentially, the inverse of the key Protestant virtue of Faith, the Faith that of itself is sufficient and necessary for the justification of man. Consequently, Infidelity bears the marks of the opposition to this central Protestant doctrine: he is compounded of both Jewish and Roman Catholic qualities. His first appearance shows him singing a nonsense song intermixed with Latin phrases from the Roman Mass; but his more immediate quality is indicated by one of his names, Mosaical Justice; indeed, like Shakespeare's Shylock, he demands justification by the law. Like the Vice of the usual morality play, he is also responsible for the temptation and fall of the heroine, Mary Magdalene. The temptation is couched in the traditional and doctrinal terms of pride, the primal sin of egoism. As Infidelity stresses to Mary,

> To be a goddesse your selfe truely you must beleue,
> And y^t you may be so, your mind therto you must geue
> All other gods beside your selfe you must despise.[7]

Finally, as must be expected, Infidelity is the enemy of Christ and all for which he stands.

But the Jew in drama did not necessarily have to be an enemy of Christianity; he could also be employed, within the strictly homiletic confines of the morality play, as a character putting defective Christians to shame by his own virtue. This is the role of Gerontus, for example, in *The Three Ladies of London* (printed 1584), a morality generally directed against the forces of greed operative in contemporary London. Mercadore, a London tradesman who speaks broken English and professes a broken Christianity, has been brought to trial in Turkey for debt evasion. His creditor, the Jew Gerontus, berates him for the crime:

> Surely if we that be Jewes should deale so one with an
>   other,
> We should not be trusted againe of our owne brother:
> But many of you Christians make no conscience to falsifie
>   your fayth and breake your day.[8]

Mercadore, rather than pay his debt of three thousand ducats, attempts to take advantage of a Turkish law that would free him of all debt if he renounced his faith and became a Moslem. As he is about to repeat the words of renunciation

---

[7] TFT (London, 1908), C3^v.

[8] R[obert] W[ilson], *The Three Ladies of London*, TFT (London, 1911), D3^v.

after the Judge, the Jew interrupts, beseeching his debtor to respect his Christian faith, and offering to cancel the interest. Mercadore persists, and the Jew finally forgives the entire debt rather than have him forsake his religion. At this point, freed from all pressure, Mercadore makes his mocking exit, saying that now he will be no Turk for all the goods in the world. The Judge provides the moral of the scene: "Jewes seeke to excell in Christianitie, and Christians in Jewisness" (D3ᵛ).

Such figurative Jewishness seems to be at the base of one of the few plays Stephen Gosson could cite without rebuke in *The Schoole of Abuse* (1579). "The *Iew* . . . showne at the Bull," he wrote, represented "the greedinesse of worldly chusers, and bloody mindes of usurers. . . ."[9] M. J. Landa, in his study of the Jew in drama, interprets this citation as an indication that the play employed the Jew as figure or symbol in a satirical invective against a current Christian evil; he cites as support the circumstantial evidence of the anti-usury laws and debates current in England from 1546 to 1578.[10] The likelihood of this interpretation is strengthened by the fact that such satirical use of the term "Jew" had been conventional at least as early as the twelfth century in the writings of St. Bernard against usury.[11]

Such manifestations of the Jew in drama point to an Elizabethan familiarity with Jewishness in a figurative as well as a literal sense, in which the Jew becomes the dramatic symbol of such Christian moral evils as greed, egoism, infidelity, and worldliness. And these moral evils are precisely the pre-eminent vices not only of the Jew of Malta himself, but of most of the characters in the play. Moreover, the Elizabethan audience had been presented with such Jewishness in contexts

[9] Quoted in E. K. Chambers, *The Elizabethan Stage* (Oxford, 1923), IV, 204.

[10] *The Jew in Drama* (London, 1926), pp. 48-49.

[11] J. L. Cardozo discusses this convention at some length in *The Contemporary Jew in the Elizabethan Drama* (Amsterdam, 1925), pp. 97 ff.

that persistently criticized Christians for not living up to their faith, and especially for the betrayal of faith for lucre. Such criticism, too, is a pervasive force in Marlowe's play; but it has been generally considered the subjective expression of the author rather than a link with the dramatic tradition that manipulated the Jew on stage within such a context. It is in the light of this dramatic tradition that *The Jew of Malta* reveals the greater consistency; the Christians come in for criticism, either directly through the words of Barabas or indirectly through the implications of their actions, to the degree that they betray their faith and approach the absolute "Jewishness"—the avarice and the egoism—of Barabas, to the degree that they substitute gold for God. It is the betrayal of Christianity and not Christianity itself that is scorned; the career of Abigail should be enough to make that clear—she is the only really admirable character in the play, and her conversion to Christianity and her Christian death are represented as the sole positive achievements in a play that deals largely with destructive issues and forces.[12] Marlowe's name for the Jew of Malta is also integral to this context of the criticism of Christian betrayal: the Barabbas of the Gospels was the notorious prisoner guilty of sedition, robbery, and murder whom the people chose to set free *in preference to Christ* in order that Christ would be crucified. Those in the play who "choose" Barabas, who seek the gold that he seeks, are those who perforce deny Christ. The reverse process is the way of Abigail.

Barabas is, of course, a literal or racial Jew as well, and as such he inherits the moral opprobrium and unpopularity attached to actual Jews by the Elizabethan audience. Part of that inheritance, as Paul Kocher has noted, includes a reputa-

---

[12] A large part of the play's alleged criticism of Christianity, including the behavior of the Friars, is directed against Roman Catholic practices, such as monasticism, and fits in with the anti-Catholic satire that had been current on the English stage ever since the Reformation. In the prologue, Machiavel lists the popes as his disciples. There is obviously no reason to interpret such slurs as a radical criticism of all Christianity.

tion as poisoner, miser, and traitor.[13] There is no escaping the Elizabethan defamation of Jews; just as there is no escaping the emblematic significance of the opening scene of Marlowe's play, which reveals the large-nosed Barabas in his counting-house, with heaps of gold before him, gloating over his "Infinite riches in a little roome" (B2). If Barabas' literal Jewishness is not enough in itself to condemn him, his presentation as an extreme embodiment of avarice in that first scene would be more than sufficient to do so. "What more may Heaven doe for earthly man," he asks, "Then thus to powre out plenty in their laps . . . ?" (B3). His highest value is defined in terms of gold, and by that criterion he judges the superiority of Jew over Christian, for Jews are richer. The theme of gold as supreme value knits together the whole play, furnishing motivation for its broad political action as well as for the comic scenes of the Courtesan's exploitation of Ithamore. The Bashaw's reply to the Governor's query about what wind has driven him to Malta is explicit:

> The wind that bloweth all the world besides,
> Desire of gold. (G)

The Jew of Malta himself stands as the quintessential embodiment of this theme.

Yet the character of Barabas and the evil he represents is not exhausted by these facets of his literal and figurative Jewishness. As Heywood's prologue for the court production proclaims,

> . . . *you shall find him still,*
> *In all his proiects, a sound* Macheuill;
> *And that's his Character* . . . (A4^v)

---

[13] *Christopher Marlowe* (Chapel Hill, 1946), p. 201. Kocher cites an anti-Leicester pamphlet of 1584 accusing the Earl of keeping an Italian and a Jew as poisoners, and refers to the record in John Stow's *Annales* (1592) that in the year 1319 more than twelve thousand Jews were killed in Germany for poisoning wells.

We do not have to take Heywood's word for it alone. Marlowe has Machiavel open the play by introducing the Jew as one of his many disciples. The popular image of Machiavelli in England, formed by the central influence of Gentillet's *Contre-Machiavel* (1576) rather than by the works of Machiavelli himself,[14] involved a host of evil characteristics beginning with the most loathsome practices of statecraft and extending to what was most vile in human nature generally. Rapacity, avarice, atheism, ruthlessness, craft and deceit, treachery, diabolism—all these were summed up in the name of Machiavelli and in the "policy" that became his notorious trademark. Under such auspices, Barabas from his very first appearance could be welcomed on stage as nothing other than total villain.

Marlowe is the first dramatist to introduce the character Machiavel upon the stage, and to give a Machiavellian the central and dominant role in a play. But the principles and dicta of Machiavellianism had been employed in drama before *The Jew of Malta*. The most notable example on the popular stage is Lorenzo in Kyd's *Spanish Tragedy*, who emerges as the arch-villain of the play, murdering Horatio, and disposing of his accomplices Serberine and Pedringano by treacherous stratagems. Like the Vice of the morality play, Lorenzo reveals himself as villain to the audience, but his principles and slogans are not so much inversions of Christian doctrine as they are examples of Machiavellian "policy":

> Where words preuaile not, violence preuailes.
> But golde doth more then either of them both.

> And better its that base companions dye,
> Then by their life to hazard our good haps.

[14] See Edward Meyer, *Machiavelli and the Elizabethan Drama* (Weimar, 1897), pp. 1-30; and Mario Praz, "Machiavelli and the Elizabethans," *Proceedings of the British Academy*, XIV (1928), 49-57.

Nor shall they liue for me, to feare their faith:
Ile trust my selfe, my selfe shalbe my freend . . .[15]

Lorenzo ruthlessly employs craft, stratagem, and violence to attain personal rather than political ends; the Machiavellian mode had been manifested in a more strictly political context in Legge's *Richardus Tertius* (acted 1579/1580). The content of this play is as slavishly dependent on the chronicles of Hall and More as its expression is dependent on Seneca; but Richard's advisers invoke Machiavellian principles which are not in the historical sources.[16] Mario Praz's suggestion that the dramatic entrance of Machiavelli upon the English stage was prompted by a further development of the Senecan tyrant[17] seems admirably to fit the situation in *Richardus Tertius*, but it is much less adequate in explaining the nature of Barabas' or Lorenzo's villainy. The moral (or immoral) principles on which they operate may bear a resemblance to the principles of the unscrupulous Senecan tyrant, but the way in which these principles are acted out is not at all similar. The dramaturgical quality and expression of the villainy of Lorenzo, and more particularly of Barabas, is drawn rather from the tradition of the morality play and the homiletic, self-demonstrative nature of the morality Vice.[18]

In *Shakespeare and the Allegory of Evil*, Bernard Spivack has outlined the specific affinities between the career of Barabas and the habitual behavior of the Vice.[19] In the second act of the play Barabas reveals the central feature of the Vice's dramatic conduct by exhibiting himself and his villainy to the

[15] Thomas Kyd, *The Spanish Tragedie* (1592), MSR (Oxford, 1948 [1949]), ll. 724-725, 1284-87. Lorenzo uses the term "policy" to refer to his own plots: see ll. 1383, 1708.

[16] Robert Joseph Lordi, "Thomas Legge's *Richardus Tertius*: A Critical Edition with a Translation," unpublished Ph.D. dissertation (University of Illinois, 1958), pp. xxii-xxvi and p. 172.

[17] "Machiavelli and the Elizabethans," pp. 63-71.

[18] See Bernard Spivack, *Shakespeare and the Allegory of Evil* (New York, 1958), p. 377.

[19] Pp. 346-353. The following section of my discussion is heavily indebted to Spivack's remarks.

audience. Even earlier, he had betrayed the favorite trick of
the Vice—dissimulation—in scenes with his fellow Jews, with
Abigail, and with Lodowick. But his meeting with Ithamore
brings out the demonstrative manner of the Vice in full force:

> *Bar.*   Hast thou no Trade? then listen to my words,
> And I will teach that shall sticke by thee:
> First be thou voyd of these affections,
> Compassion, loue, vaine hope, and hartlesse feare,
> Be mou'd at nothing, see thou pitty none,
> But to thy selfe smile when the Christians moane.
>   *Ithi.*   Oh braue, master, I worship your nose for this.
>   *Bar.*   As for my selfe, I walke abroad a nights
> And kill sicke people groaning under walls:
> Sometimes I goe about and poyson wells;
> And now and then, to cherish Christian theeves,
> I am content to lose some of my Crownes;
> That I may, walking in my Gallery,
> See 'em goe pinion'd along by my doore.
> Being young I studied Physicke, and began
> To practise first vpon the *Italian*;
> There I enric[h]'d the Priests with burials,
> And alwayes kept the Sexton's armes in vre
> With digging graues and ringing dead mens knels:
> And after that was I an Engineere,
> And in the warres 'twixt *France* and *Germanie*,
> Vnder pretence of helping *Charles* the fifth,
> Slew friend and enemy with my stratagems.
> Then after that was I an Vsurer,
> And with extorting, cozening, forfeiting,
> And tricks belonging vnto Brokery,
> I fill'd the Iailes with Bankrouts in a yeare,
> And with young Orphans planted Hospitals,
> And euery Moone made some or other mad,
> And now and then one hang himselfe for griefe,

Pinning vpon his breast a long great Scrowle
How I with interest tormented him.   (E2-E2ᵛ)

Ithamore replies to this frank avowal in kind, and Barabas
concludes:

Why this is something: make account of me
As of thy fellow; we are villaines both . . .   (E2ᵛ)

Barabas' catalogue of his past activities is almost too long
actually to have been accomplished by one who shows no signs
of great age.[20] But it really does not matter. What Marlowe
has done is to cast in the form of the Vice's conventional exposition of his activities—which do not depend on mortal limitations of space and time—the characteristic evils with which
the Jews were charged: poisoning, military exploitation,[21]
and usury. Barabas embodies them all. He shares with some
Vices the provocation of his victims to despair and suicide, although his interest is not in spiritual damnation, but merely
in the joy of destruction. This is indicative of the crucial difference in the Jew's career from that of the Vice: Barabas'
goal is the material destruction of his enemies, not their spiritual ruin; he *is* not a morality Vice, he only acts like one. Such
behavior, nevertheless, carries with it the inescapable quality
of conscienceless inhumanity, since the Vice is essentially inhuman and needs no provocation other than his own nature
for the evil he produces. Barabas' villainy, therefore, is largely
gratuitous and thoroughly cold-hearted despite his appeals
for "justice"; his speech to Ithamore makes plain that he
needs no psychological motivation for his crimes. Lust for
revenge and absolute egoism are suggested, but they really are
not sufficient to account for such spectacular evil deeds.

Barabas makes a great point of hating Christians and plotting their destruction, but the course of the play makes it quite

[20] So Cardozo argues in *The Contemporary Jew*, pp. 77-78.
[21] Cardozo records that Elizabethan travel literature described the part
Jews took in instructing Turks in the use of explosives against Christians
(p. 97).

clear that he is equally malevolent and treacherous with everyone, Christian, Turk, or Jew, including his own villainous henchman and his own daughter. This is the Vice's characteristic of aggression against everyone else. Like the Vice, again, the Jew's career is essentially an exhibition of his villainies, most of which are brought about by artful deception. Barabas uses the Vice's trick of weeping in order to persuade Mathias that the match of Abigail and Lodowick is an unhappy one as far as he himself is concerned: all part of the plot to set Mathias at odds with his friend. This setting people at odds with one another, occurring again with the two Friars, is a further characteristic activity of the Vice figure, and one in which Barabas, as well as Ithamore, delights.

Ithamore, an infidel like Barabas, is at once the Jew's darker shadow and the Vice's lighter side: darker, because of diabolic hints Marlowe gives of his character; and lighter, because of his foolish and farcical behavior, which matches the comic or farcical side of the Vice. The diabolic allusions come in two places: the scene following Ithamore's disclosure to Barabas of Abigail's conversion, and the scene in which the slave courts Bellamira the prostitute. In the first, Barabas chides Ithamore for entreating for Abigail's life, and questions his loyalty. The Turk's reply,

> Who I, master? Why I'le run to some rocke and
> Throw my selfe headlong into the sea; why I'le doe any
> Thing for your sweet sake. (F3ᵛ)

is an echo of the Gospel account in which Christ commands the evil spirits to leave a possessed man and to enter into a herd of swine, which then casts itself into the sea.[22] Barabas then promises to make Ithamore his heir, and sends him for the pot of rice with which he will poison the nunnery. Ithamore returns with a ladle as well, citing the proverb, "he that eats with the deuil/ Had need of a long spoone." Later, Ithamore's

22 Matthew viii. 28-32; Mark v. 8-13; Luke viii. 27-33.

love-speech to Bellamira, set ironically in the form of a pastoral poetic invitation, concludes with the lines,

> Thou in those Groues, by *Dis* aboue,
> Shalt liue with me and be my loue. (H2)

Ithamore swears by "his" god, the god of the underworld.[23]

From all these elements of evil, then, is the Jew of Malta concocted. So unrelieved and concentrated is the mixture that the figure of Barabas emerges as a grotesque caricature rather than a subtly realized dramatic character. To look at him from the standpoint of modern dramatic tradition is to see only a monster; to view him from the past tradition of the morality play is to see a metaphor. The truth, like the historical position of the play itself, lies in between. For Barabas is both monster and metaphor: he becomes a dramatic emblem uniting many of the worst elements in man—above all, limitless avarice, and its extension, absolute egoism—in a play which owes its structural unity to the theme of cupidity, the desire of gold. Barabas as Jew scorns all Christians, loves only lucre, and in his revenge distorts the retributive justice of the Old Law beyond all recognition. As Machiavel he works by sheer fraud and stratagem, bending all things to obey the laws of his own ego. In the manner of the Vice he takes extraordinary relish

---

[23] The diabolical characteristics of Turks in general were noted by Urbanus Regius in *An Homely or Sermon of Good and Euill Angels*, which went through three London editions in the decade 1583-1593: "A man may see a certaine image of sathan in the *Turkes*, which are the most deerest and most diligentest vesselles and instruments of sathan, to the accomplishment of all his will, lust, and desires . . . . with so deadlie and beastlie cruell hatred, are they swolne against [Christians], that they adventure and suffer at full, all manner of griefes . . . so that they may hurte and worke extreame iniurie towards the bodies and goodes of Christes true beleeuers." 3rd ed. (London, 1593), A6-A6ᵛ.

The name Ithamore probably comes from the Biblical Ithamar, who was one of the sons of Aaron. It is curious that this Old Testament family, which includes another son of Aaron, Eleazar, should have its dramatic counterpart in a "family" of the blackest villains of the Elizabethan theater: *The Jew of Malta*'s Ithamore, Aaron in *Titus Andronicus*, and Eleazar in *Lust's Dominion*.

in his deeds of villainy, delighting enormously in the virtuosity of his evil. And like the Vice, too, he is basically incapable of real suffering; discomfited, he cries out curses. As all these, Barabas represents a total inversion of the values in which Marlowe's Christian audience believed: his perverse immorality bears witness to the standards he delights in rejecting.

At the same time, Barabas continually points with contempt to the betrayal of those standards by the hypocritical Christians in the play. The traditional Christian order is vindicated by the contrasting perceptions and choices of Abigail, and perhaps, too, by the retributive justice of Barabas' end. But there is a profound, if characteristic, ambiguity in the resolution of the play's political line of action which coincides with the Jew's destruction. The Turks are demolished, the Christians restored to power, and order reigns again; the play concludes with lines more positive than any others that end a Marlowe drama:

> So march away, and let due praise be giuen
> Neither to Fate nor Fortune, but to Heauen.　(K2ᵛ)

But the lines are uttered by Ferneze, the Governor of Cyprus, one of the major Christian hypocrites of the play, who has helped to restore order only by adopting Barabas' own principles of treachery and deceit. Barabas may be dead, but his vice lives on. In the conventional resolution of the morality play, it was customary for the Vice himself to live on, representing an implicit threat to other men. Marlowe's ironic resolution embodies the familiar pattern, but gives it an emphasis that is more deeply satirical than homiletic.

T. S. Eliot is very near the truth when he calls this play a "farce of the old English humour, the terribly serious, even savage comic humour . . . . the humour of . . . *Volpone*."[24] Eliot looks at Marlowe's play from the perspective of Jonsonian

---

[24] "Marlowe," *Selected Essays*, new ed. (New York, 1950), p. 105.

drama; if he were to see it in relation to drama of the past, perhaps he would agree that in the last analysis *The Jew of Malta* remains a comedy of evil—with a Marlovian twist.

II. *THE MASSACRE AT PARIS*

Had Barabas the Jew inhabited the world of *The Massacre at Paris* he would without doubt have found much to relish in the ruin and destruction treacherously perpetrated by the enemies of Protestant Christianity. That the central figure of the play, the Duke of Guise, does not exhibit the manifest glee and delight in evil for its own sake that one would expect of Barabas is but one indication of the difference in the nature of their villainy. The broad character of their actions may be the same—intrigue, stratagem, murder by poison and dissembling—but the motivations for those actions and the mode in which they are carried through are quite distinct. The Guise, as indicated in Machiavel's prologue to *The Jew of Malta*, was looked on in England as an incarnation of the unscrupulous Machiavellian spirit, but he is a Machiavel with historical rather than metaphorical status: unlike Barabas, he does not act like a Vice. Not only do his crimes find their full "justification" in the prime political motive of acquiring the throne of France, but they also come about without the behind-the-scenes gloating and extraordinary ingenuity that characterize the deeds of the Jew. With the Guise, the end is all; for Barabas, the means are just as interesting in themselves. Furthermore, Marlowe had given to the victims of Barabas, with the exception of Abigail, a disreputable coloring which served to minimize any possible sympathy. Such is not at all the case in *The Massacre at Paris*, where the majority of victims are presented as pious and helpless Protestants, fully deserving the audience's complete sympathy. The Duke of Guise may not share the metaphorical qualities of Barabas, but he is certainly made out to be a monstrous villain.

If the quality of evil and destruction in the two plays is basically distinct, the quantity is even more so. If we can assume that the garbled and mutilated text of *The Massacre at Paris* presents the central events and actions of Marlowe's original play, it can safely be said that this is the dramatist's most luridly conceived and executed work. There is evident everywhere a mechanical reliance on swift and violent murders for sensational effects. The poisoning of the Queen of Navarre early in the play starts the long train: the Lord Admiral is wounded and then assassinated in his sick-bed; to the accompaniment of the tolling bell that signals the Bartholomew's Day Massacre, Guise stabs the preacher Loreine, Seroune and Ramus are stabbed by others, and Guise kills two schoolmasters; his next assignment is the slaughter of five or six praying Protestants. Immediately after this King Charles meets his death, probably poisoned at the hands of Catherine de Medici. Mugeroun is shot a few scenes later by the Guise's servant; then comes the Guise's own assassination, followed by the strangling of his brother the Cardinal. The play ends with the treacherous stabbing of King Henry by a fanatical Friar, who is himself killed by the dying King. In all, about twenty characters meet sudden death on stage in quick succession, and one by one the corpses are as quickly drawn off. In numbers alone this amounts to a record for any single play by Marlowe.

This general slaughter is not without its own crude principles of form and function. Although the text of this most poorly preserved of Marlowe's plays precludes any close analysis, some characteristic qualities of Marlowe's dramatization of suffering are discernible. The physiological description of suffering and death used in *Tamburlaine* appears once again; and the suffering of Guise's victims as well as his own reaction to destruction are manipulated with a view to implementing the characterization of Guise and arousing a certain response in the audience.

Most of the victims in the play die without a chance to speak more than a line; but there are some notable exceptions. The poisoned Queen of Navarre has three lines to express her suffering:

> O no, sweet *Margret*, the fatall poyson
> Workes within my head, my brain pan breakes,
> My heart doth faint, I dye.   *She dyes.*[25]

King Charles has time to be more specific:

> A griping paine hath ceasde vpon my heart:
> A sodaine pang, the messenger of death.
>
> .   .   .   .
>
> O holde me vp, my sight begins to faile,
> My sinnewes shrinke, my braines turne vpside
>   downe,
> My heart doth break, I faint and dye.   *He dies.*
>
>   (649-665)

These speeches, crude and mechanical though they are, are used, it appears, not to present a character's attitude toward death but to imply the cause of death, poison. The first case hardly needs the implication; the audience has already seen Guise sending the apothecary with poisoned gloves to the Queen, and the victim herself realizes at once she has been poisoned. But the specific mention of the brain, common to both speeches, may be derived from the account of the Queen of Navarre's death in François Hotman's *The Three Partes of Commentaries . . . of the Ciuill warres of Fraunce*, one of Marlowe's sources for *The Massacre*.[26] There it is set down that poisoning was suspected, but not detected in the autopsy "which did not open the head nor loked into the brayne."[27]

---

[25] *The Massacre at Paris*, MSR (Oxford, 1928), ll. 212-214. Subsequent references to this edition will appear in my text.

[26] Paul H. Kocher, "François Hotman and Marlowe's *The Massacre at Paris*," PMLA, LVI (1941), 349-368.

[27] Quoted by Kocher, "François Hotman," p. 352. See also H. S. Bennett's note in his edition of the play (London, 1931), p. 191.

This linking of poison with action on the brain provides a clue to the cause of the King's death later on, where no immediate cause is otherwise demonstrated. Such a hint fits in well with a speech of the Queen Mother two scenes before the King's death: she resolves that Charles must die and Henry succeed, so that she may continue to wield her own will. The implication seems conclusive: Catherine has kept her word by way of poison.

Contrasting strongly with such short, physically descriptive death speeches as these are the last words of the dying Duke of Guise:

> *Guise.* Oh I haue my deaths wound, giue me
>   leaue to speak.
> 2.   Then pray to God, and aske forgiuenes
>   of the King.
> *Guise.* Trouble me not, I neare
>   offended him.
> Nor will I aske forgiuenes of the King.
> Oh that I haue not power to stay my life,
> Nor immortalitie to be reueng'd:
> To dye by Pesantes, what a greefe is this?
> Ah *Sextus*, be reueng'd vpon the King,
> Philip and Parma, I am slaine for you:
> Pope excommunicate, Philip depose,
> The wicked branch of curst *Valois*
>   his line.
> *Viue la messa*, perish Hugonets,
> Thus *Cæsar* did goe foorth, and thus
>   he dyed.   *He dyes.*   (1230-1247)

The Duke of Guise in his moment of death not only shows himself to be above suffering and fear, but also reveals the essential qualities and ambitions of his life: presumption, aspiring pride, contempt of his enemies, and vindictiveness. There is no hint of either remorse or pain. Marlowe uses this, as he did with Barabas, to establish more firmly the inhuman quality of Guise's character. Moreover, the speech is loaded with allusions to vilify the figure of Guise in the eyes of the Elizabethan audience: Guise invokes in his last breath the names of his supporters and allies—figures hateful indeed to the England of Elizabeth—Pope Sixtus V, Philip II of Spain, and Alexander Farnese, the Duke of Parma who had subjugated the Netherlands. Finally, there is more propaganda value than consistency in Guise's cursing of the Protestant Huguenots and his salute to the Roman Mass, for, as his first soliloquy had revealed, religion had meaning to him only insofar as it could further his way to the throne of France. In short, Marlowe packs into this death-speech as many of the general and specific elements of disparagement as he can muster to brand his protagonist as totally despicable.[28]

The exploitation of the Guise's death scene for propaganda value is carried still further in the words King Henry utters over the Duke's corpse, words which stamp Guise as an enemy of England as well as of Henry himself:

> Did he not draw a sorte of English priestes,
> From Doway to the Seminary at Remes,
> To hatch forth treason gainst their naturall
>   Queene?
> Did he not cause the King of Spaines huge
>   fleete,
> To threaten England and to menace me?
>
> (1266-1272)

[28] Although many of the obviously lurid and propagandistic elements of Marlowe's drama are traceable to the matter and mood of contemporary Protestant pamphlets on the sensational subject, this dying speech of Guise is one of the few details without precedent in such sources. Marlowe did not originate the basic character of Guise, but he did see fit to employ this moment of death to underline the main elements of that character. See Paul Kocher, "Contemporary Pamphlet Backgrounds for Marlowe's *The Massacre at Paris*," *MLQ*, VIII (1947), 151-155.

This propaganda theme emerges again as the prime element in the last speeches of King Henry, whose death concludes the play. Stabbed with a poisoned knife, he shows no signs of pain or cowardice, but indulges in some last-minute orations which serve as a matched counterforce to the death-sentiments of Guise:

> Agent for England, send thy mistres word,
> What this detested Iacobin hath done.
> Tell her for all this that I hope to liue,
> Which if I doe, the Papall Monarck goes
>   to wrack,
> And antechristian kingdome falles.
> These bloudy hands shall teare his triple Crowne,
> And fire accursed Rome about his eares.
> Ile fire his crased buildings and incense,
> The papall towers to kisse the holy earth.
> *Nauarre*, giue me thy hand, I heere do sweare,
> To ruinate that wicked Church of Rome,
> That hatcheth vp such bloudy practises.
> And heere protest eternall loue to thee,
> And to the Queene of England specially,
> Whom God hath blest for hating Papestry.
>   (1512-1527)

> Weep not sweet *Nauarre*, but reuenge my
>   death.
> Ah *Epernoune*, is this thy loue to me?
> *Henry* thy King wipes of these childish
>   teares,
> And bids thee whet thy sword on *Sextus* bones,
> That it may keenly slice the Catholicks.
>   .   .   .   .
> I dye *Nauarre*, come beare me to my Sepulchre.
> Salute the Queene of England in my name,
> And tell her Henry dyes her faithfull freend.
>   *He dyes.*   (1562-1575)

It is evident that suffering and death in *The Massacre at Paris* become minor themes in a work shaped principally around the historical conflict between Protestantism and Catholicism, as seen from the contemporary English Protestant viewpoint. It is in terms of this black vs. white antagonism that the slaughter and evils of the play become intelligible: Guise, the French Catholics, and the Pope are of the devil's party; King Henry, Navarre, and the French Protestants are of God's. The general framework is thus completely orthodox from the English Protestant perspective: its outcome is as inevitable as it is orthodox—in fact, it is assured at the very start of the play by the words of Navarre:

> But he that sits and rules aboue the clowdes,
> Doth heare and see the praiers of the iust:
> And will reuenge the bloud of innocents,
> That *Guise* hath slaine by treason of his heart,
> And brought by murder to their timeles ends.[29]

> (55-59)

The opening scene which includes this prophecy by Navarre also establishes the central issues and conflicts of the play as a whole: it broaches the religious issue, links "aspiring" Guise with Papist treachery, cites his ambition and envy, and establishes Navarre as the spokesman and representative of right. From then on the play is devoted mainly to the demonstration of Guise's personal and public villainy. Marlowe does everything in his power to vilify the image of Guise, even beyond the point reached in the propaganda pamphlets of the time. The Duke is first shown preparing the poisoned gloves to kill the Queen of Navarre, a crime invented for him by the

[29] Navarre, throughout the course of the play, is the persistent spokesman for the side of Protestantism and God's justice. He continually expresses the sentiment that God will eventually secure justice for the Protestant cause, and thus serves as a moral stabilizer amidst the barbaric slaughter that pervades the play. See his speeches following lines 42, 52, 548, 582, 591, 705, 794, 805, and 936.

dramatist rather than attributed to him by any of the sources at hand.[30] The Guise's soliloquy (109-185) reveals his ultimate goal, the crown of France, and the subordination of all else to that end; the speech also aligns him with the powers of Spain and of the Pope. He gives orders for the assassination of the Admiral, who, lying wounded in his bed, is refused even time to pray, but who nevertheless manages to get out "O God forgiue my sins" (363) after he has been stabbed. His body is then thrown down to Guise, waiting below the balcony, and the Duke marks his contempt of the Protestant leader by trampling on the corpse. To bloody the figure of this unscrupulous plotter even more, Marlowe, without historical precedent, has Guise personally stab to death a Protestant preacher named Loreine, officiate at the murder of Ramus, kill two schoolmasters, and give the order to shoot a hundred Protestants swimming in the Seine—all unarmed and defenseless victims. The merciless note is maintained in his next project, the slaughter of five or six Protestants at prayer—another crime invented by the dramatist, obviously intended to increase the indignation of a Protestant audience toward the protagonist. After all this, the Duke of Guise is made the butt of mocking scorn in the episode of his being cuckolded. There is special irony in the reaction of this totally lawless and treacherous figure to the infidelity of his wife: "O wicked sexe, periured and vniust" (832). The Guise's infamous career, sullied in every possible way, ends in his assassination, and his impious death puts the last black touch on an already blackened picture of monstrous villainy.[31] With the defeat of

[30] See Kocher, "François Hotman," pp. 366-367.

[31] To say, as Paul Kocher does, that Marlowe "perversely, admires this paragon of evil more than he does any other figure in the play" ("Contemporary Pamphlet Backgrounds," p. 314) is to read into the work an attitude toward Guise which is not in the least supported by any of the play's devices and details of characterization. It may be that Kocher is confusing the degree of eloquence that a dramatist may bestow on a character with the author's admiration for that character; in his book, *Christopher Marlowe*, he actually equates the two (e.g., p. 184 and p. 204). The dangers

the arch-enemy, the forces of justice are able to rise to final prominence and victory.

The Massacre at Paris is a lurid play derived from luridly written sources. In an examination of some fifty contemporary pamphlets in both French and English dealing with the historical events upon which the play is based, Paul Kocher has found that practically every sensational action or characterization in the play can be traced directly to "the luridness of typical Protestant interpretation."[32] The play shares the extreme prejudice and propagandistic nature of these pamphlets, and differs mainly, according to Kocher, in its emphasis on the Paris massacre and subsequent events as part of Guise's personal plot rather than of a League plot.[33] The stress on the person of Guise and on the total vilification of his character goes beyond any of the pamphlets; Marlowe has heaped upon his head all the vilest incriminations available, and then added some of his own. Although Kocher tends to minimize the influence of Machiavellianism on the character of Guise, it may well be that the stage tradition of the total villain, as derived from the Vice and developed in the Machiavel (with Marlowe's Jew standing at a crucial point in this development), was in fact an operative force in leading Marlowe to make Guise both the focus of hatred and the focus of action.

For all its emphasis on the brutal and physical suffering inflicted by the Duke of Guise on his victims, Marlowe's play reveals to some small extent the sense of personal loss, that suffering of the soul rather than of the body, which gave shape to the human anguish recorded in *Dido* and, to a minor extent, in *Tamburlaine*. In *The Massacre at Paris* such loss is given

---

of this fallacious equation are manifold. Kocher's interpretation of Marlowe's portrait of Gaveston in *Edward II* as "kindly" is one evident result (*Christopher Marlowe*, p. 203); and one wonders how Shakespeare's Richard III or the Aaron of *Titus Andronicus* would emerge when viewed in the light of such a principle.

[32] "Contemporary Pamphlet Backgrounds," p. 151.
[33] *ibid.*, p. 314.

short and mechanical expression, but it is nonetheless present. Navarre offers the first instance, in his reaction to his mother's death by poison:

> My Mother poysoned heere before
> my face:
> O gracious God, what times are these?
> O graunt sweet God my daies may end with hers,
> That I with her may dye and liue againe.   (215-219)

The other instance is provoked by another murder, the assassination of the Duke of Guise; this time it is Catherine who mourns, mingling her sorrow with rage at her son King Henry:

> I cannot speak for greefe, when thou
> wast borne,
> I would that I had murdered thee my sonne.
> My sonne: thou art a changeling, not my sonne.
> I curse thee and exclaime thee miscreant,
> Traitor to God, and to the realme of France.
>
> .   .   .   .
>
> Sweet *Guise*, would he had died so thou
> wert heere:
>
> .   .   .   .
>
> And all for thee my *Guise*, what may I doe?
> But sorrow seaze vpon my toyling soule,
> For since the *Guise* is dead, I will not liue.
>
> (1320-1342)

In both instances the personal loss has provoked a wish for death, yet there is a difference in the mode of expression which relates to the character Marlowe has sketched for each person: Navarre, who consistently refers all situations and actions to God, grieves in the form of a prayer; Catherine, moved throughout by grim determination and a will to power unhindered even by family ties, concludes her role with a curse upon her son and a willful resolve hinting at suicide.[34] Even though Marlowe has not endowed these characters with any degree of complexity, he has nevertheless seen fit to match the mode of their psychological sorrow to the dominant traits which determine their nature and role. Their suffering does not really add a dimension to their characters: it merely magnifies the dimension already established. The degree to which that dimension is determined by the partisan bias of the play is obvious: faced with a similar kind of personal loss, the Protestant prays, and the Catholic curses.

Suffering and evil in *The Massacre at Paris* emerge finally as tools manipulated for propaganda purposes. Death and destruction brought about by Guise and the Catholics are evil crimes of heinous and ungodly injustice; the killing of Guise and his brother the Cardinal by forces favorable to Protestantism are virtuous acts of just retribution, and are brought about with God's help. The vivid depiction of the wholesale slaughter of helpless and pious Protestants is presented with one emotional end in mind: furious indignation. The Duke of Guise himself is the focal point of that indignation, rather than any evil for which he may stand. In this respect his villainy represents something much narrower than the villainy of Barabas, for it takes on the tone of a thoroughly personal offense inhering in a single historical figure; the universal aspects of his kind of evil, unlike the lust for gold in *The Jew of Malta*, are not stressed. The Guise's guilt is his own rather than mankind's; if there is any extension of it beyond himself, it is toward something historical and concrete—the Church of Rome—rather than toward anything universal and abstract. Evil in *The Massacre at Paris* does not inhere in the aberrations of humanity in general, nor even in the destructive ills of political humanity in particular, but primarily and principally in the Duke of Guise, and secondarily in the political forces of

[34] Marlowe may have intended here an interpretation of the Queen's actual death, which followed Guise's assassination by only a few days. See Bennett ed., p. 243, n. 161.

Catholicism. With the focus of hatred narrowed to such limits, the play remains inevitably a crude spectacle of sensationalistic propaganda.[35]

No one familiar with the history plays of the Elizabethan stage would venture to claim that propaganda—that is, the manipulation and interpretation of historical events to further certain allegiances, animosities, or notions of political doctrine —is uncommon in the genre.[36] Even so, Marlowe's play emerges as one of the most constricted of the lot, for it makes no attempt to generalize or universalize the danger of the political evils it displays: it rests content with vilification of particular events and enemies. The themes almost indigenous to the English history play from *Gorboduc* on—the dangers of unspecified royal inheritance, the evils of civil dissension, the folly of rebellion, the politically destructive nature of ambition—are noticeably absent in *The Massacre at Paris*, although the nature of Marlowe's subject matter could readily have lent itself to such treatment. The very notion of the state itself is absent; the problem of political order and its proper foundations is never suggested. In this respect *The Massacre* again stands apart from the general tendency of the history play, differing even from the plays which most resemble it in

[35] The "timeliness" of such a propaganda play was, of course, one measure of its popularity with the Elizabethan audience. Entered as a new play in Henslowe's repertoire in January 1592/1593, *The Massacre at Paris* appeared at the close of one of the fiercest anti-Catholic decades in English history, a decade ushered in by the execution of Edmund Campion and other Catholic priests, and marked by such sensational events as the Duke of Guise's plan to invade England, the discovery of the Throckmorton plot, the execution of Mary of Scotland, and the defeat of the Spanish Armada. This was the period of Elizabeth's most intense Catholic persecution, and by 1593, certainly, the strongest feelings of animosity could be triggered by the mere mention of the activities of Guise, France, Spain, or the Pope. See Philip Hughes, *The Reformation in England*, Vol. III (London, 1954), pp. 239-404.

[36] Ample witness is afforded by two important studies: Lily B. Campbell, *Shakespeare's "Histories": Mirrors of Elizabethan Policy* (San Marino, Calif., 1947); and Irving Ribner, *The English History Play in the Age of Shakespeare* (Princeton, 1957).

reliance on anti-Catholic propaganda: plays such as *The Battell of Alcazar* (printed 1594) with its exploitation of Sir Thomas Stukeley's projected invasion of Ireland with Papal and Spanish backing, or the two parts of *The Troublesome Raigne of Iohn King of England* (printed 1591), in which both monasticism and the Papacy are ridiculed, or the first part of *King Henry VI*, which offers a rough parallel to Marlowe's characterization of the Guise-Navarre conflict in its portrayal of Joan of Arc as the demonic leader of France and of Talbot as the righteous warrior of England. In these plays the evils represented by Catholic power fit into a larger view that is concerned with the just maintenance of the body politic. Marlowe's concern, as evidenced by his treatment of evil in *The Massacre*, does not extend to issues of general political significance. He presents his lurid conflict with little subtlety and with no comment other than the pious platitudes of the righteous Navarre. The scope of his artistic vision is here narrowed to its minimum.

ॐ

In *The Jew of Malta* and *The Massacre at Paris* the spectacle of evil dominates the stage, rather than the spectacle of suffering. The suffering is there, to be sure, but it is always the visible result of evil in a personal form—the evil agent. The suffering involved in these plays bears little or no resemblance to the suffering of such tragic figures as Oedipus or Lear; it contains no hints of the cosmic or mysterious, or even of the problematical. The suffering here represented is patently explicable in its cause: the evil villain. And that villain stands in each case in the direct center of the play, at a height above the surrounding characters. Some have confused that height with heroism, and have seen in the boundless and passionate ambitions exhibited by these "heroes" the romantic struggle and yearning for the infinite that characterizes the literature of a much later age.[37] They look at the Jew's goal of "infinite riches" and see more than the concrete, shining symbols of wealth and power that the Jew himself sees; into the Guise's quest for the crown of France they read a spiritual quest for individual self-fulfillment. That such interpretations are the result of a strictly modern preoccupation with the qualities of the romantic hero is, I think, clearly evident from the historical context of Marlowe's plays, which helps to define the nature of his characters. To view the Jew as a hero whose struggle is admirable and whose fall is pitiable is to fly in the face of all those qualities Marlowe has given him: his Jewishness, his Machiavellianism, his likeness to a Vice, his consummate egoism and delight in destruction for its own sake. To look at the Duke of Guise in the same way is to ignore not only his unscrupulous ambition and his links with the hateful powers of Catholicism, but also to discount the inescapable verdict of the dramatic action itself, which is a manifestly lurid exhibition of heinous crimes committed against innocent and defenseless Protestants. If such a character is intended to be "the chief exponent of Marlowe's Machiavellianism" and "ethos of living dangerously," as Harry Levin maintains,[38] then the dramatist has done everything in his power to make hateful and vile the qualities he supposedly espouses.[39] That Marlowe has capitalized dramatically on

[37] Ashley Thorndike, for example, sees Barabas as a hero "overwhelmed in the end by the inexorable destiny of human weakness." *Tragedy* (New York, 1908), p. 90. He later acknowledges that Marlowe's protagonists are evil men intent on evil deeds, but concludes that Marlowe has bestowed upon them such intensity of emotion that they are given "an elevation and a heroic interest that outlasts contemptibility or pathos" (p. 95).

[38] *The Overreacher*, p. 23.

[39] As Mario Praz has pointed out, Machiavelli never supplied "a pattern of heroism for the Elizabethan dramatists"; he only supplied "characteristics of the politic villain, who, from the very beginning, was loathed at the same time as ridiculed." "Machiavelli and the Elizabethans," p. 73. Fredson Bowers' judgment is substantially the same: *Elizabethan Revenge Tragedy: 1587-1642* (Princeton, 1940), pp. 48-49. Edward Meyer's numerous citations of Elizabethan references to Machiavelli in his monograph, *Machiavelli and the Elizabethan Drama*, leave no doubt of the universal condemnation the label carried with it.

such qualities there can be no doubt, but surely such treatment as he gives his villains does not suggest even indirectly an attitude of admiration. There is no longer any trace here of the ambivalence recognizable in the picture of Tamburlaine's bloody conquests: the stains of the treacherous and brutal crimes of Barabas and Guise are as ineradicable as they are black. They confirm beyond all reasonable doubt the stamp of condemnation impressed on these two monsters of iniquity by their very names and natures.

The Jew of Malta and the Duke of Guise stand as dramatic exemplars of consummate evil; the spirit of their ambition is as much a part of the nature of that evil as the diabolic quality of their crimes. It is an ambition itself diabolic, for the lofty images in which it is conceived are as speciously alluring as the ugly facts in which it is "realized" are hideous and painful. It is the ambition of Lucifer over again: the motive of boundless supremacy leading inevitably to painful self-destruction. Marlowe's poetic power remarkably enhances the terms of the temptation; "the Muses darling" for his verse, so Peele wrote, he was "Fitte to write passions for the soules below."[40] But to the Elizabethan audience at least, the audience for whom Marlowe wrote his plays, there was no mistaking the place where those souls belonged.

[40] Prologue to *The Honour of the Garter* (1593), ed. David H. Horne, *The Life and Minor Works of George Peele* (New Haven, 1952), p. 246.

CHAPTER IV · THE BITTER FRUITION OF AN EARTHLY CROWN: *EDWARD II*

Fire and Aire, Water and Earth, are not the Elements of man; Inward decay, and outward violence, bodily pain, and sorrow of heart may be rather styled his Elements; And though he be destroyed by these, yet he consists of nothing but these. —John Donne

I am a King, though King of miserie . . .
—Michael Drayton, MORTIMERIADOS

CHAPTER IV · THE BITTER FRUITION
OF AN EARTHLY CROWN: *EDWARD II*

WITH *The troublesome raigne and lamentable death of Edward the second*, Marlowe's dramatic focus shifts from the spectacle of consummate evil to the spectacle of tragic suffering, suffering that is deeply felt and agonizingly articulated by the protagonist himself, rather than suffering callously inflicted by him on the victims of his malice. Gone are the exaggerated inhumanities of a Barabas or a Guise; absent too are the superhuman surgings of the Tamburlainian desire for conquest. In their place are the bleaker realities of human weakness and willfulness, together with the inner and outer pains which they inevitably produce, unsoftened even by the poignancy and pathos that render the sorrows of Marlowe's Ovidian Dido bearable. From the whirl of human pettiness and pretensions, of internecine civil strife, of coarsening personalities and political degradations, the figure of a suffering king emerges, a king with neither the private nor the public virtues of kingship, a king governed by his minions and attacked by his barons, a king with nothing of the hero about him but with much of the petulant child, a king and no king. Marlowe found him in the chronicles of English history, and built around him the first of the English history plays that is at the same time a personal tragedy. How he shaped his historical source material into the form of such tragedy, a form finding its unity in the characteristics of Edward himself, has often been discussed by the critics.[1] Our own investigation will take up the particular problem of how Marlowe has given a

---

[1] See, e.g., the introduction to the edition of *Edward II* by H. B. Charlton and R. D. Waller, revised by F. N. Lees (London, 1955), pp. 31-52; Harry Levin, *The Overreacher* (Cambridge, Mass., 1952), pp. 88-90; Frederick S. Boas, *Christopher Marlowe*, rev. ed. (Oxford, 1953), pp. 175-191; and Irving Ribner, *The English History Play in the Age of Shakespeare* (Princeton, 1957), pp. 127-129.

tragic dimension to the suffering of his protagonist, a dimension not at all explicit in his sources, by presenting that suffering as the ironic result of Edward's own character and will.

In the early sections of the play, the representation of suffering is used to show the audience the nature of the king's weakness and its effects on those around him. As a king, Edward's first concern should be for the welfare of his country; as a husband his first concern should be for the love of his wife. But Marlowe has pictured him as actually working against both concerns by his fanatic affection for unworthy favorites: his wife is driven first to distraction and then to infidelity by his cruelty, his country is thrown into civil war. Edward's personal behavior leads to suffering and disorganization in the structure of the family and of the state; in the ultimate analysis it will bring about his own destruction as well.

The crucial factor in the development of his behavior and its manifold tragic results is Edward's excessive affection for his childhood friend Gaveston. Marlowe chooses Gaveston to open the play, leaving little doubt as to the nature and motivations of his character. Reading over the letter from the newly-crowned Edward inviting him to return from exile, Gaveston replies in a speech colored with erotic imagery:

> Sweete prince I come, these these thy amorous lines,
> Might haue enforst me to haue swum from France,
> And like *Leander* gaspt vpon the sande,
> So thou wouldst smile and take me in thy armes.
> The sight of London to my exiled eyes,
> Is as Elizium to a new come soule,
> Not that I loue the citie or the men,
> But that it harbors him I hold so deare,
> The king, vpon whose bosome let me die,
> And with the world be still at enmitie . . .[2]

[2] *Edward the Second*, MSR (Oxford, 1925), ll. 8-17. Subsequent references to this edition will appear in my text.

Gaveston begins to spell out his disdain for others when he is interrupted by three poor men offering him their services. This affords him a further chance of acting out his contempt, until he sees that the men may serve his utilitarian purposes. "Ile flatter these, and make them liue in hope" (46), he confides to the audience, and then in soliloquy reveals that his plans involve similar flattery of the king:

> . . . these are not men for me,
> I must haue wanton Poets, pleasant wits,
> Musitians, that with touching of a string
> May draw the pliant king which way I please . . .
>
> (53-56)

Gaveston's affection for the king, then, is hardly of a selfless nature, nor is it free from the overtones of homosexuality, as most modern critics have pointed out.[3] Marlowe has been careful to present the true worth of the king's favorite at once. In doing so, he prepares his audience not only for the basic irony of King Edward's extreme affection for Gaveston, but also for the subtler ironies of Gaveston's protestations of love, such as the one he makes at their first meeting, in which the last line carries double weight:

[3] Two notes by Paul H. Kocher, *Christopher Marlowe* (Chapel Hill, 1946), are relevant here: (1) "Edward and Gaveston use images of sexual love, like the Hero-Leander image . . . and the Danae image . . . to describe their affection, and the Queen compares them to Jove and Ganymede . . . a notorious instance of the passion which Marlowe himself had already utilized in the opening scene of *Dido*. The physical endearments go far beyond those customary between Elizabethan friends exemplified in such plays as *Damon and Pithias*, Lyly's *Campaspe*, *The Taming of a Shrew*, and *Mucedorus*" (p. 205); (2) "The flatterer of a king was regarded as highly mischievous to the state. Flattery is condemned in all treatises, including Castiglione . . . Elyot . . . Patricius. Du Bartas' comment in *Divine Weeks* . . . reflects this attitude:

> 'I'll boldly sing (bright Soueraigne) thou art none
> Of those weake Princes Flatt'rie works upon,
> (No Second Edward, nor no Richard Second,
> Un-kinged both, as Rule-unworthie reccon'd)
> Who to enrich their Minions past proportion
> Pill all their Subiects with extreme extortion . . .'" (p. 203).

It shall suffice me to enioy your loue,
Which whiles I haue, I thinke my selfe as great,
As *Cæsar* riding in the Romaine streete,
With captiue kings at his triumphant Carre.

(179-182)

Such is the man over whose retention Edward quarrels bit-
terly with his barons and earls, on his first appearance in the
play. And to aggravate the conflict by assertion of his power,
Edward heaps titles on Gaveston's head and confiscates church
property for his use. The resolution of this first conflict is victory for the nobles, exile for Gaveston, and provocation of the
king's first expression of suffering. When Edward yields to
the Archbishop's demands to sign the exile petition he says,
"In steede of inke, ile write it with my teares," and as he
signs, young Mortimer comments, "The king is loue-sick for
his minion" (403-404). The extent of his love-sickness is
revealed further in the following scene, where Edward parts
with Gaveston as one would expect the most passionate of lovers to part:

> *Edw.* Rend not my hart with thy too piercing words,
> Thou from this land, I from my selfe am banisht.
>
> . . . .
>
> Here take my picture, and let me weare thine,
> O might I keepe thee heere, as I doe this,
> Happie were I, but now most miserable.
> *Gauest.* Tis something to be pitied of a king.
> *Edw.* Thou shalt not hence, ile hide thee *Gaueston.*
> *Gau.* I shal be found, and then twil greeue me more.
> *Edwa.* Kinde wordes, and mutuall talke, makes our
>   greefe greater.
> Therefore with dum imbracement let vs part,
>   [Here they obviously embrace.]
> Stay *Gaueston* I cannot leaue thee thus.

Gau. For euery looke, my lord drops downe a teare,
Seeing I must go, do not renew my sorrow.   (437-458)

The closest analogue to this kind of parting in the plays of
Marlowe's day is to be found not in any drama of male friend-
ship, but in the second part of *Henry VI*, in which the ban-
ished Suffolk bids a sorrowful farewell to the faithless Queen.
If, as is now generally believed, Parts II and III of *Henry VI*
preceded *Edward II*,[4] and were likely to have suggested not
only verbal parallels, but also the theme of a weak king whose
country falls into civil dissension resulting in the king's murder, it could well be that the parting of Shakespeare's adul-
terous lovers provided Marlowe with a rough pattern for the
leave-taking of Edward and Gaveston.[5] In any case, the farewell is undeniably passionate, but it should be noted that the
weight of passion is on Edward's side; the extreme gesture,
the emotional outburst, the tears, are all his, while Gaveston's
remarks remain tame by comparison and even somewhat ambiguous. "Tis something to be pitied of a king" suggests an
aside rather than a word of comfort to Edward or an expression of Gaveston's own sorrow. Indeed, if the implication of
Gaveston's initial appearance means that he is actually more
an opportunistic flatterer than friend, the whole parting scene
takes on the dimension of trenchant irony, underlining the
total misdirection and excess of the king's infatuation. Such an
impression is confirmed at the end of this scene when Edward
cruelly rebuffs the Queen: "Fawne not on me French strumpet, get thee/ gone" (467-468). Gaveston utilizes this opportunity to further estrange the royal couple by planting
in the king's mind suspicion of his wife's infidelity, and nam-
ing Mortimer as the object of her affections. Despite Isabella's

---

[4] Charlton and Waller edn., pp. 10-17 and p. 218; Levin, pp. 87-88;
Clifford Leech, "Marlowe's 'Edward II': Power and Suffering," *The Critical Quarterly*, I (1959), 185.
[5] Marlowe's imagination may also have responded to the ambitious political climbers and to Richard's cruel execution of King Henry in these
plays; Mortimer and Lightborn may be extreme developments of such hints.

protestations of innocence, presented by the dramatist in the context of sincere sorrow at such maltreatment, Edward banishes her from his sight.

The sufferings of the Queen occupy the center of interest at this point: she remains alone until interrupted by the appearance of the nobles, wringing her hands, beating her breast, and lamenting her own "exile" from the king whom she still loves despite his unkindness (494-510). The younger Mortimer advises her to leave off loving such a king, but she refuses, knowing somehow that she loves in vain, yet persisting in her will to die a thousand deaths rather than cry quittance. In hope of regaining the king's favor she begs the lords to repeal their banishment of Gaveston. The repeal has been decided upon when Edward comes back on stage, mourning aloud to himself and noticing neither the Queen nor the nobles who watch him:

> *Edw.* Hees gone, and for his absence thus I moorne,
> Did neuer sorrow go so neere my heart,
> As dooth the want of my sweete *Gaueston*,
> And could my crownes reuenew bring him back,
> I would freelie giue it to his enemies,
> And thinke I gaind, hauing bought so deare a friend.
> *Qu.* Harke how he harpes vpon his minion.
> *Edw.* My heart is as an anuill vnto sorrow,
> Which beates vpon it like the Cyclops hammers,
> And with the noise turnes vp my giddie braine,
> And makes me frantick for my *Gaueston*:
> Ah had some bloudlesse furie rose from hell,
> And with my kinglie scepter stroke me dead,
> When I was forst to leaue my *Gaueston*:
> *Lan.* *Diablo*, what passions call you these [!]
>
> (632-646)

The impact of these lines is strong for a number of reasons. Beyond the eloquence of Edward's grief there is the eloquence of the stage-picture itself: all the characters on stage, who are enemies of Gaveston and hold his fate in their powerful hands, focus their attention on the mourning king, the lover of Gaveston. King Edward is the passive victim not only of his love but also of those who have reason to despise that love. He stands separated from the rest, not in antagonism or aggression—for he is not conscious of the others' presence—but in the isolation of private grief. This very isolation in brooding self-pity, this lack of awareness of others around him, are emblematic of his whole career. The distance between the king and the others is not merely one of physical space, but of psychological space as well: it is a separation by personal opposition and by the imbalance of personal power. This king is ruled by his own passions and by the political power of his nobles. The distance is increased still further by the ironic fact that the nobles have just decided to recall Gaveston, so that Edward's grief, so intensely felt and expressed, is seen by the others as soon to be over.

The poetic structure of the king's speech contributes to the whole effect. The images of the anvil, of sorrow personified, of the destructive fury, all indicate the essentially passive nature of Edward's suffering; his is not the suffering that expresses itself in terms of rage or even in terms of Stoic strength. There is irony in the emotional weight of his sorrow, not only because he is a king who looks upon himself as a weak and helpless victim, but also because we know how unworthy Gaveston is of such affection. And there is still more irony in the cognitive implications of his sorrowful words, for they reveal Edward's sentiments as basically opposed to the ideals of kingship: he would sell his crown for his friend; he would be struck dead with his own scepter. Marlowe has integrated the poetic and dramatic expression in this scene of Edward's anguish toward a final effect that is ironic rather than sympathetic; the king's sufferings emphasize his weakness, and his weakness defines the constricted quality of his kingship.

It is evident that Gaveston means more to Edward than all the world, in spite of the responsibilities and duties of his state; the sufferings of the realm are disregarded in his efforts to keep Gaveston and himself happy. Marlowe emphasizes this point on a number of occasions by juxtaposing unhistorical calamities or dangers with Edward's lack of regard for anything or anyone but Gaveston. Anxiously awaiting the return of his favorite from exile, the king greets the news that Normandy has been invaded by the King of France (an event invented by Marlowe) with: "A triflle, weele expell him when we please" (851). Immediately he turns his attention to the details of the festive triumph he has prepared for Gaveston's arrival. Shortly after, the nobles detail the grievances of the realm in an unchronological composite picture, some particulars of which have historical basis and some not:

> *Mor.* The idle triumphes, maskes, lasciuious showes
> And prodigall gifts bestowed on *Gaueston*,
> Haue drawne thy treasure drie, and made thee weake,
> The murmuring commons ouerstretched hath.
> *Lan.* Looke for rebellion, looke to be deposde,
> Thy garrisons are beaten out of Fraunce,
> And lame and poore, lie groning at the gates,
> The wilde *Oneyle*, with swarmes of Irish Kernes,
> Liues vncontroulde within the English pale,
> Vnto the walles of Yorke the Scots made rode,
> And vnresisted, draue away riche spoiles.
> *Mor. iu.* The hautie *Dane* commands the narrow seas,
> While in the harbor ride thy ships vnrigd.
> *Lan.* What forraine prince sends thee embassadors?
> *Mor.* Who loues thee? but a sort of flatterers.
> *Lan.* Thy gentle Queene, sole sister to *Valoys*,
> Complaines, that thou hast left her all forlorne.
> *Mor.* Thy court is naked, being bereft of those,
> That makes a king seeme glorious to the world,

I meane the peeres, whom thou shouldst dearly loue:
Libels are cast againe thee in the streete,
Ballads and rimes, made of thy ouerthrow.
    Lan.   The Northren borderers seeing the houses burnt
Their wiues and children slaine, run vp and downe,
Cursing the name of thee and *Gaueston.*
    Mor.   When wert thou in the field with banner spred?
But once, and then thy souldiers marcht like players,
With garish robes, not armor, and thy selfe
Bedaubd with golde, rode laughing at the rest,
Nodding and shaking of thy spangled crest,
Where womens fauors hung like labels downe.
                            (1004-1035)

The picture is bleak indeed, and is made even bleaker by the peers' threat of war if Edward will not give up the favoritism that is ruining the realm. Even the king's brother, the Earl of Kent, who has so far manfully supported the dignity of the kingship and Edward's right to rule, urges the stubborn Edward to banish Gaveston forever:

    My lord, I see your loue to *Gaueston,*
    VVill be the ruine of the realme and you ...   (1058-1059)

But Edward replies to this prophecy with the banishment of his brother instead, and then, with consummate irrationality and pettiness, greets the entrance of the Queen with: "Heere comes she thats cause of all these iarres" (1074). The deterioration of the national welfare and the indignities heaped upon the long-suffering Queen are the indexes of Edward's achievement as King of England. By setting forth the suffering of the state as well as the suffering of persons, Marlowe has indicated the multiform evil effects of the king's personal vice.
    The climactic dramatic demonstration of King Edward's persistence in considering Gaveston before the good of his kingdom comes with the report of Gaveston's execution by the

nobles. Initially, he responds to the news in the passive vein
that has marked his earlier sufferings: "O shall I speake, or
shall I sigh and die!" (1511). But suggestions from his new
opportunist-flatterer, young Spencer, that he revenge Gaveston's death with the sword, act as a catalyst on his sorrows, converting them to violent vows of extravagant revenge:

> I will haue heads, and liues for him as many,
> As I haue manors, castels, townes, and towers,
> Tretcherous *Warwicke*, traiterous *Mortimer*:
> If I be Englands king, in lakes of gore
> Your headles trunkes, your bodies will I traile,
> That you may drinke your fill, and quaffe in bloud,
> And staine my roiall standard with the same,
> That so my bloudie colours may suggest
> Remembrance of reuenge immortallie,
> On your accursed traiterous progenie . . .   (1522-1531)

It is noteworthy that active rage of this kind does not come
spontaneously from Edward; when it does come, it shows
his weakness, not his strength. Hyperbolic terms of revenge
coming from the mouth of an English king, and promising
civil war and destruction, carry with them for the Elizabethan
audience a force that the extravagancies of a Tamburlaine lack:
they indicate the will to loose on England the havoc of a
political evil ever-present to the minds of the Elizabethans,
and continually stressed in such plays as *Gorboduc*, *The Misfortunes of Arthur*, and Parts II and III of *Henry VI*. The
solidity of Elizabeth's reign, in the context of what has been
called the Tudor Myth, stood in sharp contrast to the memorable dissension of the houses of Lancaster and York: that dissension, and any analogues of it, represented to the Elizabethans the hateful alternative to their own peace and strength.
King Edward brands himself as a wicked king in holding to
what Warwick calls "A desperate and vnnaturall resolution"
(1614)—to "Make Englands ciuill townes huge heapes of

stones" rather than to dismiss his new flattering favorites
(1612). The Queen's reaction to the situation represents the
orthodox response:

> . . . a heauie case,
> When force to force is knit and sword and gleaue,
> In ciuill broiles makes kin and country men,
> Slaughter themselues in others and their sides
> With their owne weapons gorde, but whats the helpe?
> Misgouerned kings are cause of all this wrack,
> And *Edward* thou art one among them all,
> Whose loosnes hath betrayed thy land to spoyle . . .
>
> (1854-1861)

For all his early suffering, then, Edward can claim little or
no sympathy. But by the time of the great reversal, his defeat
at the hands of the Queen and Mortimer, his sufferings take
on a new quality of pathos. The general shift in sympathy
that characterizes *Edward II* is brought about in several ways:
the Queen, repeatedly rejected by Edward in her pleadings
for attention and affection, is now revealed to be in amorous
as well as martial league with Mortimer; Mortimer himself
evolves from the early Hotspur-like figure into a tyrant hardened and corrupted by ambition and power; while the Earl
of Kent, whose allegiance to one side or another has always
been governed by a rational interest in the best welfare of
the country, is now converted to the cause of the oppressed
king.[6]

After the Queen and Mortimer have secured their power, the next scene in which Edward appears is a tableau of
the fall of kings. Edward and his favorites, hiding from their
enemies in the monastery at Neath, are given assurance of the
monks' protection by the abbot; and Edward describes his
situation:

---

[6] Kent's soliloquy (1891-1910) functions as the weight that tips the
balance in favor of Edward, revealing in a few lines the three major
changes in character indicated above.

O hadst thou euer beene a king, thy hart
Pierced deeply with sence of my distresse,
Could not but take compassion of my state,
Stately and proud, in riches and in traine,
Whilom I was powerfull and full of pompe,
But what is he, whome rule and emperie
Haue not in life or death made miserable?

(1994-2000)

This is the conventional *De Casibus* theme, with the added
note of Edward's characteristic self-pity. The contrast between
past glory and present humiliation is effected visually by the
fact that Edward, hitherto seen in courtly majesty or martial
fittings, is now disguised in plain garb. The visual impact is
then strengthened by the king's pathetic action—he lays his
head in the abbot's lap, and bewails his fate with closed eyes:

... good father on thy lap
Lay I this head, laden with mickle care,
O might I neuer open these eyes againe,
Neuer againe lift vp this drooping head,
O neuer more lift vp this dying hart!   (2024-2028)

This picture of a fallen king confronts the nobles as they arrive
to arrest Edward. The Earl of Leicester, admittedly moved,
adds yet another moral caption to the scene, quoting from
Seneca:

Alas, see where he sits, and hopes vnseene,
T'escape their hands that seeke to reaue his life:
Too true it is, *quem dies vidit veniens superbum,*
Hunc dies vidit fugiens iacentem.   (2038-2041)

The visual image may have been accentuated still further by
an effective use of symbolism; Clifford Leech suggests that
the mower, whom Marlowe invents as the man who betrayed
Edward's hiding-place to his pursuers (there is no informer

in Holinshed), carries with him a scythe.[7] The stage directions do not provide this detail, but it remains as a felicitous
possibility, in which case the presence of this "gloomie fellow"
(2014) quietly but effectively suggests the cutting down of the
king—by time, as Leech believes, or perhaps even by ap-
proaching death.[8]

Edward's histrionic behavior at the arrest of his friends,
Spencer and Baldock, is quite in keeping with his earlier anguish at Gaveston's departure, and serves to emphasize his
vital dependence on his companions:

> Comes Leister then in *Isabellas* name,
> To take my life, my companie from me?
> Here man, rip vp this panting brest of mine,
> And take my heart, in reskew of my friends.
>
> (2051-2054)

A little later in the same scene he once more equates his life
with his friends (2087), just as in the deposition scene he will
equate his life with his crown (2168, 2184). But, with his capture, begins that relentless and pitiless shearing away of Edward's supports which ends in his hideous murder. The suffering of Edward from the time of his capture is the suffering
of a lost soul, a soul condemned to a kind of material damnation which deprives it of all the dignity, power and stature it
was once intended to enjoy. The *De Casibus* contrast between

---

[7] "Marlowe's 'Edward II,'" p. 193.

[8] The sickle or the scythe was the most frequent attribute of the per-
sonification of Time in Renaissance art, but from the late fifteenth century
it had been carried over as the attribute of the Death-figure as well. See
Erwin Panofsky, *Studies in Iconology* (New York, 1939), pp. 71 and 82;
Raimond van Marle, *Iconographie de l'art profane au moyen-age et à la
Renaissance*, II (La Haye, 1932), pp. 364-367.

The mower has only two lines in the scene, one to point out the fugitives,
and the other, at the scene's end, to remind Rice ap Howell that he expects
a reward. If the mower is intended visibly to resemble the figure of Time
or Death, the exchange at the end takes on a double meaning:

"*Mower.* Your worship I trust will remember me?

Rice. Remember thee fellow? what else . . ." (2107-2108)

past glory and present misery is an ever-present force in Edward's consciousness, driving him to extreme self-pity and pathetic lamentations. But it is a convention that works within his mind more than a convention of verbal or moral expression, and this is Marlowe's achievement—to give to the *De Casibus* convention a new psychological and dramatic validity, by making it a latent force behind the suffering of his fallen king, emerging time and again not in terms of the usual catalogue of past glories nor in terms of sententious warning, but rather in action, gesture, or outburst of emotion. Marlowe exploits this suffering and the impulse behind it throughout the final third of his play, alternating scenes of Edward's agony and degrading treatment with scenes involving the Queen and Mortimer. These serve to blacken their characters and shift to them the major responsibility for the king's physical afflictions.

Once Edward's friends have been led off to execution, there remain but two things his enemies must have from him: his crown and his life. The physical suffering involved in his death is gruesome enough; indeed, as Clifford Leech has stated, "No other tragic figure in Elizabethan or Jacobean times is treated in the degrading way that Mortimer permits for Edward."[9] Yet, ironically enough, Marlowe did not have to invent the details of his murder, but only to transpose them from history to the stage.[10] On the other hand, the mental agony involved in the loss of Edward's crown is Marlowe's own creation, and in the deposition scene the dramatist's use of language does more than does the final horrifying action to represent the intense anguish of the fallen king. Edward is here most eloquent in expression of his grief; of 164 speaking lines in the scene (MSR), 128 are his. His emotions range from

[9] "Marlowe's 'Edward II,' " p. 194.
[10] The main sources are Raphael Holinshed, *The Chronicles of England, Scotlande, and Irelande* (London, 1577), pp. 882-883 (Gg5ᵛ-Gg6); and John Stow, *The Chronicles of England* (London, 1580), pp. 355-358 (Z2-Z3ᵛ).

melancholy to violent rage, as he oscillates between acute
awareness of his kingship and an equally sensitive perception
of his impotence. The crown on his head becomes for him the
last external symbol of stature and dignity, and the intensity
of his self-conscious suffering becomes the internal symbol:

> The greefes of priuate men are soone allayde,
> But not of kings, the forrest Deare being strucke
> Runnes to an herbe that closeth vp the wounds,
> But when the imperiall Lions flesh is gorde,
> He rends and teares it with his wrathfull pawe,
> Highly scorning, that the lowly earth
> Should drinke his bloud, mounts vp into the ayre:
> And so it fares with me . . .
>
> . . . .
>
> But what are kings, when regiment is gone,
> But perfect shadowes in a sun-shine day?
> My nobles rule, I beare the name of king,
> I weare the crowne, but am contrould by them,
> By *Mortimer*, and my vnconstant Queene,
> Who spots my nuptiall bed with infamie,
> Whilst I am lodgd within this caue of care,
> Where sorrow at my elbow still attends,
> To companie my hart with sad laments,
> That bleedes within me for this strange exchange.
>
> (2119-2146)

Part of the great effectiveness of the lines that equate fallen
kings with "perfect shadowes" is due to the inversion of the
traditional sun-image used in Elizabethan poetic description of
the state and function of kingship.[11] Noteworthy, too, is the
similarity of the concluding image of Edward's speech to his
overheard soliloquy at the departure of Gaveston; in both he
personifies his grieving heart and sorrow, bringing them together in one image and demonstrating an inherent tendency

[11] Ribner, *English History Play*, p. 77.

to dramatize his own grief. There is a sense of soliloquy in this speech as well, though Edward is well aware of the presence of the two nobles and the bishop who have come for the crown. These men impatiently interrupt the lamentations of the king to remind him of the decision he must make, and point out that his deposition is requested for the good of the country. But the king remains in a state of vacillation, moved by personal attachment to his lost power and by the fear that Mortimer, not his son, will inherit that power. Finally, attributing the necessity to the will of heaven, he removes his crown and offers it to the nobles; but the sight of it makes him beg for a little more time:

> But stay a while, let me be king till night,
> That I may gaze vpon this glittering crowne . . .
>
> (2170-2171)

Then, in desperation, he makes a plea to the universe to stay the inevitable succession of time itself:

> Continue euer thou celestiall sunne,
> Let neuer silent night possesse this clime,
> Stand still you watches of the element,
> All times and seasons rest you at a stay,
> That *Edward* may be still faire Englands king:
> But dayes bright beames dooth vanish fast away,
> And needes I must resigne my wished crowne . . .
>
> (2175-2181)

Though the realization of this necessity grows ever more pressing, Edward is led by a last desperate self-assertion to play the "imperiall lion": replacing the crown on his head, he attempts by furious frowns to frighten the nobles, but it is a pitiful and vain attempt. The lion is brought down to the level of the beggar once more: ". . . let me weare it yet a while" (2194). This plea is met with another demand for a decision, and Edward, in a rage, flings back a negative and defiant answer. Leicester's warning that refusal will mean the loss of the prince's right reverses the king's decision, and after a moment of collapse Edward presents himself once again as the passive and afflicted victim, offering his crown in such a way as to shame even the determined nobles from their purpose:

> . . . heauens & earth conspire
> To make me miserable: heere receiue my crowne,
> Receiue it? no, these innocent hands of mine
> Shall not be guiltie of so foule a crime,
> He of you all that most desires my bloud,
> And will be called the murtherer of a king,
> Take it . . .   (2211-2217)

No one moves, and Edward suggests they call for Mortimer and Isabella to take the crown, but the very thought stirs such revulsion in his breast that he suddenly and willingly hands over the coveted crown rather than look upon his hated enemies. The final surrender completed, the external symbol of royalty lost, Edward, like Tamburlaine, face to face with the inevitable fact of defeat, comforts himself with the expectation of greater things in the next world:

> . . . now sweete God of heauen,
> Make me despise this transitorie pompe,
> And sit for aye inthronized in heauen . . .
>   (2222-2224)

In the deposition scene as elsewhere, Marlowe has heavily underscored Edward's willfulness, and he has significantly departed from his source in not making Edward realize his own responsibility for the misery he has inflicted on the kingdom, on his wife, and on himself.[12] Marlowe's Edward thinks the

---

[12] Compare Holinshed: ". . . after he was come to himself, he answered that he knew that he was fallen into this miserie through hys owne offences, and therefore he was contented paciently to suffer it, but yet it coulde not (hee sayde) but grieue hym, that he had in such wise runne into the hatred

heavens and earth have conspired to make him miserable; to him, Mortimer and the Queen are the only begetters of his calamity; "how haue I transgrest," he asks, "Vnlesse it be with too much clemencie?" (2239-2240). The nobles reply by humbly taking their leave. This blind conviction of innocence is the ultimate irony in Edward's tragedy, but it is an irony which helps to keep the response to his maltreatment from being one of total indignation.

Although King Edward's weaknesses and vices are the major causes of the disruption of state and of his initial downfall, the Queen and Mortimer bear the brunt of the responsibility for the physical indignities heaped upon the captured king in the last sections of the play. Furthermore, it is notable that Marlowe has departed from historical accounts in assigning such responsibility to Mortimer, for neither Holinshed nor Stow mentions him in connection with the appointment of Matrevis and Gurney as Edward's torturers, or with the Latin riddle that conceals the death-command for Edward. Lightborn, Mortimer's chosen agent for the execution, is totally unhistorical. Linking Mortimer directly with these episodes makes him considerably more cruel and hateful than his earlier appearances suggest, and by paralleling this coarsening in Mortimer with an increasing audacity of expression and ambition, Marlowe suggests the familiar theme of corrupting power. Mortimer prefaces his commands to Matrevis and Gurney with the boast that he himself "now makes Fortunes wheele turne as he please" (2345); after commissioning Lightborn to kill the king, Mortimer in a proud soliloquy repeats the boast of Ovid's Niobe that he is too great for Fortune to harm (2579), ironically blind to the implications of

---

of all his people: notwithstanding he gaue the lords moste heartie thankes, that they had so forgotten theyr receyued iniuryes. . . . Therefore to satisfie them . . . hee utterly renounced hys right to the Kingdome, and to the whole administration thereof. And lastlye besought the Lordes nowe in his miserie to forgiue him such offences as he had committed agaynst them." p. 882 (Gg5ᵛ). Stow also records Edward's repentance, p. 350 (Y7ᵛ).

that quotation, which in Niobe's case precipitated her suffering and destruction.[13]

It is the Queen in Marlowe's play who delegates Mortimer to do what he will with the king; indeed, it is she who makes the initial suggestion that they are not safe while Edward is alive (2329-2330). The chronicles in this case give some evidence for her responsibility, linking her with the commissioning of Matrevis and Gurney to keep Edward away from would-be rescuers and under harsh treatment.[14] Holinshed, furthermore, gives some hint of her hypocrisy and dissembling —she would send courteous and loving letters to the king at the same time that she gave commands for his harsh treatment.[15] Marlowe seizes upon this hint and develops it dramatically to blacken Isabella's character, presenting her duplicity before a messenger from the king (2310), before Matrevis and Gurney (2362-2365), and before Kent (2383). Just as he did in *The Jew of Malta* and *The Massacre at Paris*, Marlowe relies on the dramatization of ambition and duplicity to give to the characters of Mortimer and the Queen the recognizable and effective dimension of evil.

The drama now moves to the depiction of Edward's torture, which opens with the sardonic consolation Matrevis offers to the king: "Men are ordaind to liue in miserie" (2431). From Stow's history Marlowe derives the shaving of the king in channel water,[16] but he adds to this debasement the ironic touch of having Edward offer up his misery for the sake of his dead flatterers, Gaveston and the Spencers. The irony prevents too sympathetic a response to Edward's debasement; that the "distance" it effects is intentional can be confirmed, I think, by Marlowe's omission of an episode coupled by Stow with the puddle-shaving: the mock-crowning of Edward with hay.[17]

[13] Ovid, *Metamorphoses*, vi, 195 ff.
[14] Holinshed, p. 883 (Gg6); Stow, p. 335 (Z2).
[15] P. 883 (Gg6).
[16] P. 356 (Z2ᵛ).
[17] *ibid.* ". . . that wicked man *Gerney* making a crown of Hey, put it on

The inevitable suggestion here of the Biblical mock-crowning of Christ with thorns would imply a measure of value and sympathy by association which was not to Marlowe's purpose. Marlowe, as usual, is working for irony, not sympathy, in the depiction of his protagonist's suffering.[18]

Grim irony is also the keynote of Edward's murder, principally in Marlowe's introduction of the executioner, Lightborn, whose hypocritical tears and comforting words to his helpless victim veil but lightly the cruel professional pride of the artful killer. The scene of his commissioning by Mortimer reveals him to be of the school of Barabas; laughing aloud at Mortimer's suggestion that he might relent from his purpose at Edward's looks, Lightborn boasts:

> Tis not the first time I haue killed a man,
> I learnde in Naples how to poison flowers,
> To strangle with a lawne thrust through the throte,
> To pierce the wind-pipe with a needles point,
> Or whilst one is a sleepe, to take a quill
> And blowe a little powder in his eares,
> Or open his mouth, and powre quick siluer downe,
> But yet I haue a brauer way then these. (2539-2546)

The "brauer way" begins to take horrendous shape as Lightborn commands Matrevis and Gurney to prepare the tools of execution: a red-hot spit, a table, and a featherbed. His spirit of diabolic professionalism goes with his name, which, as Harry Levin has remarked, "reveals the cloven hoof; for it had also belonged to one of the devils in the Chester cycle, and is

---

hys heade, and the souldiours that were aboute him mocked him, saying, *Tprut, auaunt ur King,* making a kinde of noise with theyr mouthes, as though they had farted."

[18] In this case his treatment of Edward differs not only from the historical source but also from later poetical versions of Edward's fall: Michael Drayton's *Mortimeriados* (1596), Richard Niccols' 1610 addition of Edward's career to the *Mirror for Magistrates,* and Sir Francis Hubert's *The Deplorable Life and Death of Edward the Second* (1628) all include the mock-crowning.

neither more nor less than an Anglicization of 'Lucifer.' "[19] The red-hot spit plunged into Edward's intestines, an execution set down in historical records, is peculiarly appropriate in the hands of this Lightborn. And there is an almost pun-like appropriateness in his entrance to Edward's black dungeon, since he bears with him a light—a light which, like that of his namesake, is at the same time the herald of a fall.

But Marlowe has not stopped with investing his murderer with the symbolic hints of diabolism; he has gone further and made Lightborn perform in the manner of the morality Vice. His first words, when left alone by Matrevis and Gurney, are phrased according to one trademark of the Vice:

> So now must I about this geare, nere was
> there any
> So finely handled as this king shalbe . . .
> (2681-2683)

The phrase, centering around the conventional word *gear*, and the sentiment, inviting the attention of the audience to the skill of the Vice's stratagem and the success of his destructive purpose, are continually invoked by Vice figures throughout the morality tradition, as Bernard Spivack has noted.[20] It is the Vice's invitation to his grim game of deceit and destruction, and Lightborn indeed looks upon his encounter with Edward as macabre sport. His every phrase to the weakened and suspicious king is dissimulation as, like a Vice, he poses as the inverse of his true self. To Edward's question, he replies that his purpose is "To comfort you, and bring you ioyfull newes" (2687). As a proof of his affection and concern for the king, Lightborn offers next his tears, falling back on one of the Vice's characteristic tricks. Edward, taken in for a moment, relates the details of his heinous maltreatment, and Lightborn exclaims "O villaines!" (2703), and "O speake no more my

---

[19] *The Overreacher*, p. 101.
[20] *Shakespeare and the Allegory of Evil* (New York, 1958), pp. 190-191.

lorde, this breakes my/heart" (2716-2717). Yet Edward
sees his tragedy written on his visitor's brow, and it is with
consummate artistry that Lightborn allays his fears with a
lie that is not a lie (in light of the means by which Lightborn
is accustomed to kill):

> These handes were neuer stainde with inno-
> cent bloud,
> Nor shall they now be tainted with a kings.
>
> (2729-2731)

There follows one of the most pitifully ironic passages in Elizabethan drama, as the fatigued and tattered king faces his
fearful visitor and hopes to buy his life with his sole remaining
jewel, the last reminder of the kingship that once was his:

> One iewell haue I left, receiue thou this,
> Still feare I, and I know not whats the cause,
> But euerie iointe shakes as I giue it thee:
> O if thou harborst murther in thy hart,
> Let this gift change thy minde, and saue thy soule,
> Know that I am a king, oh at that name,
> I feele a hell of greefe, where is my crowne?
> Gone, gone, and doe I remaine aliue?   (2734-2741)

Edward does not remain alive long; his grotesque murder
takes place swiftly, within full view of the audience—the first
death in the play to take place on stage, and punctuated with
the agonizing cry recorded in history.[21]

The rest is anti-climactic. Lightborn is stabbed by Matrevis
and Gurney, Mortimer meets swift retribution at the command of young Edward (considerably antedating his actual
execution), and the drama ends in a scene of ritual expiation
as the young King Edward III offers up Mortimer's severed
head to the spirit of his murdered father.

---

[21] Holinshed, p. 883 (Gg6).

Marlowe has pictured Edward's fall and punishment at great length and with unrelieved insistence. No history play before this had dwelt so long and centrally on the suffering and destruction of a king. Edward's fall is depicted as the result of his weakness and willfulness—the result of a disordered tendency recognized as evil and destructive by all except the protagonist himself and those flatterers who profit from it. The king's early expression of suffering at the loss of his minions serves as an index of that disorder: his kingship and duties of state are not as important as his affection for Gaveston and his successors. He would rather not be king than lose these friends. There is no hint of admiration in the response to Edward's character; the fact that he is a king with prescribed duties and loyalties is one criterion by which his early actions are condemned. And significantly enough, the principal reason for the degree of sympathy that is allowed him in the latter section of the play is again the fact that he is a king. Marlowe plays upon this fact incessantly in representing Edward's sufferings; it is the frame of reference which makes possible the intense irony of those scenes of anguish beginning with the capture at the monastery.[22] Suffering as it is treated in

[22] In the abbey scene, Edward tells the abbot ". . . hadst thou euer beene *a king*, thy hart . . . Could not but take compassion of my state" (1994-1996). When Edward's friends are ordered away, the abbot remarks, "My heart with pittie earnes to see this sight,/ *A king* to beare these words and proud commaunds" (2058-2059). Edward's response to the order that he must go to Killingworth is: "Must! tis somewhat hard, when *kings* must go" (2071). The deposition scene immediately following contains a number of similar stresses on kingship (e.g., 2119-2120, 2134-2135, 2137-2140). In the beard-shaving scene, Edward calls on the immortal powers to look upon his captors wronging "their liege and soueraigne, Englands/ *king*" (2474-2475). Kent, thwarted in his attempt to rescue Edward, exclaims: "O miserable is that commonweale, where lords/ Keepe courts, and *kings* are lockt in prison!" (2503-2504). Even Lightborn's feigned sympathy comes from seeing "*a king* in this most pittious state" (2696). Edward's complaints to him emphasize the horror implied in treating a king in this way: "They giue me bread and water being *a king*" (2707); "Know that I am *a king*" (2739). (All italics mine.)

Edward II is a problem caused not only by weakness of character and the cruelty of vicious persons, but by the nature of the sufferer's inherent status and role. The tragic element in Edward's suffering is due less to his humanity than to his kingship; *Edward II* is thus the extreme articulation of the *De Casibus* theme, but without the explication of the *De Casibus* moral.

The ultimate irony of the way in which the concept or consciousness of kingship operates within the play lies in the contrast between Edward's utter disregard of the meaning of kingship before his defeat, and the intolerable anxiety he experiences afterwards *because of* his kingship. What once could not engage his concern now cannot be forgotten, and again it is the sense of loss that provokes the sufferer's most grievous pain. Too late Edward becomes fully aware of what he was meant to be, and realization of the irreparable loss of his original status plunges him into a hell of grief. His inward hell is appropriately accompanied by an outward hell—the foul lake of sewage in which he is imprisoned becomes his Cocytus; the drumming of Matrevis and Gurney, and the fiery spit of Lightborn, become the infernal instruments of torture wielded by his tormentors.

It is in part this hellish quality of his psychological and physical situation that makes Edward's suffering more akin to the suffering of Faustus than to that of any other Marlovian figure. For this king in his misery does not exhibit the pathetic tendency of Dido to compensate for loss by extravagant and wishful illusion; the circumstances of his affliction are too gross and inescapable for that. Nor does he share with Tamburlaine the gift of extravagant and voluble rage, the rage that vents itself in violent action; he possesses neither the requisite vigor nor the touch of barbaric insensitivity. Similarly out of his reach are Bajazeth's capacity for furious cursing and Zabina's lapse into self-destructive insanity. Unlike

Barabas and the Duke of Guise, he is too painfully aware of his mortality to die exulting in curses; here again, his gradual physical debilitation leaves him too weak to flame out in those last moments, except for the final scream that links his death with that of Faustus. With Faustus, too, he shares the inevitably doomed pleas to halt the movement of time; with Faustus he falls victim to his own deliberate vice. But unlike Faustus, he has not the awareness and the vision of his own culpability. That dimension of irony is reserved for the man who willed to be a demigod, to break the bonds of his own humanity. It is Edward's tragedy to be less than he was intended to be, rather than to fall in the attempt to be more than he could be. It is Edward's suffering to look back in agony at the lost chance, to yearn for the crown that he did not grace and can no longer bear. His hell is the hideous present tormented by the memory of the past; Faustus' hell is the last mortal glimpse of a future of eternal damnation. But both hells are one in the irreparable sense of loss which defines the deepest level of suffering.

Edward II is a personal tragedy set within the political context of the history play. Its political implications, even though clear to an Elizabethan audience, are strictly secondary to the stress on individual human agents and their fates. Edward's personal suffering stands out as the most memorable aspect of the play, and this suffering, unlike the suffering of King Henry VI in the third part of the trilogy that bears his name, is not linked so consistently with the sufferings of the state. Both the ritual nature and the political stresses of the plaintive molehill scene in *3 Henry VI* (ii.v) are absent from Marlowe's play; but this may be inevitable, since it is part of Henry's character to be painfully aware of the sufferings of his realm, and characteristic of Edward to ignore them.

One of the results of emphasizing the personal rather than

the political, of stressing the emotions involved in the conflict of individual wills more than the political effects of such conflicts, is to focus attention on the personal responsibility for human suffering and moral evil. The causes of suffering and of evil in *Edward II* do not lie in the mysterious structure of the universe, or even in the ineffable operations of divine power: they lie in the individual wills of human agents. There is no suffering, no pain, no representation of evil which is not manifestly explicable in terms of deliberate human action or resolve. Fate, destiny, even the Fortune which Mortimer mistakenly feels he has conquered, are but rarely evoked. It is rather the network of Gaveston's flattery, Edward's willfulness, Mortimer's ambition, and Isabella's infidelity that produces the human tribulations and cruelties in the universe of this play. That the nature of these characters is not totally malicious or unscrupulous is the significant difference in the vision of evil presented in *Edward II* from that in *The Jew of Malta* or *The Massacre at Paris*; it is a difference which makes this play more human and more credible.

But with the shift to a more credible humanity comes an accentuation of the shock value inherent in the vicious and destructive acts of man: the total villain can no longer be held responsible for everything that is evil; man's inhumanity to man stands out in starker outline. The introduction of Lightborn to execute the most heinous of the atrocities may be, after all, a concession to the other vision, a retreat to the more comfortable position of viewing the worst of evils as the work of an inhuman creature. In turning the Vice into a villain, the Elizabethan dramatist may have contributed to the simplistic vision of melodrama (if we include in that concept a somewhat unrealistic evasion of the capacity of all men to do evil) by helping to locate the source of suffering and evil in an external force completely independent of the rest of humanity, rather than in an internal principle that can invade everyone.

For the total villain is nothing but a scapegoat for the crimes of men.

Even with the presence of Lightborn there is no such scapegoat in *Edward II*. The fact of suffering in this tragedy is no more evident than the fact of human responsibility for that suffering. This, together with the retributive urgency of the play's conclusion, constitutes a view of suffering and evil that is basically moral and traditional. But with Marlowe that view needs no moralizing; the dramatization is enough.

CHAPTER V
POENA DAMNI: THE TRAGICAL HISTORY OF DOCTOR FAUSTUS

. . . they fondly thinking to allay
Thir appetite with gust, instead of Fruit
Chewd bitter Ashes . . .
                        —Milton, PARADISE LOST

Every disordered spirit shall be a
punishment to itself.
                        —St. Augustine

CHAPTER V

POENA DAMNI: THE TRAGICAL
HISTORY OF DOCTOR FAUSTUS

O N E of the points where the two worlds of Edward II and of Doctor Faustus touch each other is hidden in the devil Mephostophilis' trenchant answer to the Doctor's question whether the demons of hell have any pains to torture others: "As great as haue the humane soules of men."[1] The line cuts deep, but once it is uttered the theme is gone; there is nothing in the play to embody its meaning in action. There are fewer human figures of importance in *Doctor Faustus* than in any other play by Marlowe: men are not caught in a web of mutual betrayal or torment; rather the dramatic light focuses glaringly on one man and one man alone, a man who neither works his violent will upon others to cause them pain, nor meets his own suffering at the hands of other men. Doctor Faustus is a man who of his own conscious willfulness brings tragedy and torment crashing down upon his head, the pitiful and fearful victim of his own ambitions and desires. The irony with which Marlowe habitually invests the downfalls of his protagonists is here wrought to its finest and sharpest point; it is an irony based on theological concepts of sin and damnation, and dramatically expressed in two major patterns of action: the repetitive pattern of moral choice leading to the alternative of spiritual destruction, and the pattern of contrast between Faustus' grand imaginative designs and the actual, vacuous accomplishments of his magical career.[2] It is precisely this irony,

[1] *Marlowe's "Doctor Faustus" 1604-1616*, ed. W. W. Greg (Oxford, 1950), p. 191, l. 432. Subsequent references to this edition will appear in my text. Unless otherwise indicated, quotations are from the B-text of 1616.

[2] These themes have been given intelligent and illuminating discussion in the scholarship and criticism of recent years. See especially Leo Kirschbaum, "Marlowe's Faustus: A Reconsideration," *RES*, XIX (1943), 225-241; Robert B. Heilman, "The Tragedy of Knowledge: Marlowe's Treatment

in all its ramifications and exhibitions, which establishes the tragic dimension of the play. Unlike the rest of Marlowe's dramatic works, and indeed unlike the great majority of serious plays of Marlowe's time, *Doctor Faustus* does not rely on the representation of physical pain and destruction for its tragic effects. It is primarily and fundamentally a tragedy of the spirit.

Proportionally, the representation of suffering is not very great in *Doctor Faustus*; in addition to the agonies of Faustus' last hour, there are recurrent indications of his pangs of conscience; but that is the extent of human suffering involved. Mephostophilis talks of suffering and of the pains of hell, but with the exception of one spontaneous outburst, he is not *shown* as a suffering creature. Yet what suffering there is in the play is central to its structure and meaning; there is a definite and integral relationship between the torments of Faustus' death and the course of his career, just as there is between the nature of his suffering, as he comes to realize it, and the nature of the devil's suffering as Mephostophilis explains it to him. It is the suffering of the damned that links the human and the diabolic in *Doctor Faustus*, not the pain of hell-fire but spiritual pain. Christian theology, since the early Fathers of the Church, has designated spiritual pain as the worst punishment of the damned, in that eternal exclusion from God's presence cuts off the spirit from the divine source and end of its being, and from the vision that gives meaning and fulfillment to its existence.[3] In the terms of traditional scholastic theology, this spiritual suffering was called *poena*

---

of Faustus," *QRL*, II (1946), 316-332; W. W. Greg, "The Damnation of Faustus," *MLR*, XLI (1946), 97-107; Helen Gardner, "Milton's 'Satan' and the Theme of Damnation in Elizabethan Tragedy," *English Studies 1948* (English Association), n.s. I, 46-66; Roland M. Frye, "Marlowe's *Doctor Faustus*: The Repudiation of Humanity," *South Atlantic Quarterly*, LV (1956), 322-328; and Martin Versfeld, "Some Remarks on Marlowe's Faustus," *English Studies in Africa*, I (1958), 134-143.

[3] Michel Carrouges *et al.*, *L'Enfer* (Paris, 1950), pp. 148-174, 248-250.

damni, the punishment of loss.[4] Both concept and term remained untouched by the theological upheavals of the Reformation, and Marlowe must have encountered them during his six years at Cambridge on a scholarship intended for ministerial candidates.

There is an irony implicit in the nature of the suffering of the damned, an irony which Marlowe has exploited in dramatic terms: the inescapably logical process which brings about such punishment. The sinner, confronted with the moral choice between God's will and what is not God's will, chooses to cut himself off from God in reaching for the not-God; in doing so he brings about *by his own act* the condition of separation from God which, if not altered by the time of death, becomes the basis of damnation and the cause of eternal agony. The punishment of the damned soul is to remain eternally in the state which it has deliberately chosen.[5] Such ironical justice lies at the heart of Faustus' tragedy, and Marlowe has given it dramatic viability by stressing the Doctor's repeated choices of the not-God and by giving to his suffering the quality of *poena damni*.

[4] Thomas Aquinas, e.g., in treating the topic of damnation, writes: ". . . man's extreme unhappiness will consist in the fact that his intellect is completely shut off from the divine light, and that his affections are stubbornly turned against God's goodness. And this is the chief suffering of the damned. It is known as the punishment of loss." *Compendium of Theology*, trans. Cyril Vollert, S. J. (St. Louis, 1947), p. 188. The idea is repeated by George Gascoigne, *The Droome of Doomes day* (London, 1576), F2^v; by Myles Coverdale in *The Hope of the Faithful* (1579), ed. George Pearson, The Parker Society (Cambridge, 1846), p. 207; and is a constant theme in the preaching of John Donne. See *The Sermons of John Donne*, eds. George R. Potter and Evelyn M. Simpson, 9 vols. (Berkeley, 1953-1959), II, 99; III, 51; IV, 86; V, 80, 266-267, 388. Paul H. Kocher cites other Elizabethan echoes of the concept, *Christopher Marlowe* (Chapel Hill, 1946), pp. 116-117. See also Robert Hunter West, *The Invisible World: A Study of Pneumatology in Elizabethan Drama* (Athens, Georgia, 1939), p. 82 and p. 238, n. 45.

[5] Dorothy L. Sayers discusses briefly the application of this principle in Dante, Marlowe, Milton, and Goethe in "The Faust Legend and the Idea of the Devil," *Publications of the English Goethe Society*, n.s. xv (1946), 1-20.

I. THE NATURE OF FAUSTUS' FALL

There is no denying the fact that in *Doctor Faustus*, Christopher Marlowe, whatever his personal views of Christianity may have been, has fashioned a play that is thoroughly Christian in conception and import. Christianity was of course explicit in Marlowe's source, the English Faust-Book. But in adapting that meandering collection of anecdotes about the famous German magician, Marlowe gave it a new, concentrated, intellectual shape by reorganizing his material along the more sophisticated lines of philosophical and theological concepts of evil. As a result, his play carries much more meaning than simply, "Don't sell your soul to the devil." The moral of the English Faust-Book is little more than that.

The depiction of Faustus' motivation for adhering to magic and the service of the devil is scant and sketchy in the Faust-Book. We learn that Faustus dabbled in magic even before becoming a Doctor of Divinity, "being of a naughty minde & otherwise addicted."[6] Though "excellent perfect in the holy scriptures," he "waxed a worldly man," devoting himself to magic, astrology, mathematics and medicine (i, 136). In the interests of his worldly pleasure he "thought to flie ouer the whole world, and to know the secrets of heauen and earth" (ii, 137). And thus he began to conjure.

What Marlowe has made of this vague hint of worldly speculation can best be understood against the background of the Christian theology of sin current in his time. That theology had been given its classic and enduring formulation by St. Augustine, whose work was drawn upon by Catholic and Protestant theologians alike. The Lady Margaret Professor of Theology at Cambridge in Marlowe's university years, Peter Baro, had the highest esteem for Augustine, calling him

---

[6] *The Historie of the damnable life, and deserued death of Doctor Iohn Faustus* (London, 1592), eds. Philip Mason Palmer and Robert Pattison More in *The Sources of the Faust Tradition from Simon Magus to Lessing* (New York, 1936), ch. i, p. 135. Subsequent references to this edition will appear in my text.

"the prince of theologians";[7] and it is practically certain that Marlowe, as a student of theology, had firsthand acquaintance with his work.[8] In the view of Augustine, man, like the angels before him, was created with the power to move upward to God, in fulfillment of the purpose for which he was made, or downward to degradation and misery. "All sins," he writes in the *De libero arbitrio*, "consist in turning away from godly things which are truly lasting, and in turning towards things which are changeable and insecure."[9] "The will sins," he continues, "if it turns away from the unchangeable good which is common to all, and turns towards a private good, whether outside or below it. . . . Thus a man who becomes proud, curious, and self-indulgent, is caught up in another life, which compared to the higher life is death."[10] Thus the perverted will is the cause of all evil, and the root of that perversion lies in the impulses of pride and egoism. If the soul should go out of its way "to produce a false imitation of God, and to will to take pleasure in its own power, then the greater it wishes to become, the less it becomes in fact. And that is *pride, the beginning of all sin*; and *the beginning of the pride of man is to fall off from God*."[11]

---

[7] *In Jonam Prophetam Prælectiones* 39 (London, 1579), Tt2ᵛ.

[8] The Parker collection in the Corpus Christi College Library in Marlowe's time included an eight-volume printed edition of Augustine's works, the largest edition of any one theologian in the entire printed book collection. MS. 575, p. 5.

[9] *The Problem of Free Choice*, trans. Dom Mark Pontifex (Westminster, Maryland, 1955), I.16.35, p. 72.

[10] *ibid.*, II.19.53, p. 135.

[11] *ibid.*, III.25.76, pp. 218-219. This notion, of course, which derives from Ecclesiasticus X.14-15, was to become a theological commonplace, familiar not only to students of theology, but to all who were instructed in the barest rudiments of the Christian religion. One of the homilies officially appointed by Elizabeth to be read on Sundays throughout her realm began "Of our going frō God, the wise man saith, that pride was the first beginning: for by it mans hearte was turned from God his maker. For pride (saith he) is the fountaine of all sinne: he that hath it, shal be ful of cursinges, and at the ende it shal ouerthrow him." *Certaine Sermons appointed by the Queenes Maiestie, to be declared and read, by all Parsons, Vicars and Curates, euery Sunday and Holy day in their Churches: and by her graces*

Now it is obvious that a theological formulation such as this can apply to practically any human sin whatsoever, given enough meditation and analysis. Certainly the Elizabethan audience need not have had recourse to such ideas in order to evaluate Faustus' action in selling his soul to the devil. But the interesting thing is that when one looks at the way in which Marlowe has chosen to present *his* Doctor Faustus, as contrasted with the Faust-Book presentation, it is clear that the theological ideas and concepts involved in the Augustinian definition of moral evil are transposed *directly* into dramatic language and action. One does not have to look behind the words and actions to discover Faustus' pride, the willfulness of his falling from God, or his egoistic ambition to become his own god; they are outwardly and directly manifest in everything he says and does.

The opening Chorus describes the man, his intellectual excellence, and his fatal choice:

> . . . swolne with cunning, of a selfe conceit,
> His waxen wings did mount aboue his reach,
> And melting, heauens conspir'd his ouer-throw:
> For falling to a diuellishex ercise, [*sic*]
> And glutted now with learnings golden gifts,
> He surfets vpon cursed Necromancie:
> Nothing so sweet as Magicke is to him;
> Which he preferres before his chiefest blisse . . .
>
> (20-27)

The picture and the issue is clear enough; the allusion to Icarus, a familiar Elizabethan symbol of self-destructive aspiration,[12] is emblematic of Faustus' career, while the alternative

---

aduice perused and ouerseene, for the better vnderstanding of the simple people (London, 1582), E2.

[12] Icarus was a familiar figure in emblem books of the sixteenth century, appearing under the text "In astrologos" in Alciati and Whitney, and under "Faire tout par moyen" in Corrozet. See Henry Green, *Shakespeare and the Emblem Writers* (London, 1870), pp. 288-290. The prologue to

between "cursed Necromancie" and "his chiefest bliss" is set forth as the object of Faustus' deliberate choice.

Marlowe devotes his first scene to a careful presentation of Faustus' decision to take up magic. One by one Faustus examines the branches of higher learning as they were organized in the universities of his day: philosophy, medicine, law, and theology. One by one the fields of secular learning are rejected because their ends do not satisfy his demand—but notice what the demand is. He does not pursue knowledge for the sake of truth, but for power, superhuman power, the power over life and death. His fundamental grievance is "Yet art thou still but *Faustus*, and a man" (50). Dissatisfied with his creature status, rebelling against the limitations which define the mode of human existence, he would like to make men live eternally, or to raise the dead—secularized parodies of the activities of the Christian God. Divine learning is cast aside as well: because, as Helen Gardner's sensitive interpretation suggests, "it is grounded in the recognition of man's mortality and his fallibility."[13]

Ieromes Bible *Faustus*, view it well:
Stipendium peccati, mors est: ha, stipendium, &c.
The reward of sin is death? that's hard:
Si peccasse, negamus, fallimur, & nulla est in nobis veritas:
If we say that we haue no sinne

Thomas Preston's *Cambises* had drawn a simile between Icarus and the king to illustrate Cambises' self-will:

> "Then cleauing more vnto his wil such vice did immitate:
> As one of *Icarus* his kind, forewarning then did hate.
> Thinking that none could him dismay, ne none his fact could see,
> Yet at the last a fall he tooke, like *Icarus* to be."

Cambises king of Percia (TFT, 1910), A2. In the Induction to *The First parte of the Mirour for Magistrates* (1574) Icarus is used as an example of destructive ambition: *Parts Added to The Mirror for Magistrates by John Higgins & Thomas Blenerhasset*, ed. Lily B. Campbell (Cambridge, 1946), p. 42.
13 "Milton's 'Satan' and the Theme of Damnation," p. 49.

> We deceiue our selues, and there is no truth in vs.
> Why then belike we must sinne,
> And so consequently die,
> I, we must die, an euerlasting death.
> What doctrine call you this? *Che sera, sera*:
> What will be, shall be; *Diuinitie* adeiw. (65-75)

Faustus leaves Divinity to God, and dedicates himself to the devil. Scorning the fatality of "What will be, shall be," he performs his own act of will, and it is one of the developing ironies of the play that what he wills to be shall be.

The facile syllogism by which Faustus rejects the Scriptures and Divinity is in itself a deeply ironic comment on the Doctor's character and career. Its sophistry is really only an excuse for Faustus to turn to his true aspiration:

> O what a world of profite and delight,
> Of power, of honour, and omnipotence,
> Is promised to the Studious Artizan? (80-82)

But beyond its rationalizing function, Faustus' syllogism betrays not only a deep-seated willingness to pervert the Scriptures, but also the foreshadowing of an attitude of mind that will gradually lead him to the sin of despair. It is, in sum, the real point of his fall from God.

Faustus arrives at his fatalistic conclusion by joining together two premises which themselves are glaring half-truths, for each of the propositions he cites from the Bible is drawn from contexts and passages which unite the helplessness of the sinner with the redeeming grace of God. The first, from Romans vi.23, concludes a chapter which stresses how the Christian has been freed from the bondage of sin by Christ's redemption; in its complete form it reads, "For the wages of sinne is death: but the gifte of God *is* eternal life through Iesus Christ our Lord."[14] The second, from 1 John i.8, is also

---

[14] The translation is that of the Geneva Bible (1560).

part of an antithetical construction; the clause Faustus cites
is followed by "If we acknowledge our sinnes, he is faithful
and iust, to forgiue vs our sinnes, & to clense vs from all vn-
righteousness."[15] Faustus' error of stopping halfway in this
text could not easily have gone unnoticed by the Elizabethan
audience. The second of the official Elizabethan sermons and
homilies opened with a series of scriptural references to the
sinful condition of man, among them the very one Faustus
uses: "So doth blessed Saint Iohn the Euangelist, in the name
of himselfe, and of al other holy men (be they neuer so iust)
make this open confession: If we say we haue no sinne, we
deceyue ourselues, and the truth is not in vs: If we knowledge
our sinnes, God is faythfull and iust to forgiue our sinnes, and
to cleanse vs from all vnrighteousnesse."[16]

The sermon goes on to exhort that the state of mortal imperfection be acknowledged, but also that the mercy of God
and Christ's saving merits be relied upon to raise man from
his misery. Faustus, at this point in his career, sees only the
imperfection, not the opportunity of redemption—he scornfully casts away the whole doctrine; at a later point, consciousness of his sinfulness will be painfully present, but his self-
imposed blindness will continue to shut out the light of proffered salvation.

Faustus is blinded here by precisely the same flash of "logic"
which the devil in Thomas Becon's *Dialogue Between the
Christian Knight and Satan* (1564) employs (also in a syllogism) to tempt the knight to despair, and which in Spenser's
Faerie Queene Despair uses to tempt Red Cross to spiritual
death.[17] Faustus' desperation will be a torment to him in the
future; now it spurs him to indulge in his own dreams of pow-

---

[15] *ibid.*

[16] *Certaine Sermons*, A7ᵛ.

[17] Kocher has noted the similarity to Becon's work: *Christopher Marlowe*,
pp. 106-107; Virgil K. Whitaker has remarked on the resemblance to Spenser's: *Shakespeare's Use of Learning: An Inquiry into the Growth of his
Mind and Art* (San Marino, Calif., 1953), p. 242.

er. His attitude and decision are exact replicas of the thoughts of the reprobate described by Wolfgang Musculus, whose theological works were read and esteemed in the schools of Reformation England: "Why shoulde I trouble and trauell my selfe in vaine? and doe those things whiche doe like my mind, seeyng that I do know I am determined to destruction?"[18]

There is one final irony in Faustus' rejection of Divinity by a trick of reason, and it lies in the distinction drawn by theologians between Divinity and the other disciplines. Calvin went so far as to posit two different understandings in man, one of terrestrial things, and another of celestial ones.[19] The latter concerned the knowledge of God, his Divine Will, and man's conformity to it; but without the aid of God's grace, man's reason when directed toward these objects was totally blind and stupid.[20] Peter Baro wrote that the dignity of theology rested in the fact that only in this discipline was the Spirit of God at work as a teacher, rather than reason alone; but this Spirit would only be efficacious when the student's attitude was open and reverent.[21] Faustus' syllogism, then, is as arrogant as it is facile, and in the last analysis a destructive manipulation of thought and reason. The horror with which the sophisticated Christian looked upon such an act has been given eloquent form by John Donne, in a sermon excerpt that is itself a yardstick for the kinds of evil that Marlowe has exhibited in both this play and others: "Whilst we sin strongly, by oppressing others, that are weaker, or craftily by circumventing others that are simple, This is but *Leoninum*, and *Vulpinum*, that tincture of the Lyon, and of the Fox, that brutal nature that is in us. But when we come to sin, upon

---

[18] *Common Places of Christian Religion*, trans. John Man (London, 1578), p. 1093 (zzz3). The Parker collection in the Corpus Christi Library included two editions of the *Common Places* of Musculus. MS. 575, pp. 15-16.

[19] John Calvin, *Institutes of the Christian Religion*, II.ii.13, trans. John Allen, 7th American ed. (Philadelphia, [1936]), I, 294.

[20] *ibid.*, II.ii.19; II, 299-300.

[21] *In Jonam Prophetam*, pp. 3, 5-6 (A2, A3-A3ᵛ).

reason, and upon discourse, upon Meditation, and upon plot, This is *Humanum*, to become the Man of Sin, to surrender that, which is the Form, and Essence of man, Reason, and understanding, to the service of sin. When we come to sin wisely and learnedly, to sin logically, by a *Quia*, and an *Ergo*, that, Because God does thus, we may do as we do, we shall come to sin through all the Arts, and all our knowledge."[22]

Yet Donne's description of the "Man of Sin" does not completely cover the gravity of Faustus' decision and desire as Marlowe has presented it in this initial monologue. For Doctor Faustus aspires to be more than man. As he lingers lovingly over his necromantic books and occult characters, he foresees personal power over all the world:

> All things that moue betweene the quiet Poles
> Shall be at my command . . .
>
> .   .   .   .
>
> A sound Magitian is a Demi-god,
> Here tire my braines to get a Deity.   (83-89)

The Augustinian formulation of sin is here filled out, and the bonds that will link Faustus with Lucifer are forged by Faustus himself.[23] He repudiates his humanity, rebelling against the ultimate reality; in his aspiration to be as God he chooses the not-God. This is the essential irony of sin, and the central irony of the play. In the Christian view of the world, it is inevitable that choice of the not-God will lead not only to disappointment but also to the deepest suffering.

Faustus has made his original choice by himself: the Scriptures are thrown over for the books of magic. Marlowe now begins the pattern of reaffirmation of that choice which characterizes the structure of the play; he introduces the Good and

[22] *Sermons*, I, 225.
[23] Donne's words are again to the point: ". . . for the greatest sin that ever was, and that upon which even the blood of Christ Jesus hath not wrought, the sin of Angels, was that, *Similis ero Altissimo*, to be like God." *Sermons*, IV, 330.

Evil Angels, whose dramatic presence embodies the conflict and the alternatives that continue to face Faustus. So far Faustus has been his own tempter, and his predilection for power has weighted the issue so that the dangerous aspects of the magical books have gone unnoticed. With the Good Angel's warning, however, there can be no avoiding what is at stake: the book is damned, the act is blasphemy, and Faustus' soul is in jeopardy. But the Evil Angel cloaks the same facts in the dream that is already Faustus' own:

> Be thou on earth as *Ioue* is in the skye,
> Lord and Commander of these elements . . .
>
> (103-104)

And Faustus once more, *left by himself* to make the decision, opts for the material power that he dreams the devil can give him. His own fantastic flights of imagination put the Evil Angel's suggestions to shame: he is still his own worst tempter.

The introduction of the Angels is Marlowe's innovation; they are absent from the Faust-Book, as are Faustus' dreams of power. The Angels, in emphasizing the conflict between good and evil, bring the issue to a heightened dramatic clarity, and reinforce the impression that not only does Faustus have the opportunity to choose between good and evil, but that the choice is his own and unconstrained. Their function is to present contrasting images to Faustus' mind and will, a function which has its parallel in the theological conception of the powers and activities of spirits: the evil angel tempts by deceit, the good angel protects by admonishment, but only man can make the decision.[24] For all the supernaturalism of the context in which Marlowe has chosen to present Faustus' choice to fall from God, the burden of human responsibility emerges as the central, dominant force.

[24] See Calvin, *Institutes*, I.xiv.6-19; Urbanus Regius, *An Homely or Sermon of Good and Euill Angels . . . Translated into English by Ri: Robinson, and then first Printd 1583. Secondly printed 1590. And lastly printed. 1593* (London, 1593), *passim*.

That burden does not yet weigh heavily on the Doctor's mind. Faustus decides without even a consideration of the Good Angel's alternative; there is as yet no real conflict in his mind, which is seduced by dreams of wealth and power. Both his decision and his dreams are reinforced by the visit with Valdes and Cornelius, who elaborate on the exotic and fantastic future that awaits him, a future, ironically enough, for which they think all nations will "Canonize" them (142). Here, too, Marlowe has introduced an episode entirely lacking in his source, with the result that the essential quality of Faustus' motivation is re-emphasized with great clarity and force.

The dreams of power and wealth which infatuate Faustus, exalt his language, and lead him to conjuring are not *in themselves* heinous things; his desires bear little or no resemblance to the destructive malice of Barabas or Ithamore, or even to the usurping and ruthless political ambitions of Guise or Mortimer. One sees no victims in the wake of his imagined triumphs to bloody the image of his yearnings. And this is because Marlowe is here dealing with only one victim—Faustus himself. Faustus' desires represent, *in the context of Marlowe's presentation*, not a usurpation of legitimate political powers nor of the dignity and life of other human beings, but a usurpation upon God. His sin is the sin of angels.

That Faustus himself is unwilling to see and to recognize the nature of his sin, and the penalty it must inevitably bear, is one of the most brilliantly handled ironies of the play. In the English Faust-Book, there are discussions of Lucifer, hell, and damnation, all following the contract with the devil, and representing Faustus' morbid and pitiful curiosity about the trap into which he has already fallen. Marlowe has altered not only the nature of these discussions, but their context as well, each time with powerful ironic effect. Mephostophilis' explanation of the fall of Lucifer and the punishment of hell comes *before* the contract is made in the play, at the first interview with Faustus; in itself it is even more potent a warning than the admonition of the Good Angel. But it is a warning which Faustus, in the blind arrogance of pride, refuses to see, much less heed:

> *Faust.* Was not that *Lucifer* an Angell once?
> *Meph.* Yes *Faustus*, and most deerely lou'd of God.
> *Faust.* How comes it then that he is Prince of Deuils?
> *Meph.* O: by aspiring pride and insolence,
> For which God threw him from the face of heauen.
> *Faust.* And what are you that liue with Lucifer?
> *Meph.* Vnhappy spirits that liue with Lucifer,
> Conspir'd against our God with Lucifer,
> And are for euer damn'd with Lucifer.
> *Faust.* Where are you damn'd?
> 　　　　　　　　　　　*Meph.* In hell.
> *Faust.* How comes it then that thou art out of hell?
> *Meph.* Why this is hell: nor am I out of it.
> Think'st thou that I that saw the face of God,
> And tasted the eternall Ioyes of heauen,
> Am not tormented with ten thousand hels,
> In being depriu'd of euerlasting blisse?
> O *Faustus* leaue these friuolous demandes,
> Which strikes a terror to my fainting soule.
> *Faust.* What is great *Mephostophilis* so passionate
> For being depriued of the Ioyes of heauen?
> Learne thou of *Faustus* manly fortitude,
> And scorne those Ioyes thou neuer shalt possesse.
>
> 　　　　　　　　　　　　　　　　(290-311)

The paradoxical nature of this dialogue has been given incisive expression by Robert Heilman's description of the participants: "the nearly omniscient stealer of souls urging Faustus to save his soul; the man with the soul, thinking he is omniscient, sneering at both advice and adviser."[25] The blind-

---

[25] "The Tragedy of Knowledge," p. 321.

ness on Faustus' part, his willful rejection of what is presented to him as real, has been prepared for: the devil's initial form was too ugly for him to look upon, hence the demand (which is not in the Faust-Book) that Mephostophilis appear in the traditional form of a friar.[26] Faustus, exulting in the pliant servility of this devil he has raised, fails to be taken down a notch by the news that the real cause of his appearance has been Faustus' willingness to blaspheme God. There is no preparation, on the other hand, for the flash of pain which strikes terror to the devil's soul and momentarily forces him out of the role of tempter. Never in English drama before Marlowe had a devil acted in such a way, nor is there the slightest hint of anything like this in Marlowe's source. Dramatically, it is a striking measure—not only of the moral myopia of Faustus, but also of his own responsibility for his fall. Thematically, it is the first, intense sounding of the note of *poena damni*, the pain of loss. For Mephostophilis has defined hell by its most spiritual and agonizing suffering: alienation from God. He does so in words offering a strong parallel to the writings of St. John Chrysostom, the first of the Fathers to lay special stress on the pain of loss:[27] "Yet though one suppose ten thousand hells, he will utter nothing like what it will be to fail of that blessed glory, to be hated of Christ, to hear 'I know you not.' "[28] The works of Chrysostom had

[26] Mephostophilis in the Faust-Book takes on the friar disguise at the conclusion of a series of changes in form, none of which are at Faustus' request (ii, 138). The devil as monk or friar appears in Theodore Beza's Biblical play *Abraham's Sacrifice*, translated into English and printed in London in 1577; according to Maximilian Rudwin, *The Devil in Legend and Literature* (Chicago, 1931), p. 50, this disguise appears frequently in the fourteenth and fifteenth centuries.

[27] This parallel was first noted by John Searle in a letter to *TLS*, 15 February 1936, p. 139. Chrysostom's importance in the history of the theology of hell is indicated by Gustave Bardy, "Les Pères de l'Eglise en face des problèmes posés par l'enfer," *L'Enfer*, pp. 168-169.

[28] *Homilies on the Gospel of Saint Matthew*, A Select Library of the Nicene and Post-Nicene Fathers of the Christian Church, ed. Philip Schaff, vol. x (New York, 1888), p. 164. The passage is from section 9 of Homily

been available to Marlowe in the Corpus Christi Library at Cambridge,[29] and it may be that they served as the basis not only for this particular phrasing of the pain of loss, but, even more significantly, for the surprising central situation which produces it. In the same book of homilies on Matthew's Gospel which contains the above passage there is a description of how devils cry out against their wishes, giving testimony to their torments; thus "evil demons confess hell, who would fain have hell disbelieved. . . ."[30]

Yet in the face of all this Doctor Faustus still manages to disbelieve. Although he boasts that he confounds hell in Elysium, he can never quite forget the region whence his ministering demon comes. The very first question Faustus chooses to ask once the diabolic pact has been concluded, the first exercise of his "new-found" power, is: "where is the place that men call Hell?" (508). The answer is as orthodox as the first,[31] including this time the notion not only of an inward, spiritual state, but an external location as well; and Faustus' reaction is again that of the blind fool who wills his own blindness:

> *Meph.* Vnder the heauens.
> *Faust.* I, so are all things else; but whereabouts?
> *Meph.* Within the bowels of these Elements,
> Where we are tortur'd, and remaine for euer.
> Hell hath no limits, nor is circumscrib'd,
> In one selfe place: but where we are is hell,
> And where hell is there must we euer be.
> And to be short, when all the world dissolues,

XXIII. It is cited by John Denison in his treatment of hell's suffering in *A Three-fold Resolvtion, verie necessarie to saluation. Describing Earths Vanitie. Hels Horror. Heauens Felicitie* (London, 1608), pp. 385-386 (s-sᵛ).

[29] MS. 575, p. 4.

[30] Homily XII, section 7, p. 85.

[31] As has been pointed out by West, *Invisible World*, p. 82 and p. 238, n. 44; John Erskine Hankins, *The Character of Hamlet and Other Essays* (Chapel Hill, 1941), p. 203; and Kocher, *Christopher Marlowe*, pp. 116-117.

And euery creature shall be purifi'd,
All places shall be hell that is not heauen.
   Faust. I thinke Hel's a fable.
   Meph. I, thinke so still, till experience change thy mind.
                          (509-520)

So intent is Faustus on the prospect of unprecedented material gain that no suggestion of spiritual loss can move him now; nevertheless, as Mephostophilis prophesies, experience will change his mind. The suffering of conscience that soon begins to afflict him marks the start of that experience; his final hour is its culmination: then, hell is seen not as a fable, but as the inevitable reality. Throughout the play there is little stress on the more popular conceptions of hell as a lurid place of grotesque physical tortures, and much stress on the spiritual loss and suffering: Marlowe's hell is the hell of theology, not the hell of folklore. It is at an infinite remove from the picture of hell in the Faust-Book, which never mentions the pain of loss, but does include fire, darkness, storms, venomous creatures, brimstone, pitch, and such sensational pains as these: "there shalt thou abide horrible torments, trembling, gnashing of teeth, howling, crying, burning, freezing, melting, swimming in a labyrinth of miseries, scalding, burning, smoking in thine eyes, stinking in thy nose, horsnes of thy speech, deaffeness of thine eares, trembling of thy handes, biting thine owne tongue with payne, thy hart crushed as in a presse, thy bones broken, the diuels tossing fire brands vpon thee, yea thy whole carkasse tossed vpon muckforkes from one diuel to another . . ." (xv, 156).

Even if Marlowe's hell is not intended to terrify sinners as this one is, in the long run it is an even more terrible thing; it is a hell that gradually shapes itself into a real possibility, grounded in the personal responsibility of free human choice and the inevitable consequences of that choice.

In order to emphasize still further the importance of Faustus' choice, and the willingness with which he makes it, Marlowe has made several other significant departures from the English Faust-Book. In the play it is Faustus himself who first suggests, without any trace of fear, the diabolic contract by which he forfeits his soul; in the source, it is the devil who argues that the service Faustus desires must be paid for with that prize—and the Doctor spends some time in deliberating how to avoid the loss of his soul (iii, 139-140). Marlowe's Faustus concludes the bargain with full resolution; when his model in the source does so, it is "faintly (for his soules sake)" (iv, 140). Faustus' determination in the play is unchecked, even by the revelations about Lucifer, hell and damnation; he overrides all threats and warnings in his lust for arcane power. The imaginative dimensions of that drive are repeatedly stressed, both before and after the conjuring; yet it is not without point that Faustus' ambitions to be "great Emperour of the world" (329) through the service of Mephostophilis should be followed immediately by a comic scene in which Wagner enlists the services of a clown. This burlesque parody of the serious action serves to undercut the grandeur of Faustus' dreams, as will the Doctor's own actions later on. The comic scenes, whether written by Marlowe or another, bear that analogous relationship to the serious line of action which was a characteristic of the English stage from medieval times; fully in the tradition of the comedy of evil, they comment by implication on the nature of the serious moral problem involved in the major plot.[32] This element in the play, of course, is straight from the stage tradition; there is no hint of it in the Faust-Book.

The signing of the contract in Marlowe's play is at once more dramatic and more suggestive than in the source. The

---

[32] This aspect of *Doctor Faustus* has been given its most thorough treatment by Charlotte R. Kesler, "The Importance of the Comic Tradition of English Drama in the Interpretation of Marlowe's *Doctor Faustus*," unpublished Ph.D. dissertation (University of Missouri, 1954).

playwright has introduced with full effect the struggle of conscience and a renewed conflict between the Good and Evil
Angels to heighten both the suspense of the scene and the
sense of responsible choice on the Doctor's part. Faustus'
soliloquy before the appearance of Mephostophilis is characterized by the deep irony of inversion already operative in the
play, an inversion which gives to Faustus' worship and service
of the devil the precise qualities of the religious worship of
God. Not the Bible, but the books of magic, are "heauenly"
to Faustus; he and his fellow-magicians look forward to "can-
onization" for their practice in the black art; before the conjuring Faustus prays and sacrifices to devils; after raising
Mephostophilis, Faustus boasts of the "vertue" in his "heauenly words" (255); Mephostophilis urges him to "pray de-
uoutely to the Prince of hell" (280); and now, in the first of
his many "temptations" to repent, Faustus continues on his
inverted way:

> What bootes it then to thinke on God or Heauen?
> Away with such vaine fancies, and despaire,
> Despaire in *God*, and trust in *Belzebub*,
> Now go not backward *Faustus*, be resolute.   (392-395)

What is backward for Faustus is forward for the rest of mankind in search of the divine life. And yet the theologian of
Wittenberg is not so blind in these moments of mental trial
that he does not realize the truth about himself: "The God
thou seru'st is thine owne appetite" (398). But his new religion is more forceful than the old; to Belzebub he vows to
build an altar and a church, there to offer up the blood of
newborn babes (400-401). Such determination cannot be
swayed even by the repeated urgings of the Good Angel,
whose counsel to think on heavenly things is obliterated by the
Evil Angel's simple suggestion to "thinke of honour and of
wealth" (410). Merely the idea of wealth is sufficient to sway

Faustus; the "temptation" to repent is suppressed by his vision of the signory of Emden. The inversions continue, and Faustus calls upon the devil to bring him "glad tydings" from Lucifer (415), setting in an upside-down context the phrase with which the angels of the New Testament announced their news of Christ's birth to mankind. All these inversions, it is important to emphasize, are original with the play; they deliberately enhance the essentially ironic character of Faustus' career and of his choice.

Marlowe has not been content with providing Faustus but one chance to repent immediately before the contract; he adds the dramatic congealing of the Doctor's blood in the midst of the writing. Quite appropriately, the devil brings some fire to set the blood flowing again; but even before he is back, Faustus has rejected the warning implicit in the phenomenon. With the supremely ironic and blasphemous *"Consummatum est"* (462), Faustus completes the contract of damnation, using the very words with which Christ had completed the work of the Redemption on Calvary. Then follows the warning of the bloody inscription, *Homo fuge.* Although this happening is in the Faust-Book, it does not there provide Faustus with the repeated confrontation with a moral choice that it does in the play. Nor is the spectacle with which Mephostophilis now distracts Faustus linked in the Faust-Book with the conflict set in motion by the warning. There is every indication in the play, here as elsewhere, that the devil, even after the contract, has not clinched his case—he must still draw Faustus away from every temptation to turn back to God. As the temptations grow in importance the devil's delights grow in seductive power. Earlier in the play the idea of wealth was enough to content Faustus with evil—now the concrete symbols of wealth are needed—crowns and rich apparel. Faustus is faithful to the god of his own appetite; he rests content for the moment. His choice has been made, not once, but many times; and each time it has been his own.

II. THE IRONY OF FAUSTUS' CAREER

The sealing of the diabolic contract, though it comes early in the overall structure of the play, is nonetheless a pivotal point in Faustus' career. There is a significant contrast before and after the contract in the nature of Faustus' desires, the nature of the devil's relationship to him, and the nature of his trials of conscience. In each case the contrast is illustrative of Augustine's remark about the soul that wills to be a god, to take pleasure in its own power—"the greater it wishes to become, the less it becomes in fact." It has already been mentioned that the first request that Faustus makes is for a description of hell, a description which he refuses to accept in the very face of the being who can best describe it. The second demand is equally illuminating: Faustus calls for a wife, since, as he says, he is "wanton and lasciuious" (533).[33] Unfortunately, the devil cannot provide a *wife*, though he can supply the fairest of courtesans, since marriage is, in the Christian scheme of things, an institution divinely established by God. The Faust-Book goes so far as to state the reason explicitly (ix, 146); Marlowe presents the devil's discomfiture and the spectacle of the woman devil by which Mephostophilis dissuades Faustus from marriage. Faustus' bargain to have the devil grant him whatsoever he asks is thus countermanded from the start.

This theme of the devil's impotence to provide anything sanctioned by God is brought to a climax in the following scene with Mephostophilis, which involves the discussion of astronomy. The Faust-Book contains an astronomical discussion,

[33] Marlowe has constructed for Faustus' career a symmetrical framework of sexual desire, beginning in this demand for a wife and ending in the request for Helen. In the Faust-Book, Faustus' career has an equally inglorious yet less suggestive beginning: the first fruits of his new power are wines, foods, and sumptuous apparel stolen from the best places of Europe (viii, 145). In the morality plays, the request for a mistress or wench was a common demand following the fall of the hero into vicious ways; it occurs, e.g., in *Wisdom, Youth, Magnyfycence,* and *Lusty Juventus.*

but both its terminology and its structure are very different from Marlowe's. The play's version is quite originally introduced by a conflict of conscience—a conflict which arises appropriately enough from Faustus' meditation on the heavens:[34]

> When I behold the heauens then I repent
> And curse thee wicked *Mephostophilis,*
> Because thou hast depriu'd me of those Ioyes.
>
> (570-572)

Faustus' diabolic companion replies with much truth but little comfort: " 'Twas thine owne seeking *Faustus,* thanke thy selfe" (573). The conflict is heightened once again by the entrance of the Good and Evil Angels, and a full-scale temptation to repent is under way. Faustus' monologue reveals that such struggles have been frequent, and that each time his thoughts have moved toward God, the devils have proffered the means of suicide—"Swords, poyson, halters, and inuenomb'd steele" (591)—symbols of despair and of the spiritual death despair involves, and familiar props in the oldest of morality plays. The speech also reveals the principle of Faustus' life which is itself a major pattern of the play, the pleasure principle by which his spiritual conflicts are temporarily dissolved:

> And long e're this, I should haue done the deed,
> Had not sweete pleasure conquer'd deepe despaire.
>
> (593-594)

Here the mere remembrance of pleasure is sufficient to strengthen Faustus' resolution not to repent.

From this introductory framework of spiritual conflict, resolved as usual by Faustus himself, Marlowe moves to the astronomical discourse. Abandoning the encyclopedic but pat-

---

[34] The order of the universe, according to Peter Baro, was one of the three means by which man is recalled to God after the Fall, the other two being natural instinct and the Scriptures (*In Jonam Prophetam,* H4ᵛ).

ternless consideration of astronomy in the Faust-Book, Marlowe constructs his own discussion, proceeding logically step by step to questions of higher importance. As one critic has noted, "By a process of reasoning which resembles, and is probably intended to recall, the scholastic argument *a contingentia*, Faustus ascends from a consideration of the planets to that of the moving Intelligences; and thence to the supreme Intelligence which is the origin and mover of all."[35] But when Faustus reaches the ultimate and most significant question, "who made the world?" Mephostophilis balks and refuses to answer.[36] Once again the contract has failed; the devil who was to tell Faustus whatsoever he demanded is powerless to tell him anything that works against the kingdom of the damned; the final ends of knowledge are unapproachable. This realization stirs Faustus once more to thoughts of repentance; again the Angels make their appearance to give substance to his thoughts, and Faustus himself, now clearly showing that the mental struggle is causing him pain, comes closer to repentance than anywhere else in the play: "O Christ my Sauiour, my Sauiour," he cries, "Helpe to saue distressed *Faustus* soule" (652-653).

For the first time Faustus attempts to resolve his conflict in the direction of God, but his relationship with the devil has undergone a change to counter the new tendency in his character: his cry brings Mephostophilis and the potentates of hell, Lucifer and Belzebub, who threaten him into renewed submission. Faustus begs their pardon and makes a vow of obedience; he who would force spirits to obey his every behest now makes himself their obedient slave. Lucifer promises gratification, and Faustus' immediate pleasure is served by a spectacle of the Seven Deadly Sins. The irony of the episode is Marlowe's own, for the Faust-Book has neither the temptation

[35] James Smith, "Marlowe's 'Dr. Faustus,'" *Scrutiny*, VIII (1939), 42.
[36] The question in the Faust-Book is less to Marlowe's dramatic point: "how and after what sorte God made the world" (xix, 163).

to repentance nor the calling on Christ, nor does it include the renewed promise. It does have the appearance of the devils, and a spectacle of deformed evil spirits, whose procession does not at all please Faustus. In changing the spectacle to the Seven Deadly Sins, Marlowe has not only opened the way for some moral satire, but he has purposely and ironically presented the pageant as the visible "gratification" of Faustus. Faustus himself responds with the greatest delight, blasphemously comparing his joy in the procession with Adam's joy at the sight of Paradise on the day of his creation. Delight in the Seven Deadly Sins is a far cry from the answer to who made the world, and it is not without point that, after this episode, Faustus makes no more speculative inquiries of any kind.[37]

By means of this astronomical episode, Marlowe has presented a Faustus for whom the conflict between good and evil has become a source of suffering. No longer does the aspiring Doctor completely ignore the promise of heaven. He who was once eager with anticipation now expresses discontent with the knowledge the devil can bring him. But the devil's bait of pleasure can still numb the pain of discontent—where it cannot, the devil must now use his hook. The relationship is grounded in a theological commonplace of Marlowe's day. Lancelot Andrewes, whose lectures as catechist at Pembroke College, Cambridge, during the 1580's, drew students from many colleges and townspeople alike,[38] described the workings of Satan in terms of the bait of pleasure and the hook of violence, interpreting Augustine's words, *aut amor erit mali inflammans, aut timor mali humilians,* as "either love to the bait will entice us to evil, or fear of the hook will draw us, or at least keep us from doing of good."[39] Henry Bullinger's comment is also directly to the point: "Two things there are

[37] Heilman, "The Tragedy of Knowledge," p. 326.
[38] H. C. Porter, *Reformation and Reaction in Tudor Cambridge* (Cambridge, 1958), pp. 391-392.
[39] *A Pattern of Catechistical Doctrine* (Oxford, 1846), pp. 285-286.

that work all sins in mortal men, desire and fear. . . . Thou art promised, if thou wilt sin, to have such a reward given thee as thou dost delight in; and for desire of the gift thou crackest thy conscience, and dost commit sin. And again on the other side, though peradventure thou wilt not be seduced with gifts, yet being terrified with threatenings thou dost, for dread of that which thou fearest, commit the iniquity that otherwise thou wouldest not."[40]

But no matter what the power of the devil's hook, all theologians were agreed that man sinned of his own free will.[41] Faustus' career is henceforth characterized by the pattern of pleasure and fear: he who once set himself up as an example of manly fortitude to the spiritually tortured devil now lives in servile fear of the devil's threats of physical pain; such threats, together with the lure of new pleasures, stifle the spiritual doubts and pains that periodically afflict him. This pattern, though hinted at in the Faust-Book, is by no means developed and stressed there as it is in the play. The structure of theological ideas rather than of the diffuse folk tale operates as a formal principle in Marlowe's presentation.

The ironies which cloak the repeated exercise of Faustus' moral choice and his relationships with the devil do not exhaust the ironic pattern of Faustus' life. There remains the fundamental irony of the contrast between the actual accomplishments of his magical career and the original dreams of wealth, honor, and omnipotence which provoked that career. We are here brought face to face with the problem of the comic action in which Faustus has a part, and its relation to

[40] Henry Bullinger, *The Decades*, III, x; Harding ed. (Cambridge, 1849-1852), II, 404-405. Bullinger also comments on the worship of the devil: "The very devils . . . shall be strange gods, if we for fear shall stand in awe of them more than of God, to whom indeed our fear is due." *ibid.*, II, ii; Harding ed., I, 221.

[41] Andrewes, p. 284; Baro, *De fide, ejusque ortu, & natura, plana ac dilucida explicatio* (London, 1580), p. 12 (B6ᵛ); Bullinger, III, x; Harding ed., II, 362-368; Calvin, *Institutes*, IV.i.1; Musculus, p. 45 (C7); Regius, A7ᵛ.

the tragic action which begins in his dreams and ends in his downfall. Marlowe's authorship of the comic sections is dubious at best; yet, as W. W. Greg has pointed out, there is no reason seriously to doubt that he planned the whole, or that whoever collaborated with him carried out the plan; nor are there serious indications that later revisions substantially distorted its structure.[42] Most of the so-called "vulgar interpolations," the scenes of trickery, slapstick, and horseplay, are in the English Faust-Book; and if we look at them for what they are and not for what we think they should be, I think we will understand better the basis for Marlowe's establishing his protagonist at the start in such aspiring and grandiose terms. Like the outcome of Faustus' first requests to Mephostophilis (in scenes where Marlowe's authorship is unquestioned), the comic scenes carry out the central irony of the play: they present in visual terms the real nature of Faustus' bargain: they provide in terms of action an effective contrast to Faustus' original aspirations.

In choosing the not-God in his desire to be as God, Faustus has provided not only for his own destruction, but also for his own degradation. Instead of reaching the stature of a demigod or even commander of the world, Faustus becomes an imperial entertainer. The restless scholar hemmed in by the limits of mortality gains his satisfaction by playing practical jokes on the Papal court; the man who looked forward to controlling the lives and power of all earthly rulers now becomes the magician of the Emperor, building castles in the air, and presenting spirits that resemble great men of the past. As Faustus himself declares, "These are but shadowes, not substantiall" (1304). He who would have spirits fly to India for gold, ransack the ocean for orient pearl, drag huge argosies from Venice and bring the golden fleece from America, bids the spirits bring grapes to the Duchess of Vanholt. The warrior who would levy soldiers to defeat the Prince of

[42] "The Damnation of Faustus," pp. 99-100.

Parma and reign "sole King of all the Prouinces" (121) uses his power to grow horns on the heads of scoffing knights and to strike dumb the ignorant tradesmen and peasants whom he has swindled once before. It is true that this career of buffoonery and folly is detailed in Marlowe's source, but in that source there had been nothing about Faustus' early motivations and aspirations with which to contrast his actual career. Marlowe has himself provided the contrast by building the fantastic dream in Faustus' mind, the dream which is then belied by every dramatic action that ensues after the contract has been made with the lord of hell.

The comic scenes with Robin and Dick, which are not in the Faust-Book, also serve as ironic commentary on Faustus' bargain and use of power. With the help of a stolen book of magic, these low characters play tricks essentially no different from those of Faustus—they crave plain whores rather than distinguished courtesans, Nan Spit rather than Helen of Troy, and they steal from an inn the same things that Faustus steals from the Pope's banquet table. And, like Faustus, they are bullied by the devil. The parody makes clear in the simplest of terms what the more sophisticated touches of irony in the main action are also intended to show: a contract with the powers of evil, no matter what the motivation, leads inevitably to the loss of human dignity and order. And it is a contract that can be made by anyone.

Faustus himself is aware of the taste of ashes in the midst of the fruits his magic has produced. After selling a horse-courser an illusory horse, he is prompted to some serious meditation by the parting words of the buyer: "Now am I a/made man for euer" (1544-1545).

> What art thou *Faustus* but a man condemn'd to die?
> Thy fatall time drawes to a finall end;
> Despaire doth driue distrust into my thoughts.
> Confound these passions with a quiet sleepe:

> Tush Christ did call the Theefe vpon the Crosse,
> Then rest thee *Faustus* quiet in conceit.   (1546-1551)

Compared to his earlier mental struggles, this is indeed but a feeble stirring of conscience and spiritual concern; nevertheless its importance is enhanced by the stark contrast of a serious thought in the context of comic deceit. Even more significant is the manner in which Faustus resolves the conflict: he moves from despair to the opposite but equally dangerous alternative, presumption. Once more Marlowe has introduced, briefly but incisively, a familiar theological concept, a concept which was traditionally treated, together with despair, as one of the most serious obstacles to repentance and salvation. The official Elizabethan homily, "How daungerous a thing it is to fall from God," describes two kinds of faithless men: those who despair of forgiveness, thinking that God cannot or will not forgive their sin; and those who gamble on his mercy, hoping for last-minute forgiveness. "And both these two sortes of men be in a damnable state. . . ."[43] Lancelot Andrewes in his catechetical writings treats presumption and despair as two extremes by which men sin against hope.[44] Scholastic treatises classified presumption and despair as manifestations of the sin against the Holy Ghost, as does John Donne, since they naturally shut out the means by which the Holy Ghost can work upon men.[45] And John Woolton's *The Christian Manual* (1576) includes an admonition about presumption which bears repeating: "That saying of the Hebrew is memorable, and never to be forgotten: 'Say not, Tush, the mercy of the Lord is great, he shall forgive me my sins, be they never so many: for like as he is merciful, so goeth wrath from him also, and his indignation cometh down upon sinners.' "[46] It should be clear, then, that in these

[43] *Certaine Sermons*, E5ᵛ.

[44] *A Pattern of Catechistical Doctrine*, p. 96.

[45] *Sermons*, V, 93-94.

[46] *The Christian Manual: or, Of the Life and Manners of True Christians*, ed. The Parker Society (London, 1851), p. 145. See also pp. 109-110 on the dangers of postponing repentance.

few lines set in the midst of the more innocuous tricks of Doctor Faustus, Marlowe has deftly provided yet another index of the quality of Faustus' career and of his incorrigible habit of resolving his spiritual struggles by choosing the damnable alternative.[47]

Persistent as Faustus may be in choosing the way of destruction, he is still a man and no demon; hence, his choice, no matter how often repeated, does not become irrevocable until his death. One of the main dramatic tensions throughout the play is provided by the possibility of Faustus' repentance. If that possibility were not real, neither the admonitions and urgings of the Good Angel nor the manifest concern of the devils to lure and frighten Faustus away from godly thoughts would have any dramatic meaning or validity.[48] We have already seen how the possibility of repentance has not become an actuality for Faustus because of his despair, his presumption, his tendency to stifle spiritual conflict in sensual pleasure, and his fear of the physical violence threatened by the devils. All these factors now merge into the climactic crisis of the last act, where the Old Man urges Faustus to call for mercy and avoid despair.

The Old Man's admonition is found in the Faust-Book, but not set in a situation of conflict as it is in Marlowe's play. Faustus is at first inclined to despair, and to dispatch his own life with the dagger that Mephostophilis gives him (for which action there is no hint in the Faust-Book), but the Old Man's reminder of mercy stays him. The Doctor asks his friend to leave him alone to ponder for a while, and then cries out in mental pain:

[47] W. W. Greg, in his parallel-text edition of the play, rejects the view that the verse passage in question is by Marlowe on the grounds that "the sentimental piety and the vulgar Tush . . . are alien to Marlowe's style" (p. 370). Clearly, however, the thought of Faustus is not one of sentimental piety but one of damnable presumption; and the "vulgar Tush" is a forceful indication of Faustus' supreme arrogance at this point.

[48] See also Kocher's arguments, *Christopher Marlowe*, pp. 107-112.

I do repent, and yet I doe despaire,
Hell striues with grace for conquest in my breast . . .

(1844-1845)

But Faustus does not bring himself to the trust in God's mercy
which constitutes the fullness of repentance in the teaching of
Protestant theology.[49] His repentance is stillborn, and cannot
move beyond the conviction of sin. Nevertheless, he can and
does move himself to a thoroughly ironic "repentance" of his
disobedience to Lucifer. When Mephostophilis accuses him
of treason and threatens to tear his flesh, Faustus immediately
and without any further mental conflict surrenders himself
completely to the will of his infernal lord:

> I do repent I ere offended him,
> Sweet *Mephasto*: intreat thy Lord
> To pardon my vniust presumption,
> And with my bloud againe I will confirme
> The former vow I made to *Lucifer*. (1850-1854)

In Marlowe's play the renewed contract is suggested by Faustus himself; the Faust-Book has Mephostophilis demand it
instead. And not only are such phrases as "Sweet *Mephasto*"
and "vniust presumption" Marlowe's own ironic inversions of
the actual state of affairs, but the threefold structure of Faustus' plea for pardon is itself a parody of the threefold process
of Christian repentance: Faustus acknowledges his offence, appeals for mercy and pardon, and resolves by the renewal of his
vow not to offend his lord again.[50] Mephostophilis actually
becomes the diabolic substitute for a Father-Confessor. The
parallel could not have gone unnoticed, especially since Mephostophilis' costume is that of an old Franciscan Friar.

[49] So Kocher has noted, *Christopher Marlowe*, p. 112. The most ex-
haustive analysis of the relation of *Doctor Faustus* to Protestant doctrines
of justification is Raymond H. Reno's "The Theological Background of
Christopher Marlowe's *The Tragical History of Doctor Faustus*," unpublished Ph.D. dissertation (George Washington University, 1958).
[50] Reno, pp. 246-247.

Marlowe continues the pattern of inversion. Faustus is assigned no penance to fortify his resolution; instead he himself suggests a *pleasure*—he requests Helen of Troy as his paramour,

> To glut the longing of my hearts desire,
>
> .   .   .   .
>
> Whose sweet embraces may extinguish cleare,
> Those thoughts that do disswade me from my vow . . .
>
> (1864-1868)

The request is in the Faust-Book, but it is not there linked with Faustus' spiritual conflict; it does not come as the self-suggested reward and confirmation for diabolic repentance.[51] Furthermore, one must realize that neither Faustus nor the devil has power to resurrect actual people, but only evil spirits in the semblance of them. This has been made clear in the scenes at Carolus' court, and even recalled in the first raising of "Helen" for the scholars, which preceded the Old Man's exhortation; it is further grounded in the actual teachings of Elizabethan demonology.[52] That Doctor Faustus, at the climax of his career, should call this Helen "heauenly" (1866) is but one of the deeply ironic consequences of confounding hell in Elysium.

[51] In this scene there is a curious echoing of themes found in William Rankins' allegorical invective against the stage, *A Mirrovr of Monsters* (London, 1587), which is built around a framework of an unholy wedding between Faustus (sometimes spelled Fastus), a prosperous figure glossed as pride, and the beautiful Luxuria, who represents lechery (B4). Belzebub sends a group of maskers from hell to entertain at the wedding, and Faustus welcomes the favor from his "good Lorde," who has, he says, "heerein amplified my former reuerence, and sharpened in my minde a deeper desire to proceede in hys obedience, then heeretofore hath euer beene inserted in my hart" (G3ᵛ). The parallel is by no means precise, but it may well be that the resemblance between Marlowe's scene and this unholy union "blessed" by Belzebub and connected with an assertion of Faustus' renewed obedience to the lord of hell is more than mere coincidence.

[52] Thomas Alfred Spalding, *Elizabethan Demonology* (London, 1880), pp. 42-44; Greg, "The Damnation of Faustus," p. 107; West, pp. 94-102.

There follows what is probably the most famous poetic passage in the play, the apostrophe to Helen. Clearly this is not just poetry. In the context of the whole movement of the play, in the repeated pattern of the unalterable reality giving the lie to Faustus' dream, this speech becomes one of the most horribly ironic passages in dramatic literature. Like the previous demonic apparitions, this Helen speaks not a word. Add to this the fact that Helen of Troy was often used by Elizabethan writers as a symbol of destructive beauty and sinful pleasure,[53] and couple with it Faustus' recurrent habit of taking delight in what is most damnable. This Helen is the crowning illusory bliss of his ironic career:

> Was this the face that Launcht a thousand ships,
> And burnt the toplesse Towers of *Ilium*?
> Sweet *Hellen* make me immortall with a kisse:
> Her lips sucke forth my soule, see where it flies.
> Come *Hellen*, come, giue me my soule againe,
> Here will I dwell, for heauen is in these lippes,
> And all is drosse that is not *Helena*.

> . . . .

> O thou art fairer then the euenings aire,
> Clad in the beauty of a thousand starres:

[53] In John Pikering's play *Horestes* (1567) the love of Clytemnestra and Egistus is likened to the love of Paris and Helen (TFT [1910], C2-C3); the tale of Helen of Troy is the first to appear in Richard Robinson's *The rewarde of Wickednesse Discoursing the sundrye monstrous abuses of wicked and vngodlye worldelinges* (1574), where Helen appears in hell; *A Gorgeous Gallery of Gallant Inventions* (1578) includes a similar "tragedy" narrated by Helen in hell under the title, "The reward of Whoredome by the fall of Helen" (ed. Hyder E. Rollins [Cambridge, Mass., 1926], p. 81); in George Peele's play *The Araygnement of Paris* (1584) she is presented as a "lustie minion trull,/ That can giue sporte to thee thy bellyfull" (MSR [Oxford, 1910], ll. 527-528). Roy W. Battenhouse provides further citations in *Marlowe's "Tamburlaine"* (Nashville, 1941), pp. 166-167. The best indication of Helen's symbolic significance in the Faust legend comes from the English Faust-Book itself, which comments on the scholars' admiration for "heauenly" Helen: "Wherefore a man may see that the Diuel blindeth and enflameth the heart with lust oftentimes, that men fall in love with Harlots, nay euen with Furies . . ." (xiv, 212).

> Brighter art thou then flaming *Iupiter*,
> When he appear'd to haplesse *Semele*:
> More louely then the Monarch of the sky,
> In wanton *Arethusa's* azure armes,
> And none but thou shalt be my Paramour.
>
> (1874-1893)

What Faustus sees in Helen is not what the audience is able to see. The context of the action, the pervading fire imagery, and the diction of heavenly bliss and immortality combine to betray the perverse destructive reality beneath the form which provokes Faustus' impossible passion. The ironies implicit in each precise image and statement have been brought out by several critics:[54] Helen, whose beauty caused Troy to burn, will do the same for Faustus; the immortality offered by the kisses of a demon lover is an eternity in hell; the soul that is sucked forth cannot be given back again; hell and not heaven is in these lips; the flames of Jupiter that destroyed admiring Semele are the flames of this Helen's abode which will destroy a hapless Faustus; wanton Faustus, like Arethusa, will hold the burning sun in his arms, but not without fiery pain. The fires of hell, which, extraordinarily enough, have gone unmentioned in a play dealing so directly with hell and its punishments, now leap forth in the images of flame evoked by Helen. The imagery here is no poetic accident; it is dramatic imagery and dramatic allusion. In the total context of the scene and of the play it cuts with the razor-edge of irony; like the simple but ironic evocations of fire that characterized the speeches of Dido at the height of her fortune, these more complex images herald the final fate of the protagonist at the very moment when he seems to have reached the peak of his aspiration. The scene in which Faustus embraces the demonic

[54] Notably Kirschbaum, Heilman, and Frye in the articles cited in n. 2 above; and the author of "Marlowe and the Absolute," *TLS*, 24 February 1956, p. 116.

Helen is, in purely visual terms, the culminating emblem of Faustus' disordered union with hell.

The consummation of that union follows swiftly; in Faustus' next scene he is already looking ahead with fear and trembling to his last hours on earth. The scholars to whom he now bids farewell wonder at his melancholy, and are shocked to learn the true price of their master's fortune. In response to their exhortation to remember the infinite mercy of God, Faustus demonstrates once more the pride which refuses to recognize the possibility of that mercy:

> But *Faustus* offence can nere be pardoned,
> The serpent that tempted *Eue* may be saued,
> But not *Faustus*.   (1937-1939)

The Doctor's hyperbole is the measure of his despair; he will not recognize that he, as a man, can repent; but he will imagine an impossibility—that the serpent whose choice of damnation had always been permanent may be saved. As the term of the contract draws to an end, Faustus begins to suffer in earnest, and there is now no time to stifle his spiritual awareness in pleasure. The man who so callously dismissed the testimony of Mephostophilis about the sufferings of hell, the man who persistently yielded to the devil when threatened with physical injury, is now reduced to cowering and moaning before the prospect of the eternal spiritual pain of alienation from God:

> ... *Faustus* hath lost both *Germany* & the world,
> yea heauen it selfe: heauen the seate of God, the Throne of
> the Blessed, the Kingdome of Ioy, and must remaine in hell
> for euer. Hell, O hell for euer. Sweet friends, what shall be-
> come of *Faustus* being in hell for euer?   (1944-1948)

The Faustus for whom a hell defined by spiritual loss was once a fable now faces its inescapable reality. His fear and anxiety find expression in an illusion: he imagines he sees the devil coming to fetch him: "Looke sirs, comes he not, comes he not?" (1926). The scholars, of course, see nothing, and try to comfort Faustus, but the Doctor's despair precludes temporal comfort as well as eternal salvation.

Faustus' illusions here have no precedent in the English Faust-Book; they embody a dramatic convention in the portrayal of damned figures which can be traced back at least as far as the Chester mystery-cycle; but at the same time they represent a device which Marlowe has successfully employed in his other dramas to express the mental anguish and deepest psychological forces at work in characters under severe stress. Noteworthy, too, is another characteristic deviation from Marlowe's source: the protagonist of the Faust-Book sinks to his deepest misery when he foresees the physical tortures of hell (lx, 224-225), but the Faustus of the play is terrified rather at the thought of *poena damni*, the eternal pain of loss. The greatest sin of Marlowe's Faustus is not embodied in malicious actions, but in the perversity of his will and intellect. It is ironically fitting that the suffering which at last overcomes Faustus should operate on the same level, and afflict not so much his body as his spiritual faculties. "*Diuinitie* adeiw"—Faustus' original choice has become hardened into permanency, and that permanency is hell.

III. THE FINAL AGONY

The emotions and sufferings of Faustus in his final monologue have been prepared for by the dramatic structure of the play; they are most effective when viewed in relation to all that has gone before: Faustus' original motivations, his deliberate choice of the not-God, the repeated confirmation of that choice, the ironic limitations of his accomplishments, his continual flying in the face of fact and of reality. Faustus in the depths of his last agony brings to mind again and again the Faustus of the first act, Faustus at the height of imaginative ambition. Faustus is alone in his study when the play begins; he is alone now. After twenty-four years of voluptuous life, like the twenty-four hours of the day, he is back where he started—a creature limited by time and mortality, unable to escape the consequences and responsibilities of humanity.

The monologue begins as an intense and futile battle against time—another aspect of Faustus' rebellion against reality. The awareness of inevitability is brought home by the clock striking the hour and the half-hour, and Marlowe's art is ingenious enough to increase the effect by making the last "half-hour" shorter than the first. Faustus pleads desperately to the spheres of heaven to stand still "That time may cease, and midnight neuer come";[55] he begs the sun to rise again, but to no avail. And his most desperate and ironic cry is implicitly an evocation of the pleasure principle: "*O lente lente curite noctis equi*" (1459). This is a quotation from Ovid's *Amores*,[56] where the poet-lover makes his plea to the dawn-goddess Aurora to extend his night of pleasure. There is no doubt that the pleasure is wanton, for the poet suggests that Aurora herself would beg the horses of the night to run slowly if she were in the embraces of her young lover Cephalus rather than with her husband Tithonus.[57] The amorous connotation of the Ovidian line gives it an ironic weight in Faustus' speech, a weight which undermines the sincerity of the immediately preceding line "That Faustus may repent, and saue his soule" (1458). Aside from this, the terms in which Faustus pleads for time are much the same as those of Edward's begging to keep his crown a little longer.[58] They both ask the impossible of the universe, but in Faustus' case this is more deeply ironical because his whole career in magic has been precisely such a request for the impossible.

---

[55] A-text, l. 1454. Quotations from the final monologue are from the A-text of 1604, since, as Greg argues in his parallel text edition (pp. 85-86), it is evidently more intact in this version.

[56] I.13, line 40.

[57] See Donald C. Baker, "Ovid and Faustus: The *Noctis Equi*," *The Classical Journal*, LV (1959), 126-128.

[58] See above, p. 176.

Realizing he cannot conquer time by commands or pleas, Faustus makes a last, desperate movement toward God, and sees the vision of Christ's redeeming blood:

> O Ile leape vp to my God: who pulles me downe?
> See see where Christs blood streames in the firmament,
> One drop would saue my soule, halfe a drop, ah my Christ,
> Ah rend not my heart for naming of my Christ,
> Yet wil I call on him, oh spare me *Lucifer*!
> Where is it now? tis gone ...   (1462-1467)

It is ironic that he who refused to read the warning of his own congealing blood when he made the contract, that he who used the final words of Christ's sacrificial redemption, *Consummatum est*, to conclude the writ of his own damnation, should see the message of redemption only when it is too late —when the devil has the power to pull him down. For the last time Faustus repeats the pattern of incomplete repentance: he calls on Christ, the devil rends his heart (though for the first time in the play he is not physically present—the threat and pain are more terrifying because they are internal), and his final prayer is for the devil's mercy rather than God's: "oh spare me *Lucifer*!" The struggle raging in Faustus is here given its most intense expression, with the help of the verse structure: his attention is torn violently back and forth between God and the devil, and the two movements are present within one line in "O Ile leap vp to my God: who pulles me downe?" and again in "Yet wil I call on him, oh spare me *Lucifer*!"

As soon as Faustus redirects his attention to the devil, the vision of the redeeming blood vanishes, and is replaced by the vision of the wrath of God;[59] where mercy is rejected, justice takes over. The reversal is now complete. The Faustus who wished to become a Jove on earth, "Lord and Commander of

---

[59] See Calvin's conception of the pain of damnation, which stresses not only alienation from God, but also the experience of continual and inescapable "hostility from the Divine majesty," *Institutes*, III.xxv.12; *ed.cit.*, II, 264.

these elements," has now no power over them, though he desperately invokes them one after another, each time in the form of a *command* that has as its object the escape of Faustus into the elements themselves:

> Mountaines and hilles, come come, and fall on me,
> And hide me from the heauy wrath of God.
> No no, then wil I headlong runne into the earth:
> Earth gape, O no, it wil not harbour me:
> You starres that raignd at my natiuitie,
> whose influence hath alotted death and hel,
> Now draw vp Faustus like a foggy mist,
> Into the intrailes of yon labring cloude,
> That when you vomite foorth into the ayre,
> My limbes may issue from your smoaky mouthes,
> So that my soule may but ascend to heauen . . .[60]

(1470-1480)

And again, as the clock strikes twelve:

> O it strikes, it strikes, now body turne to ayre,
> Or *Lucifer* wil beare thee quicke to hel:
> Oh soule, be changde into little water drops,
> And fal into the *Ocean*, nere be found . . .   (1500-1504)

The invocation of the mountains and hills is a direct echo of familiar Scriptural texts, most often used to describe the last judgment and the plight of fear-ridden but unrepentant sinners.[61] George Gascoigne's *The Droome of Doomes day* (1576) quotes them in treating the unprofitable and incom-

---

[60] The address to the stars is Faustus' fantastic plea to be changed into the element of fire—by a process roughly corresponding to the Renaissance explanation of the cause of lightning. See Kocher, *Christopher Marlowe*, p. 236 (though Kocher does not link it with this passage in *Faustus*): ". . . thunder is an exhalation, hot and dry, mixt with moisture caryed up to the middle Region, there thicked and wrapped into a cloud, of this hotte matter coupled w^t moystnes, closed in the cloud, groweth a strife, the heate beatinge, and breaking out the sides of ye cloude wyth a thundrynge noyse: the fyre then dispersed, is the lightninge."

[61] Hosea x.8; Rev. vi.16; Luke xxiii.30.

plete repentance of those who will be damned: "Then shal
they begin to say vnto the hilles and mounteynes: fall vpon
vs and cover vs. They shall repent to their payne and punishment, but they shall not be conuerted vnto remission and
forgiuenesse. For it is but meete and right that they which
would not when they might, should be barred to haue power
when they would. For the Lorde hath giuen a tyme and place
for repentaunce, and they haue abused the same."[62]

Faustus, who in the first scene aspired to the status of a
deity, repudiating his humanity in one way, now repudiates it
in another, longing for extinction. His superhuman desires
become subhuman desires. He would rather be "some brutish
beast" (1493) without an immortal soul; he who took such
delight in sensuality now begs to be dissolved into unfeeling
elements. It is not the prospect of death that terrifies him—it
is the knowledge that he cannot escape the consequences of
his original choice, the choice he repeated again and again
throughout his career, the choice of the not-God. Now his
choice becomes permanent; and Faustus sees clearly that it has
been his own work:

> Curst be the parents that ingendred me:
> No Faustus, curse thy selfe . . .   (1496-1497)

Once more Faustus sees the not-God for what it really is, but
is impotent to change its shape, either through his commands
or through his imagination:

[62] Sig. D7. The passage also echoes an important thought of Augustine
in the *De libero arbitrio* which sheds some light on Faustus' helplessness to
call on God's grace at this stage in his career: ". . . a man who knows
what he ought to do and does not do it, loses the knowledge of what is right,
and the man who has refused to act rightly when he could, loses the power
when he wishes to have it" (III.18.52; Pontifex trans., p. 193). Theologians
were agreed that fear of punishment was not itself a sufficient motivation
for repentance, though it could be the beginning of repentance if used
correctly. In its extreme forms it could actually serve as an obstacle to
effective repentance. See Bullinger, *Decades*, IV, ii (Harding ed., III, 60-61);
Musculus, p. 519 (Kk4); Baro, *De fide*, pp. 124-126 (16ᵛ-17ᵛ), and *In
Jonam Prophetam*, p. 67 (I2), p. 261 (Ll3); Woolton, p. 110.

Adders, and Serpents, let me breathe a while:
Vgly hell gape not, come not *Lucifer*,
Ile burne my bookes, ah *Mephastophilis*.

(1506-1508)

Faustus is caught at last in the web of his own weaving; he is doomed to the hell of his own perverse will.

The problems of suffering and evil which dramatic tragedy of its very nature must suggest are directly met in *The Tragical History of Doctor Faustus*. The clarity and incisiveness with which Marlowe attacks these problems radically distinguish his play from the tragedies of his predecessors and immediate contemporaries. There is no discernible trace of the Senecan or neo-Senecan handling of suffering and evil, nor is the play directly in the tradition of *De Casibus* tragedy. Faustus falls indeed, but the nature and significance of his fall are not developed within the pattern of a rise to material prosperity ending in material or physical adversity; the suffering involved in Faustus' fall is not defined primarily by the contrast with preceding glories of wealth or state. Both fall and suffering are of an entirely different order and plane—the order and plane of the spiritual or supernatural. Faustus' fall at the start of the play is a restatement in imaginative and individualized terms of the archetypal Fall—the fall of man and of the angels—the fall which according to Judaeo-Christian tradition first brought evil into the world. Faustus' suffering grows directly out of the nature of his fall; it is defined by eternal separation from God, and developed not by contrast with the prosperity that has been his, but with the spiritual glory that might have been his. His career has been one long and elaborate example of the expense of greatness in a waste of shame. Because of its echo of the Fall, the tragedy of Faustus is the tragedy of man, of man not in his relationship to other men, but in relationship to God, spelled out in bold, direct, and uncompromising terms which are grounded firmly in the theology of the Christian Church. Christopher Marlowe had the genius to give a viable dramatic embodiment to those terms, a shape of action and character in action which, despite the confusions and mutilations of a problematical textual history, still maintains its power, cohesiveness, and deep irony. Marlowe's vision of evil in this play is the vision of Christian theology: Faustus' tragedy is a spiritual one; the irony which characterizes it is the irony of moral evil, the irony of sin. Doctor Faustus, by abuse of his freedom and revolt against the natural order, willfully chooses his own destruction under the guise of self-glory.

The suffering which grows out of that choice is as spiritual as the evil which produces it, an agony of mind and will. It is an agony which, by reason of the poetic and dramatic skill which created it, has become an unforgettable part of the English dramatic tradition. In its own time, it stands unmatched as an expression of deep human fear and torment; no other protagonist in surviving plays of the contemporary stage has been represented in so intense a state of suffering over so spiritual a loss. Kings and soldiers had bewailed the loss of honor, state, or power; lovers had lamented the loss of their mates; parents and children had sorrowed over the severance of domestic bonds by division or death; but no figure in early Elizabethan tragic drama had ever been driven to such torment by the prospect of the damnation of his immortal soul.

IV. *DOCTOR FAUSTUS* AND THE
MORALITY TRADITION

The supernatural context of Faustus' tragedy, and the central importance of theological concepts of evil and suffering within that context, distinguish it from all other tragedies of the time, and suggest a relationship to the English morality play. Even though Marlowe's play seems by and large to grow directly from the English Faust-Book rather than from the stage tradition of the moralities, there is no doubt that the morality tradition provided Marlowe with both a thematic precedent and devices of dramaturgy on which to draw. Hardin Craig's definition of the morality play as the presentation of man in the postlapsarian situation, where he is destined to die in sin unless he be saved by the intervention of divine grace and by repentance,[63] is certainly applicable to *Doctor Faustus*, though it by no means exhausts the meaning and effect of Marlowe's play. This general thematic import of the morality play was characteristically embodied in a dramatic structure defined by the conflict of abstract forces of good and evil over the soul of the hero, who represented all mankind. Undoubtedly the conflict between the forces of good and evil provides the major dramatic tension in *Doctor Faustus*, and Faustus himself stands (and falls) as the central figure in that conflict, the *only* human figure of real dramatic importance. But we have already reached the point where distinctions must be drawn. Is Faustus truly representative of mankind, or even of a general class of men, as the strict morality hero always was? And is the conflict of good and evil, which Marlowe has certainly heightened in his departures from the Faust-Book, the characteristic conflict of the morality?

There are many things about Faustus which would appear at first to put him outside the realm of a representative man: his uncommon intellectual attainments, his extraordinary reach of imagination and ambition, his arcane pursuits of forbidden magic, his bold and conscious arrogance in the face of the divinely established order. The dreams and desires that spur him to his fatal exercise of freedom are more superhuman than they are human; their very singularity helps to establish Faustus as one of the most individualized of Elizabethan stage characters. Nevertheless, the qualities and motivations which make Faustus an individual, especially in the way Marlowe has chosen to present them, make him at the same time a figure of more than particular or personal significance. Some critics

[63] "Morality Plays and the Elizabethan Drama," *SQ*, I (1950), 67.

have sought to identify Faustus' desires with the personal desires of Marlowe, but the whole dramatic structure with its burden of inescapable irony denies that argument. There are two aspects of Faustus' desires which give them a more universal application: the degree to which they fit the spirit of the Elizabethan age, and the degree to which they are exhibited by the most common of men. The first involves the goals of wealth, honor, and omnipotence, goals which Faustus and his fellow-magicians foresee as attainable through geographical and military exploits: India, the Orient, Spain and America, the conquest of the seas and dominion over foreign powers—all these were part of what was fast becoming a national dream for the Elizabethans. There is also the second aspect, the aspect of rock-bottom sensuality involved in Faustus' goal of a personal life of "all voluptuousnesse" (317). The universal appeal of this most common human inclination is made concrete in the comic scenes of low life which parody the learned but sensual Doctor's career. It must be emphasized that neither of these aspects appear in the Faust-Book; they are therefore indications of a conscious artistic effort toward dramatic universalization of the Faustian theme.

There is also a deeper and more general sense in which the Faustian figure stands for more than himself, and this is responsible for the enduring fascination which the figure, under one name or another, has exercised on the human imagination for centuries before and after Marlowe. It is bound up with the mythic pattern of the forbidden quest for superhuman knowledge and power, the quest which more often than not carries with it the seeds of its own destruction.[64] The application to Marlowe's Faustus has been made best perhaps by Professor Heilman: "[Faustus] is Everyman as Intellectual, with the axiological choice centered in the problem of knowl-

[64] For examples of this pattern before and after Marlowe's *Faustus*, see Palmer and More, *The Sources of the Faust Tradition*. Arpad Steiner examines the Christian awareness and interpretation of the pattern in "The Faust Legend and the Christian Tradition," *PMLA*, LIV (1939), 391-404.

edge. As Everyman Faustus embodies a perennial human aspiration—to escape inhibitions, to control the universe, to reconstruct the cosmos in naturalistic, non-theistic terms. As intellectual he is also aware of the exploit in its philosophical dimensions. In Everyman the tragic flaw—pride, wilfulness—causes blindness to the nature and destiny of man; in the intellectual, *hubris* destroys the understanding of the nature and limitations of knowledge."[65]

Marlowe has further shaped this fundamental pattern of human experience by making it grow out of a freely repeated moral choice, linking Faustus' sin with the primal or original sin of Christian theology. It is this burden and responsibility of moral choice in a Christian context which adds the final degree of universality to his figure and his career.

Faustus, then, for all his individuality, still represents humanity caught up in a conflict which, though extraordinary in its detail, is nevertheless fundamental in the experience of men. We have already seen how Marlowe has emphasized the conflict of good and evil through the two Angels who crystallize the alternatives Faustus continually faces. Their presence in the play has often been attributed to the influence of the morality tradition, and certainly to the extent that they are concrete embodiments of the conflict in Faustus' mind they appear to be a characteristic device of the morality play. But that by no means exhausts their significance and function. In the first place, angels and devils in Marlowe's time were not considered abstractions or even metaphors for the operations of the human mind; they were conceived as real spiritual beings created by God and granted certain powers and functions. Among these was the power to influence by suggestion, though not constrain, the mind of man. Now it will be noticed that Faustus never directs his attention to the Good and Evil Angels as dramatic entities; he neither speaks directly to them nor shows any sensible awareness of their physical presence.

[65] "The Tragedy of Knowledge," p. 331.

Their words are suggestive, however, of the drift of his own thought; hence their activity remains on a spiritual rather than physical level insofar as Faustus is concerned.[66]

This lack of physical interaction or even direct dialogue with the central human figure distinguishes the Angels' behavior from the characteristic dramatic activity of morality vices and virtues, and also from the dramaturgical conduct of the personified mental forces in such plays as *Horestes* and *Appius and Virginia*.[67] A further distinction lies in the absence of any interaction between the Angels themselves. In direct contrast to the conventional behavior of morality vices and virtues, they never engage in physical contact with each other, and never appear except in the presence of the human protagonist, upon whom their attention is always centered. In this they also differ strikingly from the contending personifications of human faculties in Nathaniel Woodes' *The Conflict of Conscience* (1581), where the protagonist Philologus is torn between Conscience and Sensual Suggestion. Philologus' personified conscience not only tries to persuade him to deny Sensual Suggestion, but also presents an explanation of the situation directly to the audience, and even engages in direct debate with Sensual Suggestion, during which Philologus is merely a bewildered bystander.[68]

Marlowe's use of the Angels, then, differs radically from the conventional employment of abstract or metaphorical figures in the morality plays. Even more important, however, is the fact that their very appearance in sixteenth-century English drama is unique. Nowhere in the extant morality plays dated after 1500 do good and evil angels contend for the

---

[66] See the analysis of this problem by West, *Invisible World*, pp. 102-104. The one appearance of the Angels peculiar to the 1616 text, in the spectacular scene preceding Faustus' final monologue (1995-2034) is exceptional: here the spirits call Faustus' attention to a visible heavenly throne and a picture of hell; they no longer represent two possible alternatives, but demonstrate the now inevitable consequences of Faustus' past decisions.

[67] See above, pp. 35-36.

[68] MSR (Oxford, 1952), ll. 1728 ff.

soul of man. And even among the very early moralities such angels are found in only one play, *The Castle of Perseverance* (1400-1425). If Marlowe drew his angels from a dramatic tradition rather than from theological thought regarding the nature and functions of spirits, he either made use of plays no longer extant or reverted to a much older tradition of religious drama extending through the mystery-cycles and back to the Latin drama of the medieval Church.

The first dramatic appearances of good and evil spirits in relationship with human figures are found in two Latin plays recorded in a thirteenth-century manuscript.[69] In a Christmas play the shepherds at the time of Christ's birth are urged by angels to visit the Saviour, and by evil spirits to stay away. In the second example, a Passion Play brings an angel and a demon into the story of Mary Magdalene, but only the angel speaks to Mary, moving her finally to conversion. The durability of this convention in the Magdalene story is witnessed by the English play of *Mary Magdalene* (1480-1490) in the Digby manuscript; the good angel admonishes, but the bad angel remains silent, tempting Mary only indirectly through Lechery, the personification of one of the Seven Deadly Sins. Here the spirits themselves are not paired for the dramatization of conflict and choice. This condition is more closely approximated in the Towneley Lucifer play and the Newcastle play of Noah's Ark. In the former, both good and evil angels present their arguments to Lucifer after he has aspired to usurp the majesty of God, but these are arguments after the choice has been made. In the Noah play, the strife between Noah and his wife is brought about at the devil's suggestion, but resolved by the admonition of an angel; in this case, however, the evil spirit acts upon one figure, the wife, while the good spirit acts upon the other.

The "purest" use of angels as representatives of opposing

[69] Karl Young, *The Drama of the Medieval Church*, corrected reprint ed. (Oxford, 1951), I, 535.

moral alternatives facing a single human figure is found in
The Castle of Perseverance, where the good angel assigned to
Humanum Genus heads the threefold forces of Conscience,
Confession, and Penance, as well as the subsidiary forces of
the Seven Virtues, against the evil angel, who commands the
World, the Flesh, the Devil, and the Seven Sins. Aside from
this elaborate symmetrical antagonism, the angels argue with
each other at the start of the play for the allegiance of Humanum Genus, and at the end of the play contend for the posses-
sion of his soul. It is clear that the more abstract conventions
of the morality conflict predominate in *The Castle of Perseverance*; the more impressive dramatic strife is waged outside and around the human protagonist; even the opposing
spirits direct themselves more to the argument with each other
than to the decisions of Humanum Genus. Thus, the dramaturgical conduct of the good and evil angels in the one English morality play that employs them is at a farther remove
from Marlowe's treatment of these spirits than is the non-
dramatic theological formulation concerning the activities of
angels and demons.

Both the external nature of the conflict in *Perseverance* and
its pattern of alternating victory and defeat were to become
the staple features of the battle beween good and evil in the
later morality plays, but both are foreign to Marlowe's handling of the conflict. In *Faustus*, the activities of the Angels
are confined to the attempt to sway the Doctor's will to the
side of good or evil. Unlike Humanum Genus and many of his
later counterparts, Faustus himself is never separated from
the conflict, and he himself is the only one to resolve it. In
his case there is no alternating pattern—without exception he
finally chooses the way of evil. Thus, the end result of Marlowe's staging of the Angels is to stress the Doctor's own will
and responsibility in acting against his own best interests.

The introduction of the Seven Deadly Sins is another device
in *Doctor Faustus* often linked with the morality tradition.

Here again Marlowe is indebted not to the contemporary morality play, but to the early moralities before 1500. The Seven Deadly Sins, cast in the role of militant aggressors, are found in *The Castle of Perseverance*, the Digby *Mary Magdalene*, and Medwall's *Nature* (1490-1501), and there is evidence of dramatic pageants no longer extant illustrating the Seven Sins, in documents of the fourteenth and fifteenth centuries.[70] After the turn of the century, however, the morality play characteristically exhibits a more select number of sins or vices, adapted often to the more specialized homiletic stresses of the Reformation period. But throughout the development of the tradition the vices retain both their aggressive character as destructive agents intent on seducing the human hero, and their essential strategy of deceit, disguising their vicious qualities under more attractive names. In Marlowe's play, not only are the Seven Deadly Sins presented *en masse*, which by that time had become an unusual thing in the drama, but they are also limited to one ironic episode of pageantry, and do not act as destructive agents plotting the downfall of Faustus.[71] They are presented rather as a delight and gratification to him, not in any ameliorating disguise, but in the raw, vulgar expression of their true natures (669-730). Faustus does not even get the dubious credit of being attracted to evil under the guise of an apparent good; he delights in it for what it really is, and under circumstances which present it as a "reward" for his obedience to the devil. Faustus, therefore, needs no deception to lead him to sin; he is his own worst deceiver, his own worst enemy, his own worst tempter.

[70] See Bernard Spivack, *Shakespeare and the Allegory of Evil* (New York, 1958), p. 60.

[71] A contemporary two-part play, in which the Seven Sins apparently functioned as symbolic figures in a series of scenes presenting historical and legendary characters who illustrated the Sins' effects, is known through a surviving stage "platt" or plot called "The Platt of the Second Part of the Seven Deadly Sins." There is little indication of how the Sins acted, but the play clearly had no central protagonist. See C. Walter Hodges, *The Globe Restored: A Study of the Elizabethan Theatre* (London, 1953), pp. 99-100, 182-184.

Thus there is hardly any need in Marlowe's play for the most vital of morality conventions, the character of the Vice. This arch-deceiver and chief agent of destruction is entirely absent. Faustus' chief aggressor is the devil, a devil whose language and behavior bear little resemblance either to the habitual behavior of the Vice or to that of any devil who had ever trod the English stage. The devil, as Spivack has pointed out, holds but a negligible place in morality drama;[72] he appears in only nine of the almost sixty surviving plays of the morality convention, and has a significant role as tempter in only two early plays, *Wisdom* and *Mankind* (both c. 1461-1485). For the most part he is a grotesque, ludicrous figure, descended from the roaring fiends of the mystery-cycles, and having no direct contact with the human protagonist; often he is the object of the Vice's scurrilous humor and contempt. Spivack suggests that he does not fit in with the abstract morality pattern because he is "historical" and represents too undifferentiated an evil for the homiletic purposes of the morality play.[73] In *The Conflict of Conscience* (1581), Sathan himself opens the play, and gives his reason for not partaking of the main dramatic action: his ugly shape will attract no one, he says, and so he must send out the more alluring vices to destroy man.[74] We are reminded of how Faustus recoiled, seeing the ugliness of Mephostophilis, but nevertheless persisted in his "devilish exercise" after demanding the devil to assume a more pleasing and pious shape. Marlowe's irony of a disguise that is no disguise uses an old convention in a new way and dramatically underlines the *self-imposed* moral blindness of his protagonist.

[72] P. 130.   [73] P. 132.

[74] *Ed.cit.*, ll. 1-114. The same argument is given by Sathan in Thomas Garter's *The Commody of the moste vertuous and Godlye Susanna* (printed 1578), MSR (Oxford, 1937), ll. 26-50. In the fifteenth-century play *Wisdom* Lucifer changes his form to that of a "goodly galont" when he undertakes his temptation of Mind, Will, and Understanding: *The Macro Plays*, ed. F. J. Furnivall and Alfred W. Pollard, EETS, ex. ser. XCI (London, 1904), p. 48.

Marlowe's Mephostophilis has a seriousness and intensity which is unparalleled in any previous theatrical representation of the diabolic, and unmatched in the Faust-Book as well. He is memorable not so much for the threats and the delights with which he "serves" Faustus, but for the brief yet telling witness that he gives to the pains of hell. Nowhere in the English dramatic tradition had the devil ever been used to express the suffering of damnation in this way; nowhere had the pain of loss been given such intense and lucid expression as in the words of Mephostophilis. Like the demons of which Chrysostom wrote, he cries out in testimony of his torment—and this in the face of the very man he is supposed to lead to hell. Mephostophilis' behavior in these instances is curiously at odds with the more conventional fireworks, pranks, spectacular appearances, and threats in which he and the other devils indulge in other sections of the play. Here the more typical qualities of the stage devil are thrust into the background, and he emerges as a real and suffering individual being. The dramaturgical conduct of Marlowe's devil on these occasions is closer to the theology of the diabolic and of damnation than to the behavior of any devil in the mystery and morality plays. Marlowe's theology in this case is indeed orthodox; it is based on teaching that was even older than the liturgical drama. But the originality with which he sets his theological knowledge into dramatic form is the mark of his genuine heterodoxy.[75]

---

[75] Spivack (p. 240) asserts that the "deepest suffering of the sinner in the early moralities is very little different [from that in Marlowe's *Faustus* and in Dante's *Commedia*] though it is scarcely so well expressed. He too is cut off by his sins from the divine source of his being and the vision that gives meaning to life." This may be so according to what can be *assumed* doctrinally, but when it comes to actual dramatic expression within the plays, there is nothing in the early moralities that approaches the explicit and precise formulation of the pain of loss (*poena damni*) that one finds in the speeches of Mephostophilis and Faustus—even though the directly homiletic character of the morality play invited open and precise statements of doctrine.

Marlowe makes the father of lies tell the truth to Faustus, an unheard-of tactic for any representative of evil in the morality tradition. That Faustus should proceed to his own damnation in the face of such testimony sets him at an infinite distance from any of the beguiled human victims of the Vice in the moralities. There need be no Vice in Marlowe's play, nor even a deceitful devil, for Faustus is his own destroyer. What Marlowe has done to stress this point, by his handling of Mephostophilis as well as of the Deadly Sins, is to *reverse* the normal devices of the morality play. That he knew how to employ those devices in the regular way is manifest in the dramatic behavior of Barabas and Lightborn. Here, however, he is after a different form of ironic effect, a form which emphasizes at every opportunity Faustus' *willful* blindness to the overt evil before him.

There is yet another constitutional feature of the morality play which does not appear in Marlowe's *Faustus*: explicit didacticism which takes the form of direct homiletic address to the audience. It is true that the epilogue draws a moral from the action, indeed that the action itself carries a powerful exemplary force, but *within* the play there is none of the bald didacticism directed at the audience that always characterized the morality play. The closest approach to this homiletic quality is found in the Old Man's sermon to Faustus, in the admonitions of the Good Angel, and perhaps in the self-revelations of the Seven Deadly Sins. But nowhere is the audience itself addressed openly either in general admonition or in doctrinal commentary on Faustus' actions. In the case of the speeches of the Deadly Sins, the effect is primarily satirical and comically imaginative. Marlowe has replaced homily with dramatic irony. The solidly intellectual concepts of sin and damnation, of evil and suffering, which form the basis of his play are never preached; they are dramatized. The ironic dimensions of that dramatization carry to the audience the inescapable message implicit in Faustus' career; the dramatic *exemplum* stands without need of any homiletic elaboration.

While both the character and career of Faustus exhibit a fundamental quality which is both representative and universal in human experience, and while the nature of his conflict is the familiar tension holding his salvation or damnation in precarious balance, it is clear that this conflict is not set forth in the characteristic dramaturgical mode of the morality play. The moral forces and principles that were once abstracted from man's nature and presented separately as external agents are now within his own being. The battle between good and evil is fought in Faustus' own mind, and the only true abstractions that are given life in the play—the Seven Deadly Sins—are merely symbolic ornaments rather than major movers of the dramatic action. The springs of action in *Doctor Faustus* are coiled within the moral center of Faustus' soul: his imagination, his intellect, his exercise of choice begin the movement of the play and carry it to its tragic conclusion.

Here is the tragedy of moral choice wrought to its highest pitch, simple, stark, uncomplicated by the myriad relationships of human intercourse. *The Tragical History of Doctor Faustus* stands unique among the plays of its time in that all significant conflicts, struggles, delights, decisions, and pains are packed within one man, one character who is both victim and executioner. Doctor Faustus, for all his solitary stature, is no less human than any other tragic protagonist who plays his part in a world thronged with other men. He is no less human, because he bears the paradoxical twofold burden that all men must bear: unavoidable responsibility for his freely-made choices, and final helplessness in the face of a universal order that encompasses more than can the mind of man.

Ultimately, it is precisely this burden of his humanity that is the root of his suffering. In this he is unlike all other creations of Marlowe's imagination. Dido suffers as a lover who has lost her beloved; Tamburlaine, because he loses what is dear to both conqueror and lover; the Jew and the Guise suffer when their own treachery has backfired; Edward, when his friends and his kingship are no more. But only Faustus suffers because of his humanity, because he cannot escape the consequences of his human acts of mind and will, because by those acts he has eternally separated himself from the only power that can fulfill and perfect his humanity. It is perhaps just this essentially human quality of his suffering that has made it endure as Marlowe's most powerful dramatic statement.

The quality of evil and of suffering inherent in Marlowe's Faustus establishes him as neither hero nor villain, but as man.

CHAPTER VI · MARLOWE'S VISION OF SUFFERING AND EVIL

formam lacrimis aptate meis
—Seneca

pondus meum amor meus
—St. Augustine

CHAPTER VI · MARLOWE'S VISION OF
SUFFERING AND EVIL

O N T R Y I N G to define the characteristic dramaturgical and ideological dimensions of Marlowe's portrayal of suffering and evil, one is struck at first by the sheer diversity of technique and attitude exhibited in such a small body of work. The exploitation of staged physical violence ranges from the wholesale slaughter of *The Massacre at Paris* to the single "hellish fall" of Doctor Faustus; the focus of suffering which in Part I of *Tamburlaine* falls solely on the protagonist's victims is confined in *Edward II* to the victimized protagonist; the isolable evil of *The Jew of Malta* and *The Massacre at Paris*, incarnated in an external villain, becomes inextricably part of human nature—the "enemy within"—in *Doctor Faustus*; the tableau-like formality of the death scenes of Zenocrate and Tamburlaine gives way to the grotesquely violent but symbolic character that marks the ends of Barabas and Edward; the psychological effects of grief range from pathetic illusion to malicious cursing, from madness and wild rage to passive self-pity, from Stoic resolution to Christian resignation, from despair to hateful revenge. It is evident, too, that Marlowe's diverse treatment of suffering and evil is in part a result of his dramatic eclecticism; for he has made use of the full range of the dramatic traditions and conceptions of tragedy available to him.

Marlowe's plays, in the minor scenes in *Dido* and *Faustus*, carry over from the mysteries and moralities the quality of the comedy of evil; in the behavior of Barabas, Ithamore, and Lightborn, reminiscent of the Vice, that quality is given a new twist of mordant irony. The allegorical dimension of evil in the Vice figure of the moralities is not altogether lost in Barabas, the human symbol of the avarice and egoism which infect every level of action in *The Jew of Malta*. The morality conflict between spiritual good and evil lies at the heart of

Doctor Faustus, while the more particular devices associated with this dramatic form are often reversed in the play in order to focus attention on the moral energies, choices, and blindness within Faustus himself. The characteristic emotions of the suffering wicked in the mystery-cycles, wrath and despair, are carried over into Marlowe's usage, but in an entirely new context. The element of Herodian rage in Tamburlaine's fury is undercut, not by the familiar elements of the Christian myth which provide for the ultimate defeat of evil, but by the ironic helplessness of even the mightiest of conquerors in the face of disease and death. Faustus' despair is indeed the despair of the spiritually damned, but it is a condition of his being which springs from the dramatic pattern of his repeated actions and choices throughout the play; it is not the despair *ex machina* of the older religious plays. It also functions as an operative force in the persistent tension generated by the uncertain state of Faustus' soul.

The sense of retributive justice that pervades the handling of suffering in the morality plays and the plays which borrow from that tradition is also felt in Marlowe. Suffering and destruction brought on by the character's own action or perversity is at work in one degree or another in the fates of Barabas, Guise, Edward, Mortimer, and Faustus, affording one major means of making their suffering intelligible. The "hybrid" plays, *Cambises*, *Horestes*, and the like, also provided Marlowe with dramatic precedent for the secularization of the Vice figure: in characters like Barabas and Lightborn, physical rather than spiritual destruction becomes the prime object of professional pride.

The motif of the inevitable fall from material prosperity which characterized *De Casibus* tragedy is given sensational embodiment in the deaths of Cosroe, Bajazeth, Zabina, and Tamburlaine himself in the two parts of *Tamburlaine*; it is epitomized in the rise and fall of Mortimer, and reaches its most subtly modulated expression in the histrionic suffering of the deposed Edward II. The *Mirror for Magistrates'* persistent urging of the responsible will rather than Fortune as the determining cause of tragic downfall is also converted into dramatic terms in Marlovian tragedy, where the network of evil is always traced to its source in the willful desires and ambitions of human agents; the careers of Barabas, Guise, Mortimer, Edward, and Faustus are effective demonstrations of this principle.

The confluence of non-dramatic *De Casibus* tragedy with the morality tradition and with the Elizabethan theoretic view of tragedy provided Marlowe with a major structural pattern: the parading of a character with a morally shocking nature through a series of incidents which demonstrate dramatically his destructive or evil quality. The Jew of Malta and the Duke of Guise are the most obvious examples; there is more procession than plot involved in the exhibition of their villainies. The same can be said of the career of Faustus, though here the moral nature of the protagonist is more complex, and the incidents which lead him to his tragic destruction are ranged in order of increasing intensity and deepening ironic significance. Tamburlaine's career is equally pageant-like; as his victories and ambitions swell to greater and greater proportions, the violence and destruction wrought in their wake become more and more evident; his honor is mirrored in blood, and the irony of his accomplishment is reflected in the gold coffin of Zenocrate. *The Tragedy of Dido* represents a variant of this essential framework; Cupid, representing love, provides the motive force behind the exhibition of destruction. *Edward II* is more complex; its structure is clearly divided into two parts with different aims, but the pattern in each part is roughly equivalent to the pattern of repetitive, illustrative incident which is basic in the other plays. In the first part, the object of demonstration is Edward's failure to give proper attention to either his kingdom or his wife; in the second, every scene involving Edward develops his suffering over his lost kingship, while each of the other scenes puts Mortimer's tyrannical ambition on display in the blackest of terms. It is, by the way, this characteristic tendency of Marlovian tragedy to put evil on exhibition—a tendency derived ultimately from medieval traditions—that impedes any critical approach which operates either on an Aristotelian theory of tragedy, with its demands for an admirable hero, or on a romantic-humanist theory, which exalts and values the rebel and the individualist. Although most of Marlowe's major figures are indeed individualists, one of the persistent measures of their distinction is a whole-hearted indulgence in thought and action which to the Elizabethan audience was patently evil and reprehensible. In Marlovian tragedy it is not the universe that is destructive, but the heart of man.

Unlike many *De Casibus* tragedies, Marlowe's plays do not demand the psychological punishment of remorse for those whose deeds are so clearly evil and destructive. With the great exception of Faustus, Marlowe's protagonists exhibit no sign of self-condemnation, no matter how guilty they may appear to the audience. Their lack of conventional conscience is notorious, and it cannot always be attributed to the heritage of the conscienceless Vice or Senecan tyrant. Edward II, whose torment is so closely allied to the *De Casibus* theme of lost glory, is not allowed by Marlowe to exhibit awareness of his own partial responsibility for his fall that the chronicle sources are so careful to point out. This omission achieves a measure of ironic detachment from the final plight of the king, and such ironic distance seems to be Marlowe's goal with other characters as well. The fearful dreams of Shakespeare's Richard III or the agonies of Lady Macbeth, both of which embody dramatically the conventional idea of retributive remorse, have no counterpart in Marlowe's representation of suffering. One may interpret this lack as an index of Marlowe's own contempt for conventional moralizing devices, but it would be more consistent with Marlowe's general dramatic technique to attribute it to his concern for establishing and maintaining ironic distance. Marlowe's Jew is less human than Shakespeare's Richard, though both bear the hereditary marks of the Vice; Marlowe's Guise and Mortimer, and even Tamburlaine, are less human than Macbeth, though all become bloody tyrants. At least one measure of the difference in Marlowe's figures lies in their total lack of human fear. To the degree that they lack such humanity they also lack dramatic sympathy; and thus the physical retributions that finally destroy them come with a greater sense of justice.

Marlowe's representation of suffering and evil owes less to Seneca and to English classical drama than to native tragic traditions of medieval origin. In the most "classical" and academically oriented of his plays, *Dido Queen of Carthage*, there is little Senecan flavor, except perhaps in the lurid quality of Aeneas' narration of the fall of Troy; Virgil and Ovid provide the predominant themes and bases of expression. *Tamburlaine* remains the most Senecan of Marlowe's works, but only in occasional parallels of character conception and expression, such as the physiological description of physical pain, the Stoicism of Agydas and Olympia, and the Herculean fury of the stricken Tamburlaine. Although Marlowe shares in the general debt which Elizabethan tragic drama owes to Seneca for the use of classical allusion, hyperbolic imagery, the five-act structure, and carefully elaborated rhetoric, neither of the *Tamburlaine* plays bears much resemblance to the conscious imitations of Senecan style found in the academic tragedies. For all *Tamburlaine*'s emphasis on eloquence, there is more dramatized action involving suffering and death in the play than in any of the academic efforts, just as there is an obvious lack of sententiousness or explicit moral comment by a chorus. Though the theme of ambition makes a startling appearance in Marlowe's plays, it has little to do with the political contexts of evil established in the English classical drama. Marlowe has even less to do with the basic Senecan situations of the sufferer tormented by overpowering passion, or by the suicidal wish to inflict punishment upon himself for some semi-voluntary or involuntary crime, and actual suicide is conspicuously absent from the plays except for *Tamburlaine* and *Dido*. Finally, the fundamental Senecan theme of Stoical resistance to an inevitably hostile universe is also conspicuous for its absence in Marlovian tragedy; in Marlowe's tragic vision the root of hostility, evil, and destruction lies in the will of man.

Marlowe shares with Kyd the wholesale exhibition of violence and death on stage, but the most tragic of his plays—*Faustus* and *Edward II*—do not depend primarily on such sensational exploitation of external suffering. The motive of revenge, vital in Kyd's *Spanish Tragedy*, is used by Marlowe chiefly in *The Jew of Malta*, but with differences greater than any similarities: in *The Spanish Tragedy*, revenge is an obsession which drives the distraught but innocent parents of Horatio to frenzy and insanity; in *The Jew*, revenge is but one of the fine arts of destruction practiced with cold and ingenious calculation by the malicious Barabas—the difference is that between the impassioned Senecan revenger and the inhuman morality Vice. The kind of mental suffering Kyd exploits is in a long tradition of domestic pathos: the lament of a father or mother for a lost child—a stock situation in both the native and Senecan dramatic traditions. Kyd gives it poetic and dramatic elaboration and makes it part of the motive force of his play; Marlowe, on the contrary, hardly ever touches it. Where Kyd and Marlowe are most alike is in turning poetry into drama, the verbal image into the visual image, metaphor into action. The sorrow of their characters is given more than precise poetic articulation; it is dramatically activated. Though there are still traces of the self-contained, set lament in both *Tamburlaine* and *The Spanish Tragedy*, one can see new life breaking out in dramatic gesture, such as the mourning Tamburlaine's splintering his lance on the ground in the effort to

free the furies who might bring back Zenocrate, or Isabella's
cutting down the arbor in which her son was slain. Marlowe's
dramatic articulation of suffering is most effectively realized in
the last scenes of *Edward II* and *Faustus*: the hell of grief that
the deposed king feels is mirrored in his physical situation—
helplessness before his diabolic torturers; similarly, when the
aspiring Faustus tries to leap up to his God, he falls, Icarus-
like, back to earth—the earth that will not harbor him.

Despite all that is diverse and derivative in Marlowe's
dramatic depiction of suffering and evil, there emerge from
his plays certain central preoccupations and techniques which
are the true measure of his originality. At the heart of Marlovian tragedy one finds the persistent expression of the sense
of loss, the persistent dimension of irony in human aspiration
and destruction, and persistent emphasis on human responsibility for suffering and evil.

It has been truly said that in the development of English
tragedy Marlowe's heroes were "the first to die dramatically,
significantly, revealing in their deaths the deepest meaning
of their lives."[1] It might be more accurate to say that they reveal in their greatest sufferings the deepest meaning of their
lives, and the greatest suffering in each case is not always death.
Dido's deepest grief is the cause of her death, but it is not the
prospect of death that causes her deepest grief—it is the loss of
her lover. Tamburlaine's greatest fury—his way of expressing
suffering—is sparked by the death of Zenocrate, and by the
temporary loss of his own convictions of superhumanity. The
Jew of Malta is struck most severely by the loss of his gold;
Guise, by the frustration of his ambition. Edward's most extravagant sorrow results from separation from his unworthy
favorites, and especially from the loss of his crown. In *Doctor
Faustus*, the greatest suffering of hell is revealed as what
theology calls the pain of loss: the pain that Faustus will

---

[1] Herbert J. Muller, *The Spirit of Tragedy* (New York, 1956), p. 155.
See also Theodore Spencer, *Death and Elizabethan Tragedy* (Cambridge,
Mass., 1936), p. 223.

not credit until he feels it for himself, until he experiences its foreshadowing during his last terrible hour on earth; for him it is not death, but the loss beyond death, that is most tormenting. Essentially, it is the pain of loss, either in its precise theological definition or in an analogous form, which constitutes the greatest anguish for each of Marlowe's protagonists; the pain of loss is central to the Marlovian vision of suffering.

If Marlowe's theological training entered into his view of human experience, as I think *Doctor Faustus* demonstrates, it provided him with a conception of the causes of pain in the human soul which could be fruitfully developed in dramatic tragedy. The pain of loss is the greatest of all known sufferings because it represents the alienation of the creature from the Creator, the interminable separation of the human soul from the one Being in which it could have found perfect fulfillment. The nature of the suffering is defined by the nature of the sufferer. This principle can be transposed by analogy to human experience which does not involve the supernatural, and to any human relationship grounded in love or desire, in which the object of love or desire promises a certain fulfillment and the privation of that object results in frustration or pain.[2] The soul is weighed in the balance by what delights her, as St. Augustine put it, which is another way of saying that what a man loves tells most about what that man *is*. The converse is equally true: what makes a man most acutely suffer reveals his nature—his own particular nature is defined by the nature of his suffering. Here is a principle rich in potential for dramatic characterization. The suffering of a dramatic figure can define the precise nature of his character, if what makes him suffer

---

[2] That Marlowe himself made the conscious application of the pain of loss as it defines the suffering of hell to the purely human level is revealed in *Edward II*, where Gaveston on two occasions likens his separation from the king to this suffering (MSR [Oxford, 1925], ll. 154-155, 436), and where Edward testifies that the thought of his lost kingship makes him feel a "hell of greefe" (ll. 2739-2741).

most is distinct from what makes others suffer most. In Marlowe's handling of suffering, the limiting and distinguishing factors are the nature of the loss which causes his characters' greatest pain, and the mode of reaction to that loss.

Marlowe's handling of the suffering of loss functions not only in the definition of character, but also in the definition of dramatic theme. His protagonists' deepest griefs reveal their greatest values, and in each case these values constitute the central thematic significance of the play. In Dido's case, the love of Aeneas is all-important; the play is concerned with the winning and losing of that love—in it centers the dramatic interest and dramatic irony. Tamburlaine's greatest affliction is the sickness which proves him to be a man; his whole career has been a series of stupendous efforts to prove himself lord above all men—his audacious ambition is the theme of the play. When the gold which is Barabas' god is taken from him, the Jew weeps and rages in torment; but practically everyone else in the play worships at the same altar. The ambition of the Duke of Guise is less infectious; the propagandistic nature of the drama keeps the disease from spreading to the "good side." Nevertheless, his pitiless climb to power constitutes the center of the play, and his fatal stumbling *en route* causes him the most agony. Edward's favorites and Edward's crown are the foci of dramatic interest in *Edward II*; the struggle for Faustus' soul is the central conflict of *Doctor Faustus*. Over and over again, that which is lost represents the central thematic issue.

The pain of loss helps to define the character of Marlowe's protagonists insofar as they are the victims of suffering. But figures like Tamburlaine, Barabas, Guise, and Mortimer are also defined by another kind of suffering, the suffering they inflict on others. Aside from Barabas, whose Jewishness, Machiavellianism, and resemblance to a Vice automatically define his destructive and malicious nature, the driving force behind these figures is material ambition, the material ambition which critics have singled out as the quintessence of the Renaissance spirit and the burning thirst of Marlowe himself. If an examination of Marlowe's plays from the perspective of suffering and evil accomplishes anything, it should certainly help to point out the inadequacies of this characterization. If one considers only the words on the printed page, it is perhaps understandable that one should be swept away by the grand poetry and rhetoric which express the desires of the characters. But there is a rhetoric of action in the drama which must be heeded as well; in a wider context which includes awareness of that rhetoric, the theme of ambition takes on a different note. As Tamburlaine soars to the heights of aspiration he plunges a dagger into the heart of his cowardly but curiously rational son; his march to fame leaves kings and queens in bloody heaps behind him; it terrorizes mothers into slaying their own sons, leaves riddled corpses on city walls, and disposes of conquered kings as so many beasts of burden that have outlived their usefulness. The ambition of the Duke of Guise leaves an even more congested wake of bloody corpses, all good pious Protestants, defenseless and innocent. Mortimer's rise is established by the subjection of Edward to pitiful torments, and confirmed by one of the most gruesome executions of the Elizabethan theater. This is suffering with dramatic point, suffering that pricks the bubble of ambition's enchantment, suffering which does more to underscore the destructive fruits of ambition than the most sententious of moralizing choruses. It is the tool of a dramatist with an eye for irony rather than a concern for moralizing; but it is no less moral for all that.

It has become something of a commonplace to seize upon Marlowe as the symbol of the "pagan Renaissance," or as one writer puts it, a dramatist who "beat the drum for that kind of self-reliance and autonomous glory that permitted one to rise above both good luck and disaster to achieve the complete realization of personality."[3] How well does this judgment fit the dramatic spectacle of human destruction that Marlowe's aspiring heroes leave behind them? Does the rhetoric of his dramatic action permit one to rest in admiration of the self-reliance of a Mortimer or a Barabas? Or does anything in *The Massacre at Paris* point to the author's beating a drum for the Duke of Guise? It seems to me that no one who takes into account the full dramatic experience of Marlowe's plays, and the historical context of their original presentation, can give an affirmative answer to these questions. On the contrary, Marlowe's staged suffering clearly underlines the irony of the kind of human "fulfillment" to which his major characters aspire.

Marlowe's sense of irony is at work in more ways than one in his treatment of suffering and evil. It is nowhere more evident than in the dramatic shape he gives to the catastrophic downfalls of his major characters. I fail to see the "self-reliance and autonomous glory," the rising above good luck or disaster, or "the complete realization of personality" in Dido's pitiful grief and suicide, in the vengeful curses of the dying Guise, in the spectacle of Barabas thrashing about in his caldron, hurling his invectives and boasts of malicious deeds at those around him, in the ragged and tormented Edward's last moments with the grim and mocking Lightborn, or in the desperately fearful end of Faustus as he pleads with the elements to hide him from the dreadful wrath of God. The final suffering of these characters does not embody that victory of the spirit or that sublime sense of the transcendent human individual upon which rests the romantic or heroic humanist theory of tragedy; Marlowe is not wont to stress the splendor of defeat, but the deep ironies of defeat.

[3] Herschel Baker, *The Dignity of Man: Studies in the Persistence of an Idea* (Cambridge, Mass., 1947), p. 302. Paul H. Kocher's picture of a Marlowe "oblivious to the needs of the whole body social and immersed in egocentric dreams of power" is substantially the same (*Christopher Marlowe* [Chapel Hill, 1946], p. 192).

In *The Massacre at Paris* and *The Jew of Malta*, the ironic appropriateness of the traitor betrayed is effective, though somewhat mechanically contrived. In *Dido*, the suicidal catastrophe is foreknown, and Marlowe depends on that foreknowledge when he inserts the imagery of fiery destruction into the love-pleadings of Dido, thereby stressing the irony of her particular destructive aspiration. By introducing the element of illusion into the sufferings of both Aeneas and Dido, Marlowe again emphasizes the irony of their situations, revealing their pitiful helplessness, rather than any spiritual resilience, in the face of affliction. And finally, Dido's pain of loss is given its most agonizing twist by her recognition of her own measure of responsibility for it.

Illusion is a mark of Tamburlaine's suffering, too, and once more it is used to stress his helplessness in the face of death, his unwillingness to accept the conditions of mortality even when they press closely upon him. His response to pain is indeed extraordinarily audacious, but the very fantasy of his daring and of his extravagant action is its own ironic comment on the little even the strongest of men can accomplish against inevitable human limitations. He "overcomes" the pain of loss by pretending the loss does not exist.

In *Edward II* and *Doctor Faustus*, Marlowe's irony cuts deepest of all. The suffering of the damned, with its inherent ironies, is at work in both plays, at a spiritual level in *Faustus*, and at the analogical material level in *Edward*. In the aspiring pride that leads him to repudiate his humanity, Doctor Faustus, like Lucifer, brings on his own damnation and is himself the cause of his worst suffering. His career, which begins in the flush of superhuman desires, progresses through the satisfaction of strictly mundane requests and the exhibition of illusory pranks, and ends in the inevitable reality of eternal loss. The grand dream is reduced to limited and spiritually destructive accomplishment; the inflated aspiration sputters out in the cravings of *cupiditas*. There is cupidity in Edward's "sin" as well: in the indulgence of his flattering and self-seeking favorites, he repudiates his kingship. Like the repudiation of Faustus, Edward's bears the seed of his own punishment: after his fall from power, it is the loss of the very thing he repudiated—his kingship—which torments him most. Like Faustus, too, he engages in a pitiful fight against time, because his closest links are with the temporal rather than the timeless. His final aspiration is as ironic as the aspirations of all the others; he yearns for what is essentially unattainable.

The ironic dimensions of Marlowe's representation of suffering and evil reveal the underlying reality beneath the fanciful aspirations of man. Marlowe's tragic vision is defined, not so much by awe for the powerful and rebellious individual, as by the trenchantly ironic display of the limitations, frustrations, and destructive effects of aspiration and power. The theme itself is neither original nor heterodox in the history of English tragedy, but the *mode* of its elaboration and communication is. No English dramatist before Marlowe had demonstrated with such spectacular effect the ironic force of the rhetoric of action in counterpoint with the rhetoric of language; the dream of the poetic word is consistently confronted with the reality of the dramatic action. No earlier playwright had ever put dramatic irony to such remarkable and responsible work in English tragedy.

To reveal the ironies of human aspiration is not to discount the naked forcefulness of will inherent in Marlowe's protagonists. His heroes are defined by the strength of both their sufferings and their desires. But within the total context of each play, the revelation is clear that it is just this force of will that explains and makes intelligible the panorama of calamity, destruction, and evil exhibited upon the stage. The root of tragedy is in the will of man. Here lies the dramatically intelligible cause of evil in Marlovian drama.

"It is of the essence of tragedy," writes Helen Gardner, "that it forces us to look at what we normally do not care to

look at, and have not invented for ourselves."[4] Yet the suffering and the evil that Marlowe's drama forces us to look
at are above all examples of what man *has* invented for himself, for here the human will is always the observable agent
of destruction and pain. The problem of suffering is resolved
in the mystery of iniquity; there is a Barabas here, but no Job.
The guiltless sufferer is never the primary subject of Marlowe's concern; wherever there are innocent sufferers, there
too is the human agent. And yet, not Barabas but Faustus is the
most significant embodiment of the mystery of iniquity in Marlowe's plays; he is his own afflicter; the complexity of his
moral nature is more like that of every man, and out of it he
spins the thread of his tragic fate. In Faustus' career Marlowe has best fused two characteristic elements which appear
throughout the plays: the irony of self-destruction and the
sense of retributive justice. They are united dramatically much
as they are united conceptually in the theological formulation
of damnation. One major reason that we accept the justice by
which Marlowe's tragic protagonists are destroyed is the dramatist's careful working out of human self-will as the cause
of human catastrophe.

Once again, Marlowe's essential view of the causes of evil
in human experience is no different from the orthodox Christian one; his distinction lies in the dramatic skill in converting his theoretical knowledge into effective theater. Unlike
the tragic figures of the *Mirror for Magistrates*, his characters
do not talk about free will and human responsibility as the determining forces in life; instead they demonstrate the idea by
acting. The total action of Marlowe's dramas reveals his conception of tragic fate, a conception that he shares ultimately
with both Dante and Shakespeare. It is the conception, as Hardin Craig describes it, "arising out of Christianity and in its
typical form unknown to the ancient world, [which holds] that

[4] "Milton's 'Satan' and the Theme of Damnation in Elizabethan Tragedy,"
English Studies 1948 (English Association), n.s. I, 61.

catastrophe is the result of guilt and is a function of character and conscience."[5] Craig contrasts this view with the Greek formulation of human calamity as an irresistible and sometimes inexplicable manifestation of divine order, which calls for a response of heroic acceptance; and with the Senecan view that disaster lies in the very nature of things, so that man can be victorious only in attitude, in his ability to meet fate with courage. There is an inkling of the Senecan attitude in Marlowe, but it crops up in the least admirable of his figures, Barabas, Guise, and Mortimer. Their final posturings of "resolution," however, do not find justification in the context of any hostile universe—their catastrophes are wrought in an ordered universe in which evil of its very nature works toward its own destruction. The Christian conception of tragic fate remains predominant.

In Marlovian tragedy evil erupts into dramatic action through personality, and the suffering that it produces is nearly always deeply personal and individually felt. The tragedy in Marlowe's plays is always the tragedy of individuals; it does not reach cataclysmic proportions, as Shakespeare's does. Bernard Spivack has characterized the Shakespearean vision of tragedy as one in which "evil in its greatest magnitude expresses division and disorder." The tragic deeds of Shakespeare's great tragedies, he notes, all have social, metaphysical, and cosmic overtones: "They violate the nature of man, the nature of society, the nature of the universe. It is in this deep sense that they all receive their great condemnation as *unnatural* acts."[6] Marlowe does not share the breadth and scope of this vision; his emphasis is largely, if not wholly, on personal aberration. But there is a sense in which he tries to give a dimension of universality to the personal crimes and weak-

[5] "The Shackling of Accidents: A Study of Elizabethan Tragedy," *PQ*, XIX (1940), 12. See also Charles T. Harrison, "The Poet as Witness," *SR*, LXIII (1955), 541-547.
[6] *Shakespeare and the Allegory of Evil* (New York, 1958), p. 49.

nesses of his characters. Dido's self-destructive yearning for an unattainable love is echoed in Anna and Iarbas, so that she becomes a symbol for the destructive effects of love, the central theme of the play. Tamburlaine, as one of the greatest conquerors, becomes, as Theodore Spencer points out, "a type of all conquerors,"[7] whose march to fame must lie through fields of blood. Barabas is himself a dramatic emblem of the self-seeking greed that pervades *The Jew of Malta*. In *Edward II* Gaveston, Baldock, and Spencer are all cast in the same mold of the flatterer, while Mortimer and ambition become practically synonymous. And Faustus, of course, is framed in the shadow of Lucifer but shaped with the fuller dimensions of Everyman. Marlowe's characters, in other words, are often fashioned as concrete universals: for all their unarguable individuality they still hint at an allegorical dimension and the dramaturgical heritage of the morality tradition.

When we have acknowledged the fact that in Marlowe's plays suffering and evil are the result of human responsibility, that Marlowe's tragic characters, unlike those of the Greeks, knowingly push themselves and others into disaster by their own driving wills and desires, we are left with an important question: does Marlovian tragedy as a whole imply or assert a faith in man? When Tamburlaine's soaring words are matched against his deeds and Faustus' godlike aspirations with the illusion and sensuality of his career, when the powerful and individual wills of Barabas and Guise result in wholesale treachery and slaughter, and the dissensions, cruelties, and betrayals of the world of *Edward II* are spread upon the stage, how can one characterize Marlowe as the Elizabethan herald of romantic humanism? Is not his vision of human tragedy more akin to the judgment of the Earl of Gloucester in Shakespeare's *Lear?*—"Machinations, hollowness, treachery, and all

[7] *Death and Elizabethan Tragedy*, p. 227.

ruinous disorders, follow us disquietly to our graves."[8] But there is a difference: Marlowe stresses above all the human habit of cloaking these manifestations of disorder and perversity in eloquently expressed "ideals" and high-sounding language. Faustus' speech to Helen is the masterpiece of this kind of irony. For Marlowe, the tragedy lies, not in the inevitable falling off of human achievement from the ideal, but in the travesty of the ideal that the deeds of men so often represent, and in the illusory aura of nobility with which man persistently invests his base desires. It is the tragic view of the ironist who sees in man the responsible cause of his own undoing, who presents man as a destructive agent who, by the abuse of freedom and will, persistently betrays others and inevitably betrays himself. One of the few characters in Marlowe's plays whose suffering brings new insight or deepened wisdom makes a relevant judgment: ". . . experience, purchased with griefe,/ Has made me see the difference of things," says Abigail; "I perceiue there is no loue on earth."[9] Marlowe's image of man may have heroic proportions, but the giant's deeds inspire neither faith nor optimism. Inwardly and inherently, it is the image of a fallen giant.

All three of the central components of Marlowe's vision of suffering and evil—the pain of loss, the irony of human aspiration, the root of evil in the will of man—are conceptions which were essential elements in the Christian theological formulation of the nature and destiny of man. Whatever Marlowe may personally have felt about Christianity, he clearly drew from its doctrines the ideological bases for his portrayal of the dark side of human existence. Whether or not he found the formulations of Christian theology ratified in human experience is a matter of speculation, but there is little doubt that he found in them the potentially effective themes for

[8] *King Lear*, I.ii, in *William Shakespeare: The Complete Works*, ed. Peter Alexander (London, 1951), p. 1078.

[9] *The Famous Tragedy of The Rich Ievv of Malta* (London, 1633), F2ᵛ-F3.

creating vital dramatic experience. By his dramatic genius for transforming thought into action, by his poetic genius for the formulation of functional blank verse, and by his highly developed sense of irony, he succeeded in bringing these themes to theatrical fruition in tragic drama which, though rooted in tradition, was unmistakably powerful and original. This tragic power was greatest in the plays which most clearly compressed and explicated all three themes: *Edward II* and *Doctor Faustus*.

To say that Marlowe gave dramatic life to conceptions involved in Christian theology is not to say that he wrote as a theologian, nor even that he dramatized the Christian view of human suffering in its entirety. There are few "fortunate falls" in Marlowe's plays, few examples of the suffering that clears and deepens human perception and insight, or of the suffering that redeems. One finds in Marlovian tragedy a clearly definable vision of evil, but little vision of good. Marlowe may share with Dante the Christian conception of tragic fate, and the idea that sin and its punishment are essentially identical, but there is little inclination in his work to move beyond the circles of the inferno. For Marlowe the inferno extended into the world of men; although his dramatic universe is humanistically oriented, it remains a world where one must say with Mephostophilis: "Why this is hell: nor am I out of it." In the end, Peele's judgment is still the fitting final word: Christopher Marlowe's unique province was to give undying dramatic voice to the sufferings of "the soules below."

INDEX

Major entries are indicated in italics.

Beza, Theodore, 205n
Bible, the, 16-18, 125, 127, 129, 132, 135, 141, 142n, 180, 195n, 197-199, 206, 209, 210, 212n, 228
Blenerhasset, Thomas, 44n
Boas, Frederick S., 82n, 161n; on Marlowe as divinity student, 6; on *Dido*, 76n, 80n, 84; on *Tamburlaine*, 107, 114
Boccaccio, Giovanni, 42, 43, 59, 60, 86
Bonfinius, 114
Bowers, Fredson, on revenge in *Spanish Tragedy*, 70n; on Machiavelli, 157n
Brooke, C. F. Tucker, on *Dido*, 76n
Buckingham, Henry, Duke of, 47
Bullinger, Henry, 118n, 214-215, 229n

Cade, Jack, 43-44
Callimachus, 114
Calvin, John, 200, 202n, 215n, 227n
Cambises (Preston), 33-35, 38-42, 113, 197n, 248
Cambridge University, 11, 56, 71, 90; theology at, 3, 6, 7, 193-195, 206, 214; see also Corpus Christi College
Camden, Carroll, Jr., 90n, 93n
Campaspe (Lyly), 163n
Campbell, Lily B., 42n, 47n, 49n, 155n
Campion, Edmund, 155n
Cardozo, J. L., 134n, 140n
Carrouges, Michel, 192n
Castiglione, B., 163n
Castle of Perseverance, The, 30, 41, 236-238
Catholicism, 117, 155n, 194; satire against, 132, 135n, 156; in *Massacre at Paris*, 148-151, 154-157
Chambers, E. K., 17n, 76n, 134n
Charlton, H. B., and R. D. Waller, on *Edward II*, 161n, 165n
Chaucer, Geoffrey, 42

Chester plays, 12-13, 20, 180, 225
chorus, 50, 52n, 54, 55, 59, 63, 70, 196, 251, 256
Chrysostom, St. John, 205-206, 240
Churchill, George B., 56n
classical tragedy, English, 56-62, 82n, 86, 108-109, 113, 155, 170, 251
comedy: allegorical, 27-28, 35, 208, 217, 233; in the Vice, 27, 34, 35, 239; in *Dido*, 84-85, 247; in *Faustus*, 208, 215-217, 233, 247; in *Jew of Malta*, 141-144, 247; in *Tamburlaine*, 103
comedy of evil, 11, 14-16, 24, 34, 144, 208, 247
Conflict of Conscience, The (Woodes), 32, 235, 239
Corpus Christi College, Cambridge, 6; Parker collection in library, 6, 118n, 195n, 200n, 206
Corrozet, Giles, 196n
Costello, William T., S.J., on Cambridge curriculum, 6n, 90
Coventry Corpus Christi Plays, 12, 17-18
Coverdale, Myles, 193n
Craig, Hardin, on morality plays, 24n, 232; on conceptions of tragic fate, 260-261
Craik, T. W., 24n
Cunliffe, John W., 49n, 86n
Cupid, 59, 83, 84, 85, 86, 249

damnation, 12-14, 20-21, 30, 32, 36, 45, 140, 225, 227n, 260; in *Edward II*, 173, 184-185, 253, 254n, 258; in *Faustus*, 13, 191-193, 203, 204, 208, 210, 219, 224, 225, 227, 231, 240-242, 247, 258; see also Hell
Damon and Pithias, 163n
Dante, 193n, 240n, 260, 264
Decameron (Boccaccio), 59, 60, 86
De Casibus tragedy, 8, 42-49, 56, 61, 62n, 99, 120, 230, 248-250; in *Spanish Tragedy*, 64-65, 94; in *Tamburlaine*, 88, 89, 94-98,